Summer Suffragists

Woman Suffrage Activists in Scituate, Massachusetts

Lyle Nyberg

Published by Lyle Nyberg, www.lylenyberg.com
Scituate, Massachusetts, 2020

ISBN: 978-1-7354745-0-2 (paperback)
ISBN: 978-1-7354745-1-9 (Kindle)
ISBN: 978-1-7354745-2-6 (hardcover)

Library of Congress Control Number: 2020914084

Cover: Illustration by Susannah Green using (1) "Peggotty Beach, Third Cliff in Distance, Scituate, Mass.," Tichnor Brothers postcard, early 1900s, author's collection, and (2) "Pennsylvania on the picket line," Harris & Ewing photo, 1917, Library of Congress. Author photo by Kjeld Mahoney.

Inside: Map by John Roman, using photos from start of chapters (credited). Most other images are in the public domain, edited for clarity and size, and converted to black and white.

CONTENTS

CONTENTS iii

FOREWORD v

PREFACE vii

INTRODUCTION 1

Scituate 3

The Suffragist Connections 6

The Suffrage Summer Capital? 8

1 THE WOMAN SUFFRAGE MOVEMENT 11

Timeline 12

The Early Years 14

The 1900s 18

Onward 26

2 INEZ HAYNES IRWIN & WILL IRWIN 27

Early Suffragism and Scituate Summer Scene 28

Inez's Later Suffragism 37

Will Irwin 42

Inez's Family and Life in Scituate 50

3 CARO MOORE & MARY MOORE FORREST 57

4 MEYER BLOOMFIELD 65

Background 66

Suffrage Activism 67

Professional Career; Industrial Reformer 71

Family Life on Third Cliff 74

5 BEATRICE FORBES-ROBERTSON HALE & SWINBURNE HALE 77

Early Years and Suffrage Work 78

Hale Family in Scituate, An Overview 86
Beatrice Arrival in Scituate 87
Touring America, 1914–1919 92
Later Times in Scituate 106
Marital Problems 115
Swinburne's Other Women 124
Swinburne and Marie, Divorce, and Demons 129
Epilogue 133
6 THE GLADES 137
7 JUDITH WINSOR SMITH & SYLVANUS SMITH 141
Background and Life in East Boston 142
Suffrage Activities 146
Early Summers at Old Scituate Light 153
Stowaway 155
Summers in Scituate 157
The Oldest Suffragist Orator in the World 168
The Smith Cottage in Scituate 172
8 WOMEN VOTE 179
Ratification 179
Voting 181
Recognition 185
Reflections, and Onward 187
NOTES ON SOURCES 193
NOTES 197
INDEX 263
ACKNOWLEDGMENTS 271
ABOUT THE AUTHOR 273

FOREWORD

The book title, *Summer Suffragists: Woman Suffrage Activists in Scituate, Massachusetts*, nicely gives away the topic of Mr. Nyberg's new book, but there is so much more than the suffrage movement in Scituate discussed in the book. What will be surprising to people who are fairly well versed in Scituate history is that there was a sophisticated effort by multiple women and their husbands to bring to fruition the right to vote nationwide in 1920.

Scituate has a unique, varied, and fascinating history. Some of it has been widely written about, but other aspects of the town's past are not well known. For example, the influx of Irish to Scituate beginning in the late 1840s is well understood and documented. Even a cursory look at the town from that time period will show a rapid increase in the Irish population here and the reason for it is obvious. Harvesting Irish moss, a red algae seaweed, could provide the Irish immigrants a living wage. Beginning in the latter part of the 1800s artists began to come to Scituate, spending the warmer part of the year here. All of these groups seemed to want to be in the same general area of the town, namely along and near the coast.

Mr. Nyberg has successfully brought to the forefront the Scituate suffragists in a way that is both fascinating and enlightening for the reader. He starts off featuring Inez Haynes Irwin, nationally known feminist and suffragist and ends the book with Judith Smith, another important figure in the right to vote movement. Mr. Nyberg has successfully uncovered many diaries, photographs, and other documents relating to both Scituate and national organizations involved in the women's right to vote effort. He is known for his deep, wide-ranging research and that is clearly obvious in this book. *Summer Suffragists: Woman Suffrage Activists in Scituate, Massachusetts*, is now the authoritative source for this topic in Scituate and surrounding towns.

David Ball
President, Scituate Historical Society
Author of many books on Scituate's history

PREFACE

I started researching the history of my neighborhood. It expanded to cover much of my town, Scituate, and most of its history from even before English settlers arrived in the early 1600s. My work came to the point where I had enough material and enough words for two books.

This is not one of them.

All that expanding research had uncovered quite a few significant suffragists who spent summers in Scituate. Some were almost literally in my back yard, since four suffragists lived three houses away from mine. But all these suffragists stayed in my draft writings until two factors spurred this book.

First, in early July 2019, I discovered Judith Smith's deep connection with Scituate. Surprisingly, she and her family spent many summers at the iconic, but abandoned, Old Scituate Light. Later, the family built a cottage near the lighthouse. Judith is a treasure of a suffragist, a South Shore native who spent most of her life working with well-known suffragists and leading key suffrage organizations. She spent 50 years working for suffrage for women until she was finally able to vote for president in 1920.

I found and read Judith's papers at the Drew Archival Library of the Duxbury Rural and Historical Society. In addition, I reviewed the Judith Smith collection at the Massachusetts Historical Society, the most extensive collection of her papers.

I am happy to share this discovery, and others, with you.

The second factor spurring this book, and giving it urgency, was the centennial of America's adoption of the 19th Amendment in 1920. This gave women the vote. It was a remarkable achievement for democracy. It was achieved through the fight and persistence of Judith Smith and others who are profiled in this book.

This is more than a local history book. Yes, Scituate was the summer home of a surprising number of nationally recognized leaders of the suffrage movement. This book tells the stories of their summers in Scituate. But they went back to their homes in Boston, New York City, and Washington, DC. There and elsewhere they fought for the women's right to vote. This book tells the stories of their fight as well.

They were involved in many of the key events of the suffrage movement, such as speeches, parades, political campaigning, picketing, and protesting. This book explores these events and these suffragists' personal stories, nearly all of which appear here for the first time. Their stories bring the suffrage movement to life. It is relevant to our times, when the right to vote and the right to protest are still under siege. I hope we will remember their fight and persistence, and keep improving our democracy ourselves.

Lyle Nyberg
Scituate, Massachusetts
August 2020

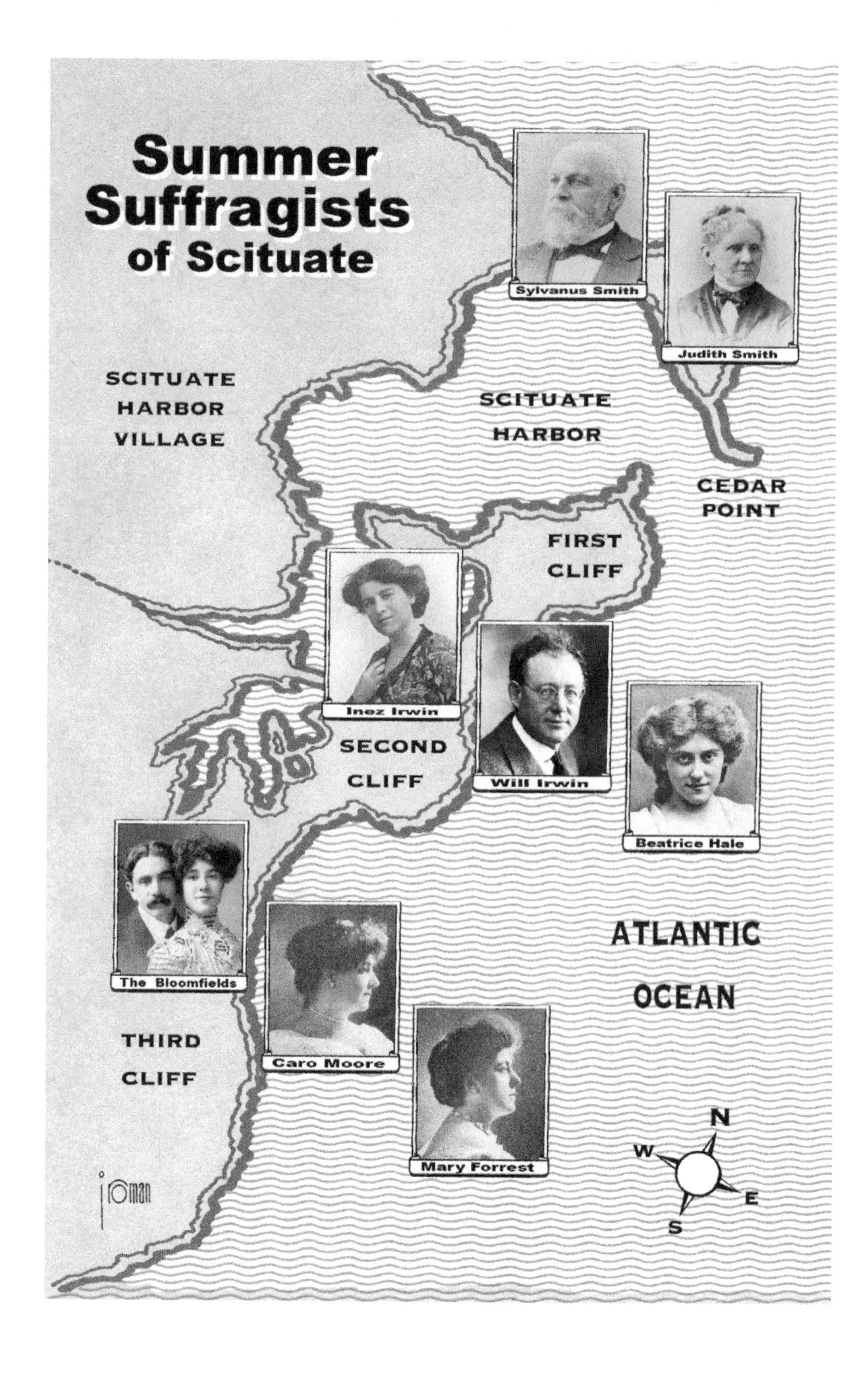
Summer
Suffragists
of Scituate
Sylvanus Smith
Judith Smith
SCITUATE
HARBOR
VILLAGE
SCITUATE
HARBOR
CEDAR
POINT
FIRST
CLIFF
Inez Irwin
Will Irwin
SECOND
CLIFF
Beatrice Hale
The Bloomfields
Caro Moore
Mary Forrest
ATLANTIC
OCEAN
THIRD
CLIFF
N
W
E
S

Introduction

Scituate, Massachusetts, was the summer home of a surprising number of nationally recognized leaders of the suffrage movement to give women the right to vote. This book tells their lesser-known stories as suffragists and describes their unique relationships with Scituate, a seaside town southeast of Boston. What were the odds that so many of the country's leading suffrage activists would summer on Scituate's shores?

Let's introduce these suffragists of Scituate, women and men:

- *Inez Haynes Irwin.* An early suffragist and feminist. In 1900, she founded the College Equal Suffrage League with her Radcliffe classmate Maud Wood Park. She was a leader of the militant National Woman's Party and wrote the party's history. She also wrote fiction, including the popular Maida books for children.
- *Will Irwin.* A muckraking journalist and writer, he became the second husband of Inez Haynes Irwin and joined her in the suffrage movement.
- *Caro Moore.* An organizer of the groundbreaking 1913 suffrage procession in Washington, DC, and one of 59 profiled in the procession's official program.
- *Mary Moore Forrest.* Caro Moore's stepdaughter, also profiled in the 1913 procession program. She was a founder of the National Woman's Party, and a member of its National Advisory Council along with Inez Haynes Irwin.
- *Meyer Bloomfield and Sylvia Bloomfield.* Both Meyer and his wife Sylvia were early suffragists and social reformers. Meyer was a noted lawyer, social worker and industrial reformer. He was on the original board of the Boston Equal Suffrage Association for Good Government, and an original member of the Massachusetts Men's League for Woman Suffrage.
- *Beatrice Forbes-Robertson Hale and Swinburne Hale.* An actress and suffrage speaker in her native England and across America,

Beatrice was in the same feminist club (Heterodoxy) as Inez Haynes Irwin. She was mother of the "suffrage twins," whose beach nudity caused a scandal. Her husband Swinburne Hale was an early suffragist and officer of the Men's League for Woman Suffrage in New York.

- *Judith Winsor Smith and Sylvanus Smith.* Both shipbuilder Sylvanus and his wife Judith were early Massachusetts suffragists. Judith was a key member of the Massachusetts Woman Suffrage Association, and the New England and American Woman Suffrage Associations. She was a close friend of leading suffragists Lucy Stone, Alice Stone Blackwell, and Julia Ward Howe. She gave public speeches into her 90s, fighting for the vote for women. She lasted the entire fight and lived to vote in 1920.

These were key suffrage activists in Boston, New York City, and Washington, DC.

They came to Scituate for diverse reasons. They were not a colony, more of a confluence. They already had a web of connections with one another outside of Scituate, mainly in Boston and New York City. They had some social connections with one another, and with the upper class, but most were not listed in the Social Register. They were more united by their dedication to progressive interests and movements. They were a microcosm of the suffrage movement.

They represented both wings of the suffrage movement. The mainline suffragists had long-time suffragist Judith Smith, who was central to suffrage organizations, and nationally known lecturer Beatrice Forbes-Robertson Hale, who said that picketing the White House was counter-productive. The more militant suffragists had Inez Haynes Irwin (Beatrice's friend) and Mary Moore Forrest, leaders of the National Woman's Party. The NWP promoted picketing the White House and demonstrating against the President during his visit to Boston.

These suffragists had a web of connections outside of Scituate. At the center of the web was Inez Haynes Irwin. She was an early and important suffragist. Her presence and spirit attracted others to Scituate. These connections are explored below in more detail.

During the prime years of woman suffrage activism, 1890–1920, Scituate developed as a popular summer destination. Like other summer residents, the suffragists came to escape the summer heat of the city, and to enjoy the cooling breezes, ocean views, and beautiful beaches.

While the main point was to relax, many of the suffragists continued their suffrage activity. They may not have known that Scituate lacked the strong anti-suffrage activists of other towns along Boston's South Shore like Cohasset — that is, apart from those in the Glades enclave in Scituate's secluded far north, next to Cohasset.

Few newspapers reported on this summer suffrage activity, and then only briefly. Scituate's hidden history as a summer retreat for suffrage activists is told here for the first time.

Drawing on the suffragists' diaries, letters, and journals, never before published, this book tells the stories of these fascinating summer suffragists of Scituate, and provides rare glimpses into the summer life of this small seaside town one hundred years ago. Biographical sketches cover their summer lives in Scituate, their personal lives, and their suffragist lives. They promoted the woman suffrage movement, and their actions helped lead to the 1920 adoption of a constitutional amendment giving American women the vote.

Scituate

Scituate was a small seaside town with only 2,500 permanent residents in the early 1900s. The population doubled or tripled in the summer. Summer vacations were long, at least for those who could afford it. The season lasted from late May to early October.

The entrance to Scituate Harbor has two peninsulas that reach like arms trying to hold in the harbor waters. The north arm is Cedar Point with its iconic old lighthouse. The south arm is First Cliff.

Moving south along the shore, First Cliff connects by a beach to Second Cliff. Second Cliff connects by Peggotty Beach, a crescent beach, to Third Cliff. Third Cliff no longer connects to Fourth Cliff.

Third and Fourth Cliffs were separated by the storm of 1898, and now the North River exits between them. The four cliffs have been a recognized feature of Scituate since its founding in the 1630s. They are represented on the town seal used since the early 1900s.[1]

In those days, Scituate was often called "Old Scituate." It had a particular reputation as a quaint seaside New England town. Americans knew the town for its picturesque industry of gathering Irish moss from the shores. Scituate had "The Old Oaken Bucket" homestead made famous by Samuel Woodworth's poem, first published in 1817. Scituate had the picturesque old lighthouse at Scituate Harbor, built in 1811. This was the scene of the popular story of Rebecca and Abigail Bates, daughters of the lighthouse keeper. They were famous as the "American Army of Two." During the War of 1812, they scared away a British warship by playing a fife and drum, pretending to be an American army.[2]

PEGGOTTY BEACH, THIRD CLIFF IN DISTANCE, SCITUATE, MASS.

Peggotty Beach, view from Second Cliff toward Third Cliff. Tichnor Brothers postcard 109971, early 1900s. Author's collection.

In addition to these historical sites, the town had scenic and recreational features for summer visitors. Scituate was "a quiet old marine village looking out on the ocean through a wide harbor-mouth," said a travel guide from the 1870s. Scituate had "singular and desolate bluffs," along with "good bathing" at Peggotty Beach.[3]

Scituate was also a haven for artists. The Americus Club of "well known professional people, actors, artists, &c.," camped on Second Cliff in the 1870s. In the late 1800s and early 1900s, a colony of painters lived and worked in Scituate. They included Dawson Dawson-Watson, Thomas Buford Meteyard, and Alice Beckington. Meteyard and Beckington had painted in Monet's Giverny. Meteyard left Scituate for England, but Beckington stayed on. She became a member of suffragist and author Inez Irwin's circle of friends. By 1903, Inez daily visited artists Beckington, Theodora Thayer, Matilda and Josephine Lewis, and Mabel Stuart. Inez posed for them. She found these artists to be denizens of a magical world.[4]

Inez and others then made Scituate a literary center in the early 1900s. Jacques Futrelle was a journalist who became a famous writer of detective stories. Gelett Burgess was a popular writer and humorist. He was a friend of Inez, and he was the one who introduced her to his friend and roommate Will Irwin. Soon after, in 1905, Inez introduced Will to Scituate. Will was a journalist and writer of short stories and serialized novels for popular magazines. Will and Inez's relationship later grew into marriage. Gelett was a frequent guest of theirs in Scituate. And, of course, Inez (whose first husband Rufus Gillmore was also a journalist and author) was herself a rising author.

A 1916 guidebook said:

> The old town of Scituate, or Satuit, has retained much of its oldtime atmosphere and simple beauty, and is the summer resort of many literary and artistic people.
>
> ...
>
> This coast, because of the high contrasting colors of marsh, sea, and cliffs, is a favorite resort of artists, who have transformed many old barns in the neighborhood into studios.
>
> ...

> On Second Cliff are the summer homes of a considerable literary colony, including Mrs. Inez Haynes Gillmore; Will Irwin; Gelett Burgess, ...[5]

In addition, Scituate was only an hour's train ride away from Boston, which was within easy reach from New York City by train or by boat.[6]

The Scituate suffragists were summer visitors. Like other visitors, some developed family attachments to the town or became residents.

The Suffragist Connections

The suffragists found different places to spend their summers along Scituate's shores. They were close to one another geographically. They chose shore communities at Cedar Point, Second Cliff, and Third Cliff. From any of these places, they could walk to the commercial center at Scituate Harbor village. Fresh fish and lobsters were abundant.

While atmosphere, beauty, company, and lobsters were good reasons for anyone to spend summers in Scituate, the suffragists had more specific reasons.

Judith and Sylvanus Smith had a connection that allowed them to stay at the keeper's cottage of the iconic old Scituate lighthouse starting in 1873, even though the federal government had long since abandoned it.

Inez Irwin came in 1901 when her family rented a cottage on Peggotty Beach on Second Cliff for summers.

Inez's presence attracted others, such as her future husband Will Irwin, and her friend and fellow suffragist Beatrice Forbes-Robertson Hale.

Beatrice and Inez are the best examples of connections among these summer suffragists. Both belonged to a small feminist club called Heterodoxy formed in 1912 in Greenwich Village. Other members included Inez's sister Daisy Thompson and suffragists such as Charlotte Perkins Gilman, Fola LaFollette, Frances Maule Bjorkman, and Inez Milholland. Milholland led the March 3, 1913, suffrage parade in Washington, DC, on a white horse.[7]

Beatrice witnessed and reported on that parade. In addition, Beatrice appeared in New York City's May 4, 1912, suffrage parade. In that parade, her husband Swinburne Hale marched together with Inez's future husband Will Irwin representing the New York Men's League for Woman Suffrage. Beatrice began coming to Scituate for summers the following year, 1913.

Later came Caro Moore and her stepdaughter Mary Moore Forrest. Mary was one of the leaders with Inez of the National Woman's Party. Caro's husband (Mary's father) William Moore represented Scituate and neighboring towns in the Massachusetts legislature in 1909–1910. In addition, he joined the Massachusetts Men's League for Woman Suffrage in 1910 with Meyer Bloomfield. Meyer and his family later moved next door to Caro and Mary for summers in Scituate.

Meyer's fellow members in the Men's League included Garrisons and Blackwells. They were well acquainted with Scituate summer suffragist Judith Smith through the Massachusetts Woman Suffrage Association.

In addition, Meyer was active in the Boston Equal Suffrage Association for Good Government (BESAGG) from its founding in 1901 by suffragist Maud Wood Park and others. Maud Wood Park was a classmate of Inez Haynes Irwin at Radcliffe, and together they founded the College Equal Suffrage League. Maud went on to lead the congressional lobbying effort of the National American Woman Suffrage Association to obtain approval of the woman suffrage amendment. Maud later became the first president of the League of Women Voters. Maud and Will Irwin early on became friends, perhaps through his relationship with Inez starting in 1905.

Years later, Inez wrote Maud that, "I have seen so many types of people fall under your fascination. ... The whole Filene family. All the Bloomfields."[8] This shows that Inez knew of Maud's involvement with the Bloomfields starting with Meyer Bloomfield's activism in BESAGG with its founding in 1901. When Inez wrote the letter in 1938, the Bloomfields were her summer neighbors on the next cliff.

There were few degrees of separation among these summer suffragists of Scituate. There were many connections.

The suffragists were too few and too separate to be called a suffragist colony. But their presence was more than coincidental. They shared connections with one another, and they shared connections with the wider suffrage movement.

Some had connections with Maud Wood Park, as described above. Another Scituate summer suffragist, Judith Smith, knew major early suffragist Mary A. Livermore. Livermore was an intimate friend of Inez's Aunt Lora, and was the first editor of the *Woman's Journal* founded by Henry Blackwell and Lucy Stone. Judith Smith, in addition, worked closely with national figures Lucy Stone, Julia Ward Howe, and Alice Stone Blackwell. All of them were major suffragists who considered Judith a dear friend.

These suffragists had connections with one another. Some connections were recorded, others implied. This book fills in some of the gaps in their recorded interactions in and about Scituate. Their connections with others in the wider suffrage movement are also explored.

The Suffrage Summer Capital?

Such a cluster of suffragists in a small town was uncommon. Only a few other places can claim similar groups. We consider them below.

Wianno was a summer center of powerful suffragists at the turn of the century. Wianno is in the village of Osterville in the town of Barnstable, Massachusetts. Its location on the south shore of Cape Cod served as a haven for Anna Howard Shaw (1847–1919), who was president of the National American Woman Suffrage Association from 1904 to 1915. In Wianno, she had a house built in 1892 and she spent summers there until about 1908, when she built a house in Pennsylvania. Her companion Lucy E. Anthony was the niece of Susan B. Anthony, who visited them in Wianno. Wianno was also the summer retreat of the family and descendants of abolitionist and suffragist William Lloyd Garrison.[9] Additional summer suffragists included Mrs. Horace L. Bearse, Ellen B. Dietrick, and Elizabeth B. Chace. Chace was president of the Rhode Island Woman Suffrage Association, and she summered in Wianno from 1877 to 1898.[10]

Shoreham, New York, claimed in a plaque installed in 2017 to be the "Summer Capital of the Suffrage Movement." The town lies on the north shore of Long Island. Harriot Stanton Blatch (1856–1940), a noted suffragist and daughter of famed suffragist Elizabeth Cady Stanton, had a bungalow there, starting in 1902 and lasting through at least 1915.[11]

Chilmark on Martha's Vineyard, Massachusetts, was a retreat for the Blackwell family. Edna Lamprey Stantial owned a home adjoining that of Alice Stone Blackwell.[12]

In Newport, RI, wealthy Alva Belmont threw open her summer mansion, Marble House, to benefit suffragists in 1909. In 1910, a *Woman's Journal* article noted that the traditional watering place of Bar Harbor, ME, was "strangely backward" with no suffrage promotions, even though ardent supporters spent summers there.[13]

Among these summer clusters of suffragists, Scituate ranks well in recognition. The *Woman's Journal*, published from 1870 to 1917, mentioned Scituate 97 times, Chilmark 47 times, Wianno 21 times, and Shoreham 8 times.[14]

Scituate likewise ranks well in quantity and quality of its summer suffragists. Although some of them stayed for decades, we focus on summers from 1914 to 1920. Those were the most active years of the suffragist movement.

In those years, anywhere from five to eight of these suffragists summered in Scituate. Many were nationally prominent. Three held national offices in suffrage organizations (Smith, Irwin, and Forrest). Seven marched in suffrage parades in Boston, New York, or Washington, DC. Seven received press coverage in large newspapers. Scituate's summer suffragists gave public speeches, none more than Beatrice Forbes-Robertson Hale, who traveled through the country.[15]

Several of Scituate's summer suffragists were mentioned frequently in the *Woman's Journal*. Beatrice's name, for example, appeared more than 140 times. Judith Smith's name appeared 327 times, about the same as noted suffragist Maud Wood Park (who did not spend summers in Scituate). Inez Irwin, notably, organized college women to the suffrage cause, along with Maud Wood Park. Inez later wrote the history of the National Woman's Party. Inez is the most prominent example of Scituate's suffragists.[16]

This book takes a close look at the places where these Scituate suffragists lived, worked, and frolicked. These places included Scituate, of course, but also Boston to a great degree.

Boston was a center of the woman suffrage movement in America, along with New York City and Washington, DC. Boston was home to many important suffragists, such as Julia Ward Howe, Lucy Stone, and Maud Wood Park. It was home to many important suffrage institutions, such as the Massachusetts Woman Suffrage Association, founded in 1869, and the *Woman's Journal*, founded in 1870 and published weekly in Boston until 1917. During critical periods of the suffrage movement, Boston was the year-round home to many of Scituate's summer suffragists, including Inez Haynes Irwin, Meyer Bloomfield, and Judith Smith.

Scituate suffragists played an important role in the long and tough fight to allow American women to vote. That fight played out over more than 100 years. It culminated with the 1920 adoption of the 19th Amendment to the US Constitution. Allowing women to vote had profound effects on the nation and American towns like Scituate.

This book opens with an overview of the "woman suffrage" movement (as it was called back then). Further chapters cover these particular suffragists (not "suffragettes," which was a term used in Great Britain). Speaking of terminology, a woman's first name is used where possible. But back then, they were often known by their husband's first name, as in Mrs. Thomas Nelson Perkins. At the other end of the spectrum was Alice Stone, who specifically kept her maiden name when she married Henry B. Blackwell. This book closes with a brief look at the adoption of the 19th Amendment, and what happened when women got the vote.

1

The Woman Suffrage Movement

Suffrage picketers in front of the White House, 1917. Harris & Ewing photo, probably January 24, 1917, "Pennsylvania on the picket line." Courtesy of Library of Congress.

Putting the suffragists of Scituate in context requires a review of America's woman suffrage movement (as it was called then) — its times, events, people, and organizations. This is complicated for a number of reasons. The movement lasted a long time, roughly from the mid-1800s through the 1920 adoption of the 19th Amendment to the US Constitution. The movement involved many people beyond the familiar names. The movement had many national, state, and local organizations promoting woman suffrage. To summarize, here is a timeline and an overview of the woman suffrage movement in America.

Timeline

- 1830s. Anti-slavery movement became active
- 1840s. Woman suffrage movement became active. Seneca Falls convention was held in 1848, and included Lucretia Mott and Elizabeth Cady Stanton.
- 1850. First national women's rights convention held October 23–24 in Worcester, MA; Lucy Stone (1818–1893) helped organize.
- 1853–55. First US women's rights newspaper, *The Una*, published in Providence, then Boston
- 1869. Woman suffrage movement split in two. The National Woman Suffrage Association (NWSA), based in New York, was headed by Susan B. Anthony and Elizabeth Cady Stanton. The New England Woman Suffrage Association (NEWSA) was formed in 1868 by Julia Ward Howe and Lucy Stone. It had overlapping leadership with newly formed American Woman Suffrage Association (AWSA), based in Boston and headed by Lucy Stone.
- 1870. Massachusetts Woman Suffrage Association (MWSA) was formed, led by Lucy Stone, Julia Ward Howe, and others. Lucy Stone and Henry B. Blackwell launched the *Woman's Journal*, aligned with AWSA and MWSA.
- 1878. Susan B. Anthony resolution was introduced in Congress to allow American women to vote
- 1879. Massachusetts law allowed women to vote in school committee elections
- 1890. Lucy Stone's daughter Alice Stone Blackwell (1857–1950) persuaded AWSA and NWSA to combine into the National American Woman Suffrage Association (NAWSA). NAWSA sought suffrage at the state level.
- 1895. Massachusetts held non-binding referendum and decided not to allow women to vote in municipal elections, with anti-suffragists active
- 1900. Maud Wood Park (1871–1955) and her Radcliffe classmate Inez Haynes Gillmore (later Irwin) organized the College Women's Suffrage League

- 1901. Maud Wood Park and others formed Boston Equal Suffrage Association for Good Government (BESAGG). Meyer Bloomfield was on original board.
- 1908. Maud Malone and Bettina Borrmann Wells led the first American suffrage parade, held in New York City
- 1910. Harriot Stanton Blatch organized the first large-scale American suffrage parade, held in New York City
- 1912. America's largest suffrage parade, May 4, in New York City (followed by larger torchlight parade there in November)
- 1913. Alice Paul (1885–1977) organized the first woman suffrage procession in Washington, DC, perhaps the city's largest parade to that time, with NAWSA's Congressional Committee. Alice Paul and Lucy Burns formed the Congressional Union for Woman Suffrage (CUWS) as an adjunct to NAWSA. Alice Paul created *The Suffragist* journal.
- 1914. Feminist mass meetings were held at Cooper Union in New York City
- 1914 and 1915. Woman suffragists held parades in Boston
- 1915. MA, NY, NJ, and PA held referendums and voted against woman suffrage. Suffragists and anti-suffragists were particularly active. NAWSA elected Carrie Chapman Catt as president.
- 1916. Alice Paul formed the Woman's Party, which became the National Woman's Party (NWP) in 1917, when CUWS was merged into NWP. The NWP took a more militant approach. Suffrage focus shifted to a US constitutional amendment.
- 1917. NWP suffragists began picketing the White House on January 10.[17] US entered World War I in April. Picketing continued. Some picketers were jailed, went on hunger strikes, and were force-fed.
- 1919. White House picketers were arrested and jailed for setting watch fires. NWP organized a "Prison Special" train tour of various cities by 26 suffragists who had been imprisoned. NWP suffragists protested during Pres. Wilson's visit to Boston. They were arrested, jailed, and sentenced, and they served time, the last suffragists to do so in the US and the only ones outside Washington, DC. Pres. Wilson called

Congress into special session, which passed the Constitution's 19th Amendment allowing women to vote.

- 1920. The 19th Amendment was ratified by enough states to take effect. NAWSA became the League of Women Voters.

The Early Years

In the beginning, women had the vote in what became America. They had powerful voices in Native American communities, and could participate in governance in the English colonies. Some colonies, and, later, the new American states, individually, took away woman suffrage. The US Constitution provided no express right to vote. Instead, each state could decide who could vote. One example is Massachusetts. Its 1780 constitution, the oldest constitution still in effect in the world, gave limited suffrage to women. Even that was eliminated by an amendment in 1820. On the other hand, Wyoming was the first US territory to give women the vote, and when it was admitted as a state in 1890, it was the first in a string of mostly Western states that enfranchised women. Thus, when America adopted the 19th Amendment, women in much of the country did not gain the vote, they regained it.[18]

The woman suffrage movement grew out of the anti-slavery movement of the 1830s. The movements were intertwined. As journalist-author Elaine Weiss summarized,

> … race was an issue in suffrage from the very beginning because it comes out of the abolition movement. They're almost sibling causes that grow up together with many of the same participants. The women we think of as the foremothers, Stanton and Anthony, Lucretia Mott and Lucy Stone, are really abolitionists first. They come to suffrage through their experiences and this idea of universal personhood and universal suffrage. And they really expect to get it after the Civil War ….[19]

Rev. Samuel J. May (1797–1871) was one of America's early abolitionists. He was a prominent reformer in many causes, including equal rights for women. He was the minister from 1836 to 1842 at the South or Second Parish of Scituate. This was in South Scituate, which separated from Scituate in 1849 and was later renamed Norwell. The church, now known as First Parish of Norwell, is in Norwell's center. In 1845, a few years after he left Scituate, Rev. May preached what was probably the first suffragist sermon.[20]

In 1848, in Seneca Falls, NY, a group of women held the first women's rights convention. The group included Lucretia Mott and Elizabeth Cady Stanton. The convention adopted a Declaration of Sentiments, modeled on the US Declaration of Independence. It endorsed a woman's "inalienable right to the elective franchise."[21]

The famed social reformer and women's rights activist Susan B. Anthony (1820–1906) was born in Adams, MA. (Interestingly, her mother's mother, Susannah Richardson Read, was from Scituate.) In 1851, Susan met Elizabeth Cady Stanton, who became her lifelong friend. Together, they founded a number of women's rights organizations, including the National Woman Suffrage Association (NWSA). She led NWSA's successor, the National American Woman Suffrage Association (NAWSA). In 1878, Susan arranged for the introduction in Congress of the first draft of her resolution giving American women the right to vote.[22]

The suffrage movement split in two after the Civil War, largely over race. The 15th Amendment to the US Constitution was proposed to enfranchise black men. Some believed the amendment must also enfranchise women. Others decided to support the amendment, to achieve a partial victory, with women to gain the franchise later. The abolitionist position was "the women's hour is not now." America ratified the 15th Amendment in 1870.[23]

By then, two rival organizations had formed. The National Woman Suffrage Association (NWSA) headed by Anthony and Stanton was based in New York. It focused on a national amendment allowing women to vote. The American Woman Suffrage Association (AWSA) was based in Boston. Its leaders included Julia Ward Howe, Lucy Stone, and Mary A. Livermore. The New England Woman Suffrage Association (NEWSA), already formed in 1868, had overlapping leadership with AWSA. These leaders worked with abolitionists to support the 15th Amendment. AWSA sought suffrage at the state level.[24]

Portrait of Lucy Stone, by J. Notman, in *History of Woman Suffrage*, vol. 2 (1881), pp. 760–761

In 1870, Lucy Stone, Lucy's husband Henry B. Blackwell, Julia Ward Howe, and Mary Livermore formed the Massachusetts Woman Suffrage Association (MWSA). In the same year, Lucy and Henry founded the *Woman's Journal.* Mary Livermore was its first editor, until she resigned in 1872 to go on the lecture circuit, and then Lucy and Henry took over as editors. The journal was aligned with AWSA and MWSA. The journal shared offices in downtown Boston with AWSA, NEWSA, and MWSA.[25]

The *Woman's Journal* became an important voice for the woman suffrage movement. It was published weekly in Boston from 1870 until 1917, when it was merged into a similar publication in New York City. At the start, its offices were in a block across the street from the Massachusetts State House, including 3 Park Street from 1888 to 1908.

Lucy and Henry's daughter, Alice Stone Blackwell, graduated with honors from Boston University's College of Liberal Arts in 1881, and then she began to help her parents edit the *Woman's Journal.* She eventually became its chief editor.[26]

The lighter colored building (or paired buildings) in the center, between the domed Massachusetts State House and the Park Street Church, was 3–5 Park Street, Boston, home of woman suffrage associations and the *Woman's Journal.* Chickering photo, *One panoramic photo of Park St. Station, showing Park St. Church and State House in distance, Boston, Mass.*, about 1903. Courtesy of Library of Congress.

In 1890, Alice Stone Blackwell persuaded the rival national groups to combine into the National American Woman Suffrage Association (NAWSA).[27]

Meanwhile, the woman's hour still had not come. The movement had some modest gains. Massachusetts, for example, passed a law in 1879 that allowed women to register and vote in school committee elections, though not general elections. Even this limited right to vote encountered obstacles. In 1880, a Scituate woman wrote to the *Woman's Journal* to say:

> They told me when I reached the door of the town hall that they were not voting just then for school committee, and should not for some time, they did not know when. A little after I asked again, and this time they said they had got past that.[28]

Married women had to register under their married names. Lucy Stone, who kept her maiden name, was not allowed to vote.[29]

Massachusetts men as a whole were not in favor of women's rights. For example, Scituate voters, all men, in 1882 voted "Not to ask the Legislature to extend to women the same rights of holding office &c as male citizens." They also voted "Not to grant to women the right to hold town offices and vote in town affairs on the same terms as male citizens."[30]

Despite this kind of opposition, by 1886 a hundred or more women served on school committees in Massachusetts. In March 1886, Scituate voters elected Emily Jacobs to the school committee for three years. In March 1891, they elected Carrie Litchfield to that committee.[31]

In 1886, among other years, the MWSA held a suffrage festival and bazaar to raise funds. Scituate women helped as local members of the large general state committee. They were Sarah E. Welch, Louisa F. Bonney, C. M. Allen, and Mary F. Prouty, all from prominent local families.[32] Later local suffragists reportedly included art teacher and newspaper writer Sally Bailey Brown.[33]

In 1895, Massachusetts held a referendum to allow municipal suffrage for women. Women could vote on this referendum. Suffragists called it a "mock referendum" because it was non-binding. Anti-suffragists urged women to stay away from the polls. Only about four percent of women voted, but those who did almost universally supported it. Among male voters, however, less than one-third lent their support, leading it to fail. The Scituate vote was also negative: 85 yes, 104 no, 70 blanks.[34]

The 1900s

As these numbers in the 1895 referendum suggest, an anti-suffrage movement grew during the late 1800s. The country's oldest and strongest anti-suffrage movement began in Massachusetts in 1882. In 1895, some prominent women formed the Massachusetts Association Opposed to the Further Extension of Suffrage to Women (MAOFESW). The association spent large sums to oppose municipal suffrage for women in the 1895 referendum. Many members believed that women belonged in the home, and they would lose their femininity if they joined the coarse, corrupt, and cigar-filled world of politics. Many also questioned whether the government should force suffrage on women, who might not want it. The anti-suffrage movement attracted many prominent women. In 1909, one of the MAOFESW's vice presidents was Miss Agnes Irwin, Dean of Radcliffe College, a women's liberal arts college affiliated with Harvard. The MAOFESW later changed its name to the Women's Anti-Suffrage Association of Massachusetts.[35]

The MAOFESW published its official organ *The Remonstrance* annually from 1890 until 1908, then quarterly until 1920. In 1914, its title lengthened to *The Remonstrance Against Woman Suffrage*. It did not carry the names of officers of the association until 1896, and it was edited anonymously by a man, Frank Foxcroft. Among the MAOFESW's other publications was a 1911 pamphlet "Opinions of eminent persons against woman suffrage."[36]

By 1911, the headquarters of *The Remonstrance* was at 687 Boylston Street in Boston, known as the Kensington Building. This was just up the street from the headquarters of its rival, the *Woman's Journal* (along with MWSA and BESAGG), at 585 Boylston Street, known as the Chauncy Hall Building. The latter building also housed MWSA and the Boston Equal Suffrage Association for Good Government (BESAGG).[37]

In 1913, a Boston newspaper had a Special Equal Suffrage Section, edited by BESAGG (so beware the political slant). One article gave reasons why woman suffrage would be harmful:

> Because if women had the franchise they would not use it.
>
> Because if women had the franchise they would do nothing else but vote all the time, and their homes and husbands and children would be neglected.
>
> Because women are such angels that they should not meddle in politics.
>
> Because women are so easily corrupted that they are not fit to have a hand in politics.

> Because it is more modest for a woman to use her sex influence in wheedling men into passing any law she is interested in than it is for her to drop a little paper ballot in a box.
>
> Because the ignorant foreigner, the unlettered negro and any man, no matter if he can only make his mark on a ballot, is so much more capable of deciding questions of government than even the most highly educated college-bred woman.[38]

Meanwhile, back in 1900, Maud Wood Park and her Radcliffe classmate Inez Haynes Gillmore (later Inez Haynes Irwin) organized the College Women's Suffrage League. It was a big success, resulting in chapters at many colleges. Maud devoted her life to the woman suffrage movement. She was at first involved with MWSA, and later took key roles at the national level with NAWSA starting in 1916.[39]

With few legislative successes, the woman suffragist movement turned to parades to attract attention to the cause. In 1910, Harriot Stanton Blatch, the daughter of suffragist Elizabeth Cady Stanton, organized the first large-scale suffrage parade in America. This was a march down Fifth Avenue in New York City. Suffragists held six more parades there in the next seven years.[40]

Suffragists held the most significant parade on March 3, 1913, in Washington, DC. Alice Paul convinced NAWSA and its Congressional Committee to sponsor the parade. She organized the procession, as it was called, and she had only three months to prepare. It became a defining moment for her and vor the movement. The parade was held the day before the inauguration of Woodrow Wilson as President. With more than 5,000 marchers, it was the largest parade ever held in the nation's capital, and attracted an exceptionally rowdy crowd. The parade and the crowd's mistreatment of the marchers produced much positive news coverage for the woman suffrage movement.[41]

The 1913 parade is discussed in more detail in the chapter on Scituate suffragists Caro Moore and Mary Moore Forrest. Both were key members in organizing and conducting the parade. Other chapters discuss similar parades held in Boston in 1914 and 1915 that involved Scituate suffragists.

Though Washington, DC, was an important battlefield, New York City was the main center of the suffragist and feminist movements at this time. In 1914, the feminist Heterodoxy group of Greenwich Village held "Feminist Mass Meetings" at Cooper Union. Topics went beyond the right to vote. Handbills announced that the first meeting featured ten-minute speeches by 12 people, including Will Irwin. The second meeting included speeches by Beatrice Forbes-Robertson Hale on "The Right of the Mother to Her Profession," and Charlotte Perkins Gilman on "The Right to Specialize in Home Industries."[42]

Irwin, Hale, and Gilman all had Scituate connections and later chapters discuss them in more detail. Here it is worth mentioning that Irwin and Hale belonged to the Men's League for Woman Suffrage. It began as a New York organization about 1909 and quickly grew into a national organization. A Massachusetts Men's League for Woman Suffrage began in 1910. Meyer Bloomfield and William Moore were original members. They, too, had Scituate connections. Men such as these played a key role in promoting woman suffrage.[43]

In 1915, because of suffragist activism, several populous states held referendums to allow women to vote. This spurred the anti-suffragists into action. In Massachusetts, the MAOFESW mailed a pamphlet to every voter titled "The Case Against Woman Suffrage." It said the Socialists were behind the suffrage movement, and it quoted eminent persons saying that suffrage would be a loss to women and an injury to the state. At a rally at Faneuil Hall in Boston, one speaker said woman suffrage "would interfere with the sacredness and happiness of the home. He believed that woman is too noble and too pure to be drawn into the vortex of politics." Given these sentiments, on November 2, 1915, Massachusetts voters, all male, rejected woman suffrage by almost two-thirds of the vote. New Jersey, New York, and Pennsylvania also rejected similar referendum proposals that year for full suffrage for women.[44]

These rejections showed the strength of the anti-suffrage movement. By 1915, the MAOFESW had grown to nearly 37,000 members. That was a significant proportion of the 58,000 members claimed that year by their rivals, the MWSA. In late 1916, about 100 delegates from the Massachusetts anti-suffrage association took a special train to Washington, DC, to attend the convention of the National Anti-Suffrage Association.[45]

About this time, the woman suffrage movement split, again. Alice Paul led a group out of NAWSA and took a more militant approach. In 1913, she and Lucy Burns formed the Congressional Union for Woman Suffrage (CUWS) as an adjunct to NAWSA. In 1916, Alice Paul formed the Woman's Party, which became the National Woman's Party (NWP) in 1917, when CUWS merged into NWP. NWP was then NAWSA's rival as a suffragist organization. While both soon focused on a US constitutional amendment, their methods to achieve it differed.[46]

NAWSA tried to establish a positive relationship with President Woodrow Wilson. When Wilson ran for reelection in 1916, he addressed a NAWSA convention in September. He affirmed his commitment to woman suffrage but refused to endorse a federal constitutional amendment, instead leaving suffrage up to each state.[47]

The NWP took a more confrontational approach. When voters narrowly reelected Wilson later in 1916, it freed him from campaign pressures for a federal suffrage amendment. Alice Paul wanted to maintain political pressure for suffrage. She mapped out a plan to picket the White House and discussed it with only a few other people at NWP, including Harriot Stanton Blatch. Harriot was the daughter of pioneering women's rights activist Elizabeth Cady Stanton, and she was herself a long-time suffrage activist.[48]

When NWP representatives met with Wilson on January 9, 1917, he told them he could not dictate to his political party on the federal amendment, and he abruptly left the room. Disappointed suffragists returned to NWP headquarters. There, Harriot Blatch gave an impassioned speech, saying Wilson controlled his party, and the NWP had to keep the federal amendment question before him all the time. Harriot asked:

> Won't you come and join us in standing day after day at the gates of the White House with banners asking, "What will you do, Mr. President, for one-half the people of this nation?" Stand there as sentinels — sentinels of liberty, sentinels of self-government — silent sentinels. Let us stand beside the gateway where he must pass in and out, so that he can never fail to realize that there is a tremendous earnestness and insistence back of this measure. Will you not show your allegiance today to this ideal of liberty? Will you not be a silent sentinel of liberty and self-government?[49]

Harriot Blatch was most ardent for picketing the White House and she led the picketing at first, according to Alice Paul in later interviews. The idea of suffragists picketing was fresh but not unprecedented. The New York shirtwaist strikers of 1909 held mass meetings and picketed, and some of the picketers were imprisoned. Alice Paul herself engaged in similar activism in England in 1909 — demonstrations leading to imprisonment and hunger strikes. In any event, picketing would prove to be one of the most dramatic phases of the suffragist movement.[50]

Credit for the idea of picketing the White House probably belongs to Harriot Blatch. In her history of the National Woman's Party, Inez Haynes Irwin does not say who came up with the idea. But in her unpublished autobiography written in 1950, Inez takes credit for the idea:

> Alice said, "Mrs. Irwin, can you think of any method by which, every time the President of the United States appears in public, we can draw attention to the suffrage fight?" Fresh from California and the labor rights I saw there, I said instantly, "Why don't you picket him?" Less than a week later, as we sat down to breakfast, Bill [Irwin] took up his newspaper, exclaimed, "Alice Paul has taken your advice, Inez." The first four pickets in the long campaign of picketing had appeared at the gates of the White House.[51]

The picketers appeared at the White House gates on January 10, 1917, the day after NWP's disappointing meeting with President Wilson. These "silent sentinels" appeared every day except Sunday for months, then most days, well into 1919. This was called "the first political protest ever conducted at the gates of the White House."[52]

At first, bystanders ignored or were amused by the picketing, which was peaceful. Things changed after the US entered World War I in April 1917. Many felt the picketing was unpatriotic and detracted from the war effort. Even Harriot Blatch opposed wartime picketing. The picketing continued. Police arrested some of the picketers. Mrs. Agnes H. Morey of Brookline, MA, and her daughter Katharine Morey were among the first ones arrested. Some of those arrested were jailed and they engaged in hunger strikes. Authorities force-fed them. On the night of November 14, 1917, guards at the Occoquan Workhouse brutalized and attacked suffrage prisoners. One of the prisoners was Eunice Dana Brannan, daughter of the *New York Sun* publisher Charles A. Dana. (Dana spent part of his college years teaching in Scituate.) Newspaper coverage of this "Night of Terror" created sympathy for the picketers. Eventually, President Wilson supported a constitutional amendment for woman suffrage.[53]

With Wilson's support, the Susan B. Anthony amendment to allow women to vote came before Congress (again) in 1918. The resolution narrowly passed the House on January 10. US Congressman Peter F. Tague, a summer resident of Scituate, voted against the resolution, as did a majority of the Massachusetts delegation. In the Senate, on October 1, it fell two votes short of the necessary two-thirds.[54]

One Senator voting "no" was John W. Weeks of Massachusetts. He was up for reelection, and both NAWSA and MWSA campaigned against him. On November 5, he lost the election in favor of David Walsh, a suffrage supporter and former governor.[55]

Meanwhile, Congress moved slowly in considering a constitutional amendment to give women the vote. On January 4, 1919, five NWP suffragists, including Alice Paul, set watch fires in front of the White House and were arrested for lighting fires on government property. The watch fire demonstration was repeated February 9, and picketers were arrested and imprisoned. Then the NWP organized a "Prison Special" tour of various cities by train with 26 suffragists who had been imprisoned. The tour left Washington, DC, visited various large cities out to California, and returned through Boston, Hartford, and New York.[56]

In Boston, on February 24, 1919, NWP suffragists demonstrated during President Wilson's visit to Boston. Alice Paul was there, at NWP local headquarters at 9 Park Street, near the State House. When the presidential entourage passed by that location, there were only half a dozen suffragists, because, according to a newspaper report, "the greater part of the Suffragists were locked up." Nineteen suffragists spent the night in jail. They included Katherine Morey, mother of Agnes Morey, both of whom had been arrested for picketing in front of the White House. The next day, sixteen suffragists refused to pay fines and the court sentenced them to eight days in jail. They served time, although eventually all were released after others paid their fines. But three of them protested their release, and Katherine Morey had to be carried out of jail.[57]

This kind of pressure from the NWP may have led President Wilson to call a special session of the new Congress in May 1919 to vote on the suffrage amendment and other matters. The House of Representatives took up the amendment May 21, just as the MWSA opened its annual convention. At the convention, MWSA president Alice Stone Blackwell announced that:

> a telegram had just been received from Mrs Maud Wood Park, Congressional chairman, at Washington, that for the first time the suffragists have the needed two-thirds majority in both houses of Congress for the passage of the nation-wide Woman Suffrage amendment.[58]

Later that day, the House of Representatives passed the suffrage amendment, 304–89. Congressman John F. Fitzgerald ("Honey Fitz") of Massachusetts, who had temporarily replaced Peter Tague, voted in favor. On June 4, 1919, the Senate passed the amendment, 56–25. Counting absent members and those paired (for and against), the

Senate vote was actually 66–30. Maud Wood Park of Massachusetts, representing NAWSA, was one of the few chosen to attend the signing ceremony. Then the amendment went to the states for ratification. Ratification is discussed in the last chapter.[59]

Onward

Two books tell the stories of Massachusetts suffragists. The first book is by Susan Ware, *Why They Marched: Untold Stories of the Women Who Fought for the Right to Vote*. Some of the untold stories are about Massachusetts suffragists. They include Alice Stone Blackwell, Molly Dewson, Polly Porter, Claiborne Catlin Elliman (who rode through Massachusetts on horseback in 1914), and Maud Wood Park.[60]

The second book is by Barbara F. Berenson, *Massachusetts in the Woman Suffrage Movement*. It tells the stories of Lucy Stone, her husband Henry B. Blackwell, and their daughter Alice Stone Blackwell. It also tells the stories of Julia Ward Howe, William Lloyd Garrison, and many others who played important roles in the fight for woman suffrage.[61]

These books demonstrate the importance of the suffragists of Massachusetts and their Massachusetts-based organizations. But neither book provides details about the suffragists discussed below and their important roles in gaining woman suffrage.

2

Inez Haynes Irwin & Will Irwin

Inez Haynes Gillmore Irwin (1873–1970) was an important figure in the woman suffrage movement. She is the most famous suffragist who spent summers in Scituate. With Maud Wood Park, she founded the College Equal Suffrage League in 1900, and she wrote the history of the National Woman's Party (NWP) in 1921. She was a prolific and popular writer, including the "Maida" series of children's books. Some of her books had feminist themes.[62]

Inez Haynes Gillmore (later Inez Haynes Irwin), about 1902. Sarony Studios, New York City. Courtesy of Yale Collection of American Lit., Beinecke Rare Book and Manuscript Library (box 33, series III).

Others have written at length about her suffragism, feminism, and writings, and her life in Greenwich Village, but nobody has published an exploration of her summer life in Scituate and deep connections with the town. Inez had family in Scituate, and it became her year-round home later in life.

This chapter discusses how Inez became involved in the suffrage movement, married and divorced journalist Rufus Gillmore, married journalist Will Irwin, and established a summer residence on Second Cliff that hosted prominent writers, artists, and other important figures of America. The chapter explores Inez and Will's summer lives in Scituate and their contributions to the suffrage movement.

Early Suffragism and Scituate Summer Scene

Inez may have been destined to be a suffragist. She was born in Rio de Janeiro into a family from the Boston area. Her parents moved there to seek a fortune in the coffee trade. It did not work out, and the family returned to the Boston area.[63] The family was open-minded, and some of Inez's aunts were early suffragists.[64] So was her father, according to Inez in a 1913 interview:

> My father, who was the friend of all the oppressed, and who, fifty years ago, as warden of the Massachusetts State Prison [in Charlestown], made that institution the model prison of the world, was an ardent suffragist. His sister, one of the first women clergymen of the country, entered a divinity school when she was over fifty, graduating at the head of her class — the only woman in it — and taking charge immediately of two parishes, talked, lectured and preached equal suffrage to the end of her last days.[65]

Inez's aunt Lorenza (called Lora by her nieces) preached in Rockport, northeast of Boston, including the town's Pigeon Cove area, as well as in churches in Maine. She was a lifelong supporter of women's suffrage. While she was librarian of the Waltham public library, she became intimate friends with two important suffragists: Rev. Olympia

Brown and Mary A. Livermore. Lorenza died in 1899, when Inez was attending college.[66]

Inez attended Boston schools and was a special student at Radcliffe College in Cambridge, Massachusetts, from 1897 to 1900. Her stepsister Blanche had graduated from Radcliffe. Inez's Radcliffe classmate Maud Wood Park said that Inez had the most vivid personality that she had run across.[67]

Looking back in 1913, Inez said:

> At Radcliffe College I became the intimate friend of Maud Wood, now Mrs. Park, who was quite as ardent a suffragist as I; more ardent, in fact, for, since her graduation, Mrs. Park has given her whole life to the movement, whereas I have worked for it only at intervals. At first we were the only suffragists in the college but we proselytized endlessly. Before we left in 1899, we had gathered a little band about us. The next year, Mrs. Park evolved the idea of a College Equal Suffrage League, to be made up of college graduates living about Boston who were believers in suffrage. That league grew steadily. In time other leagues came into existence in other cities and affiliated themselves with us; now the College Equal Suffrage League is a national institution.[68]

In 1897, her first year at Radcliffe, Inez Haynes married Rufus H. Gillmore (1879–1935). He was a newspaperman who became general manager of Boston's *Commercial Bulletin*, and he later wrote detective stories.[69]

In 1900, Inez and Maud Wood Park arranged a set of two dramatic performances to raise money for the College Equal Suffrage League. The first was "The Weathervane of Love" by Rufus Hamilton Gillmore, Inez's husband. The performance had four actors, including Inez Haynes Gillmore and Walter Haynes, Inez's brother. The second performance, "The Judgment of Minerva," had 16 actors and other performers, including Maud Wood Park and Mary Livermore Norris. Mary was named after her famous suffragist grandmother, Mary A.

Livermore, who had been an intimate friend of Inez's Aunt Lora. Carl Ruggles contributed music. He was a composer who later became a close friend and frequent guest at Inez's summer bungalow at Second Cliff in Scituate.[70]

Inez and her family first came to Scituate in 1901, when its seaside land was being developed for summer cottages. That included Second Cliff. It was just over the causeway from Scituate Harbor village. The causeway included a wooden bridge. (It was replaced in 1930 by a bridge with cantilevered beams of reinforced concrete and piers of granite.) Second Cliff is next to the ocean, and is connected to the beautiful Peggotty Beach.[71]

The Haynes family came to Scituate by happenstance. Inez's brother Harry E. Haynes (1860–1958) had long worked at a famous sporting goods store in Boston. A woman from Scituate came into the store and Harry asked her if there were any cottages for rent on the beach. She said there were two. Hers was rented, but William Supple's cottage was available. Family members visited the cottage, reported back to the rest of the family, and they decided to rent it for the summer of 1901.[72]

The cottage was at Peggotty Beach. It was one of three cottages marked on a 1903 map as belonging to W. E. Supple. At the time, there were few people at the beach, at most 20 on a Sunday. The Haynes family had it almost to themselves. During this time, Inez was writing each morning, typing away on a Remington typewriter, a practice that would continue for her long writing life.[73]

Harry's work at a sporting goods store reflected a broader interest in hunting. He was a prominent member or guest of the Massachusetts Rifle Association by 1890. In 1903, he took his brother-in-law Rufus Gillmore deer hunting for two weeks up in Maine, along with four other friends. Rufus gave a dinner for Harry in 1905 when he left the sporting goods firm for a position with a New England agency of another firm. Harry would eventually work for gun firms, including Savage Arms, and was considered a leader in developing firearms for sportsmen.[74]

The family rented at Peggotty Beach for a while. In 1906, Walter Haynes rented a cottage, and Inez and her husband Rufus rented

Supple's cottage. But in 1907, they made a more serious commitment to summer life in Scituate. Starting that year, Inez's brother Harry bought four lots on Second Cliff. The lots were bounded by what is now Peggotty Beach Road, Crescent Avenue, and Bridge Avenue. Later, Inez bought two lots adjacent to her brother's property in 1910, and two more lots adjacent to hers in 1911. These lots were also between Peggotty Beach Road and Crescent Avenue. They were less than a quarter mile from Peggotty Beach.[75]

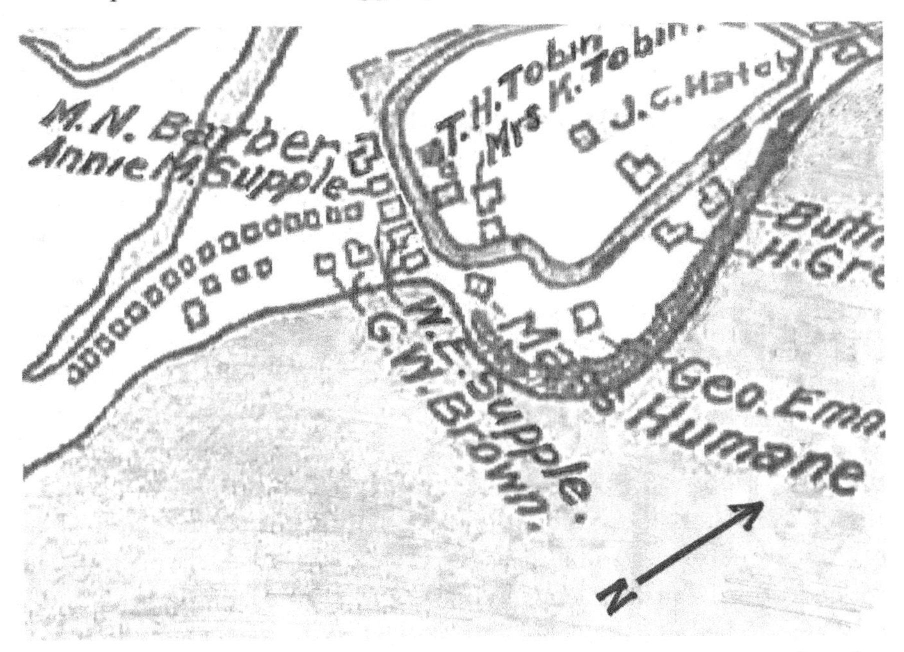

Haynes family's first cottage (W. E. Supple, center) at Peggotty Beach and ocean (bottom), in this modified detail from the 1903 *Atlas of Plymouth County*. Courtesy of State Library of Massachusetts.

Others who were important to Inez also committed to Scituate in 1907. Many were journalists, like Inez's husband, or writers, like Inez. These people require some background information.

One important figure in Inez's social circle was Charles H. Copeland (1874–1913). He was a *Boston Post* reporter from Cambridge. He made friends with Jacques Futrelle, another *Boston Post* reporter. In 1893, Jacques invited Charles to his home in Georgia, where Charles fell in love with Jacques' sister Elberta. They married and settled in Cambridge. He became president of the State House News Service. In

1900, they moved to Scituate, where they had a summer house on Second Cliff. Later, they had a home in town on Meeting House Lane, just across the causeway from Second Cliff. The Copelands provided their home on Meeting House Lane as a meeting place for writers and artists, and they were active in an artist colony that had developed there. In 1905, their barn became a summer school to promote craftsmanship. In 1907, Elberta purchased the Meeting House Lane property.[76]

Another important figure was Elberta's brother Jacques Futrelle, who evidently spent some time at his sister's place in the early 1900s. He retreated there after burning out while reporting on the Spanish-American War. He returned to journalism at the *Boston American*, and then left in 1906 to write novels. He soon became a famous writer of detective stories. Like Harry Haynes, he bought lots on Second Cliff in 1907.[77]

By 1908, Jacques and Harry built rambling bungalows across Bridge Avenue from each other. Jacques' place was called "Stepping Stones." By 1912, Inez built a bungalow next door to Harry's. The property had a small pond hidden among tall bushes, fed by what Inez believed was the only spring on Second Cliff. She named the pond "The Fairy Pond." She later stocked it with goldfish and added water lilies. Then on her property she added gardens with annuals. Her bungalow had six bedrooms, a maid's wing, a library, and a large living room 43 feet by 23 feet. The bungalow had wide, covered piazzas (porches) on three sides.[78]

Yet another important member of Inez's circle was Gelett Burgess, who played key roles in these three bungalows in a row. Gelett designed Harry's bungalow (and may have built it). He also designed Inez's bungalow, built by William (Bill) Supple, who owned the beach cottage in which the Haynes family members first stayed. For all we know, Gelett also designed the house that Jacques built.[79]

Gelett Burgess had a fateful and roundabout journey to Scituate. Gelett and Will Irwin connected in San Francisco. They wrote together, including a book published in 1904. When both moved to New York, they shared an apartment. In December 1904, Gelett gave a tea for his friend Inez Haynes Gillmore, who was visiting from Boston. That was how Will met Inez. Gelett would later be part of their summer circle in Scituate. He was an artist, art critic, poet, author, and humorist. He graduated from MIT and worked as a draftsman, but he was not noted as an architect.[80]

Jacques Futrelle house (Stepping Stones), left, and Harry Haynes house, right, in view from causeway to Second Cliff. Postcard published by C. W. Frye, early 1900s. Courtesy of Scituate Historical Society.

Harry Haynes hosted Will Irwin at his new summer home on Second Cliff during the summer of 1908. One day, they went swimming at Peggotty Beach in high surf. They almost drowned. An undertow kept them from returning to shore. It swept Harry a half mile down the coast, nearly over to Third Cliff, but he was able to reach the shore. Will was still struggling. Harry tied a long rope around his waist and swam out to get Will. People on the beach hauled them back to shore.[81]

The Gillmores established a well-known summer social scene in Scituate. Their visitors ranged well beyond the suffragists of Inez's earlier years. They included a composer, a cartoonist, and a sculptor. Composer Carl Ruggles visited them often, including 1912. He became a lifelong friend after meeting Inez in 1897. During one of their visits to Scituate, Carl and his wife Charlotte became friends with Boardman

("Mike") Robinson, a painter and cartoonist, and his wife Sarah, a sculptor, who were staying on First Cliff. In 1911 and 1912, they visited the Robinsons.[82]

Harry Haynes owned the large house just to the right of center. His sister Inez owned the next house to the right. "Second Cliff from Causeway, Scituate, Mass.," postcard, not postmarked, published by W. N. Seaver, early 1900s. Original is colored. Courtesy of Scituate Town Library.

Carl Robinson worked with Inez in New York City and was in favor of woman suffrage. He first studied art at the Massachusetts College of Art in Boston. He was a founding member of Barn House, a communal summer home on Martha's Vineyard. Robinson was a cartoonist for the *New-York Tribune* and *The Masses*, a left-wing monthly magazine published from 1911 to 1917. Max Eastman was the editor of *The Masses*, and Inez was fiction editor. Max was also the founder of the Men's League for Woman Suffrage. Not many years after summering in Scituate, Robinson would draw a cartoon sympathetic to picketing suffragists.[83]

Two tragic deaths occurred in 1912–1913. Jacques Futrelle died at the age of 37 while traveling on the *Titanic*, which sank. His wife, who was also on the *Titanic*, survived. She returned to their house on Second Cliff, Stepping Stones. Then in 1913, Charles Copeland died at age 39. Within two years, his wife Elberta lost both her brother Jacques, and her husband Charles. Charles had been active in Scituate's artist colony, and he bridged the evolution to Scituate's literary colony. Attendees at his funeral in Cambridge included Inez, Inez's husband Rufus Gillmore, and Inez's future husband Will Irwin.[84]

The Gillmores gathered their summer guests on Second Cliff in an area known as "The Writers' Roost," according to writer Marilyn Ziffrin. The visitors were divided into two groups: the "regulars" and the "once-in-a-whiles." In 1913, the regulars were:

> Mr. and Mrs. Rufus Gillmore, Samuel Merwin and Mrs. Merwin, Will Irwin, Mrs. Jacques Futrelle, Ralph Renault and Mrs. Renault, Carl Ruggles, the composer, Franklin Clarkin and Robert [Swinburne] Hale and his wife, Mrs. Beatrice Forbes-Robertson Hale. The once-in-a-whiles, who manage to creep out from New York for a week or two at a time, include Franklin P. Adams, Samuel Hopkins Adams, Boardman Robinson, the cartoonist, Gelett Burgess, Maude Radford Warren and Miriam Finn Scott.[85]

Inez's sister Edith "Daisy" Haynes Thompson (1875–1977) described summer life with Inez and company. Her fabulous reminiscences appear on the Scituate Historical Society's website, captioned "I Remember Scituate by Daisy Thompson." She mentioned all their noted visitors, saying:

> We became intimates of this charming group and our society soon took on a cosmopolitan atmosphere. Other painters and writers were weekend guests – Dawson Watson, a painter from London, Bliss Carmen and Frederick [Richard] Hovey, two poets, Gelet [Gelett] Burgess and Beatrice Forbes-Robertson Hale, niece of Forbes-Robertson Hale, the Shakespearean actor, and a well known actress and authoress in her own right and married to Swinburne Hale, the poet. We entertained simply and charmingly – garden parties, masquerades for which the painters designed fascinating costumes, beach parties – at that period

fifteen people on the beach was a mob – tea and tennis parties.[86]

Daisy dropped names of other noted people who visited Inez in Scituate. They included Fola LaFollette, suffragist and member of Heterodoxy; Wallace Irwin, poet and writer (and Will's brother); Josephine Hull, actress (a native of Newtonville, MA, who attended Radcliffe about when Inez did, and performed in the stage and film versions of *Harvey*); and Sinclair Lewis, author.[87]

Causeway and wooden bridge leading to First Cliff and Second Cliff (foreground), and Peggotty Beach. Scituate Harbor village in background. "The River and Town, Scituate, Mass." postcard, unknown publisher, early 1900s. Courtesy of Scituate Historical Society.

Inez's group organized an annual tennis tournament, with the prize being the "Second Cliff invisible cup." For Labor Day 1913, the *Boston Globe* reported (probably tongue-in-cheek), that the tournament committee included "Mrs Inez Haynes Gillmore, Scituate's best tennis player; Rufus H. Gillmore, Scituate's worst player; Will Irwin, Samuel Merwin, Reinald Werrenrath and Franklin Pierce Adams."[88]

Meanwhile, back in May 1913, a trade journal reported that Inez and her husband Rufus both had publishers in the same building in New York, adding that:

> Mrs. Gillmore has just left the city for the summer at her Scituate, Massachusetts, bungalow, where she is in touch with literary and artistic people, including Alice Beckington, Samuel Merwin, Franklin P. Adams, Will Irwin, Adriana Spadino, Gelett Burgess, Edna Kenton, Maude Radford Warren, Mrs. Jacques Futrelle and Boardman Robinson. Mr. Gillmore has been making a tour of Kentucky and other Southern states.[89]

Beatrice Forbes-Robertson Hale was not listed, but she would join Inez in Scituate later that summer, as discussed in a separate chapter.

The Gillmores' departing in opposite directions at the start of the summer reflected the state of their marriage. They divorced in 1913 or 1914. Inez had spent a year in California to establish her residence (San Francisco) and a base for her divorce. She continued to use her Gillmore married name for some of her writings.[90]

Inez's Later Suffragism

In the midst of personal turbulence, Inez did not neglect her suffrage activities. In 1910, she participated in the first large-scale suffrage parade in America. This was a march down Fifth Avenue in New York City. This led to more suffrage parades, and the one in 1912 attracted 20,000 participants and half a million spectators.[91]

Inez was one of about 17–25 members who formed the Heterodoxy club in 1912 in Greenwich Village. The club met to debate ideas. It aimed to develop more radical concepts of feminism. Most charter members had met as suffrage workers. They included Charlotte Perkins Gilman, Inez Milholland, and Beatrice Forbes-Robertson Hale. During her membership, Inez wrote a feminist novel *The Lady of the Kingdoms* (1917).[92]

In July 1913, Inez joined a group of suffragists taking an automobile tour of Massachusetts on the way to Washington. Suffragists came from around the country to join a demonstration at the Capitol in favor of a constitutional amendment allowing women to vote. A parade of automobiles representing all states traveled down Pennsylvania

Avenue to present the suffragists' petition, with 200,000 signatures, to their Senators.[93]

The years 1914–1915 were important for the woman suffrage movement, particularly in New York and Massachusetts. In 1914, suffragists held a parade in Boston. It was probably inspired by the 1913 parade in Washington, DC, discussed in more detail in the chapter on Caro Moore and Mary Moore Forrest. The Boston parade took place May 2, 1914, and it had between 7,000 and 12,000 marchers, including members of the Massachusetts Men's League for Woman Suffrage. The parade attracted a crowd of 250,000. Noted persons gave speeches afterwards, including ex-congressman (and future governor) Samuel W. McCall.[94]

In 1915, the suffrage movement in Massachusetts reached a crescendo. A state referendum slated for November asked voters to approve women's suffrage as an amendment to the US Constitution. Suffragists were active in Scituate at this time. In June, local newspapers mentioned that Mrs. Beatrice Hale (subject of a separate chapter) was on Second Cliff for the season, while also reporting:

> The Woman's Suffrage League held a meeting at the Idle Hour theater on Monday afternoon June 7th. Miss Etta Seaver the president of the League opened the meeting and introduce [sic] Mrs. Inez Haynes Gilmore as the speaker of the afternoon. Mrs. Gilmore gave a talk on Suffrage as it impressed her in California.[95]

Etta Seaver was the daughter of Unitarian minister Nathaniel Seaver and his wife. Etta graduated from Smith College in 1892. She lived in the family home on First Parish Road, next to the Methodist Church, and was "actively interested in suffrage and other social movements of the day."[96]

In July, the suffrage publicity campaign continued, and the town's most prominent citizen, Thomas Lawson, announced he was a suffragist:

> The regular meeting of the Equal Suffrage League was held on Monday at the home of Mrs. Edward C. Newcomb. Mrs. Inez H. Gillmore gave a talk on

> "Reminiscences of a Suffragist." After the address there was a social hour and dainty refreshments were served by the hostess.
>
> Mr. Thomas W. Lawson, in a recent interview with a member of the Scituate Equal Suffrage League, claimed to be a suffragist. He invited the league to visit his place and mentioned that his daughters were suffragists and active workers in the cause and suggested that they be called on to assist the work in Scituate.[97]

More local suffrage activism happened later that summer of 1915:

> On Tuesday several of the Suffrage League motored to the Town Hall, where the [primary] voting was taking place, and distributed suffrage literature among the voters there assembled. Miss Seaver and Miss Stenback [Stenbeck] were among the workers.
>
> The suffrage rally, held at the Idle Hour Theatre on Friday evening, August 17, in spite of the intense heat, was well attended. Mrs. Beatrice Forbes Robertson Hale and Mr. Will Irwin were the speakers of the evening, and remarks were made by the Rev. Mr. Stambaugh and others.
>
> … Miss Kelley and Miss Annie Kelley have closed their house on Kent street, and are in Cambridge for the winter, where they are very active in suffrage work.[98]

The site of some of this activity, the Idle Hour theater, was owned by Inez's brother Walter Haynes and his wife Margaret. It was located on Front Street in the Scituate Harbor village.

Suffrage activities occurred around the state. In August 1915, it was Suffrage Day at Fenway Park when the Boston Red Sox played the Cleveland baseball team.[99]

On October 16, 1915, suffrage supporters held a "Victory" parade in Boston with 15,000 marchers. They included the Massachusetts Men's League for Suffrage. Its members assembled at Berkeley and Marlborough Streets at the start of the parade. The parade had 30 bands. Half a million people viewed the parade. At the time, supporters were positive. For example, in Scituate, according to the *Boston Globe*,

> Miss Etta Seaver, president of the local Suffrage League, feels confident of an overwhelming success at the polls in November. A careful poll of the town, she says, gives every indication of a large majority for the women.
>
> Miss Ella Waterman of the anti league, while not sure of carrying Scituate, says the vote against suffrage will surprise those in its favor.
>
> Both sides have been active in the town, the suffrage league numbering more than 50 prominent women, with a somewhat smaller anti faction.[100]

The Victory name was premature. On November 2, in spite of all the pro-suffrage activity, the referendum was rejected by almost two-thirds of the state's voters. Only one town voted in favor: Tewksbury, with a vote of 149 to 148. Scituate's vote was resoundingly negative: 130 yes, 351 no, blanks 45. The state was not alone. In 1915, New Jersey, Pennsylvania, and New York also rejected similar referendum proposals for full suffrage for women.[101]

In the same trip to the polls, Massachusetts voters defeated incumbent governor David I. Walsh, a Democrat who fought for woman suffrage, and they replaced him with Republican Samuel W. McCall. (Evidently McCall was also in favor of woman suffrage.) In Scituate, the vote was 281 for McCall, who had Scituate connections, and 166 for Walsh, with fewer amounts for other candidates.[102]

After the state referendum defeats, suffragists focused on a national solution, an amendment to the US Constitution.

Inez Haynes Irwin played a role in the national efforts. By 1915, she was one of 27 members of the Advisory Council for the Congressional Union for Woman Suffrage. Members were listed on the masthead of the organization's paper *The Suffragist.* Other council members included Charlotte Perkins Gilman, Helen Keller of Massachusetts, and Mary Hutcheson Page of Massachusetts. After the Congressional Union became the National Woman's Party, Inez was a member of the party's National Advisory Council. She was listed on the masthead of the 1920–1921 editions of the party's paper *The Suffragist.*[103]

As World War I started, later to involve America, Inez traveled in Europe with her husband Will Irwin, who was reporting on the war. In 1918, Inez returned to Scituate and in September she was to give a talk in Boston at the Wilbur Theater, "A Woman at the Front." The talk was to benefit the canteen work for the war effort by the Boston Equal Suffrage Association for Good Government (BESAGG). Inez's talk was evidently postponed at the request of the government's Emergency Health Committee, presumably due to the influenza pandemic then hitting Boston.[104]

After the war, and after the pandemic, Inez wrote the biography of her party, *The Story of the Woman's Party*, published in 1921. A historian recently called the book influential, and worth deconstructing. The book came at a critical time for the NWP, boosting both its spirit and its revenue.[105]

Inez was mainly a popular writer. Over many years, she wrote the well-liked *Maida* series of books for children.[106] In 1933, she returned to feminist themes with the publication of *Angels and Amazons: A Hundred Years of American Women*, which included a history of the suffrage movement.[107] In 1950, she wrote an unpublished biography, *Adventures of Yesterday.* Her later mystery novels were "a paean to Scituate … all set in the fictional town of Satuit, a gracious New England village replete with history, beautiful historic homes, antiques, and very nice people who occasionally kill someone."[108]

Will Irwin

Will Irwin (1873–1948) was a nationally known journalist, muckraker, and writer. He was a noted war correspondent in World War I, the author of many stories for *Saturday Evening Post* and other popular magazines, and the biographer of Herbert Hoover. To borrow his wife Inez's description, he was a reporter, newspaper editor, magazine editor, war correspondent, short story writer, poet, novelist, dramatist, and historian.[109]

Will was born in Oneida, New York, and grew up in Colorado. One of his early jobs was delivering newspapers, on a pony, in winter blizzards with temperatures below zero.[110]

Will Irwin, about 1921. Photo by Orren Jack Turner (probable). Courtesy of Library of Congress.

Will attended Stanford University and became a reporter in San Francisco. In 1904, he co-authored a book with Gelett Burgess, *The Picaroons*. Also in 1904, he moved to New York City to work for *The Sun*. Will's biggest story was the 1906 San Francisco earthquake. He covered it in New York for *The Sun* based on limited telegrams and his own memories of the city. His series of stories was called "The City That Was."[111]

Will's relationship with Inez, and thus with Scituate, began early. In December 1904. Inez visited New York City. Her friend Gelett Burgess gave a tea for her. There, she met Gelett's roommate, Will. Will and Inez were attracted to one another. The next month, Inez, with her husband Rufus, again visited New York, and met with Will during the visit. Soon afterwards, Will accepted Inez's invitation to visit Boston, where she showed him around historic sites. During 1905, they wrote each other, and Inez invited him to visit at the Haynes family's summer home in Scituate. When he visited in July, Inez introduced him to history and life in New England. In September, she returned to New York City. She walked to the offices of *The Sun*, where Will worked. Will called her.[112]

At the time, Will was married, and he had a child. He was divorced about 1907. By 1909, he spent summers in Scituate, staying with the Gillmores on Second Cliff. His friend and former roommate, Gelett Burgess, designed the summer bungalows in Scituate for Harry Haynes, Inez's brother, in 1907–1908, and for Inez by 1912. Soon after Inez built her house, Will bought lots on Prospect Avenue, the next street over from Inez and her brother Harry. Inez was divorced in 1913.[113]

During this time, Inez and Will both lived in New York City, except for summers in Scituate.

Will was involved in the woman suffrage movement early on. Colorado, where Will grew up, gave women the vote in 1893, the year before Will went out to Stanford University. Will said he "inherited woman suffrage from my mother, so to speak." By 1908, Will was friends with Maud Wood Park, Inez's college classmate and a leading suffragist. Maud was a founder and the executive secretary of the

Boston Equal Suffrage Association for Good Government. In 1911, BESAGG arranged a writers' afternoon to raise funds for the suffrage campaign in California. Among the first agreeing to help were Inez Haynes Gillmore and Will Irwin.[114]

Back in New York City, woman suffragists were holding parades, an innovation in suffrage activism. Will said he skipped the first suffrage parade (meaning the one in 1910 or 1911). But he was in the second one, on May 4, 1912, and he led the men's division part of the way. "One felt like an early Christian in the arena," he said. The suffragists had to overcome two special obstacles: (1) that voting would "unsex" women, at a time when the popular image of a suffragist was a hatchet-faced character, and (2) that suffragist activity with its parades was a source of merriment for men. Will reported on the parades:

> Past the masculine scoffers, prepared to behold an aggregation of freaks, there marched for hours and hours a column of conventionally dressed women excruciatingly normal in demeanor and bearing a remarkable resemblance to the mothers, sisters, wives, and sweethearts whom the spectators had been loving all their lives. So far as New York was concerned, this pageantry took the laugh out of the topic.[115]

Reports of the number of men who marched ranged from 619 to 2,000. By any measure, the men were a good complement of the 10,000 or more marchers, and far more than the 100 or 200 men who marched the year before. One man who marched said, "The street crowds were far different in their reception of us than they were last year. Today's reception was splendid and shows the rapidly changing public sentiment toward suffrage." One newspaper said the parade "was probably the greatest procession of the sort that has ever been held in this country, if not on two continents."[116]

Inez, who participated in at least one of these parades, probably encouraged Will to become a significant supporter of women's suffrage. He was a featured speaker for the "First Feminist Mass Meeting" on February 17, 1914, at Cooper Union in New York City. On August 17, 1915, he spoke at a suffrage rally in Scituate.[117]

Like many others, Will fell in love with Scituate. He became one of its greatest storytellers.

He described the scene in Scituate about 1913 as follows:

> So although this ancient harbor town is only thirty miles from Boston, and although a few of its permanent residents commuted to business, it was still remote, picturesquely simple and agreeably true to old-fashioned Yankee type. Just as Provincetown became afterward the summer capital of Greenwich Village, so in the five years before the First World War a group of authors, artists and musicians, mostly New Yorkers in the winter, lived from May to October in Scituate "talking about work and — occasionally — working." Inez Haynes Gillmore and the lamented Jacques Futrelle first came to live on Second Cliff, only a hundred yards or so from the intimate Peggotty Beach. By natural attraction, others gathered round them.[118]

The others who gathered, according to Will, included Leroy Scott, novelist, Carl Ruggles, composer, Boardman Robinson, painter, Jesse Lynch Williams, writer, Samuel Merwin, novelist, and Franklin P. Adams, columnist. The "dark, comely Adriana Spadoni [was] a delicious narrator of stories about the Italian immigrants. … And tall, golden-blonde, heroically formed Beatrice Forbes-Robertson Hale, once leading lady with the company of her uncle Sir Johnston Forbes-Robertson, [was] at this time lecturing and fighting for equal suffrage." Beatrice had "a pair of girl twins startling in their beauty."[119]

Will also mentioned Inez's niece Phyllis Duganne, a precocious writer who sold a story to the *Saturday Evening Post* at age nineteen; Sam Adams, Al Thomas, and Edna Aug; and Josephine Lewis and Alice Beckington, "painters and survivors of an earlier group which, like this, relentless time broke to pieces. Perfectionists, they had restored and transformed a seventeenth-century farmhouse into a gem."[120]

Will and other members of this group played tennis on a court at Harry Haynes's place, adjacent to Inez's place. The court was next to Peggotty Beach Road. (A mid-century modern house now occupies the spot.) This was one of only three lawn tennis courts in town. Inez's friends the Copelands had another one at Meeting House Lane. Will was impressed that, "Robert Haven Schauffler — once doubles champion of Italy! — came over from his wooded estate in Greenbush." Schauffler was a musician, writer, and athlete, and he would become a war hero in World War I. His estate in Greenbush, a part of Scituate, was named Arden.[121]

Will wrote a 1914 magazine article that gave national exposure to Scituate for its summer beach scene. The title was "Togo, Mayor of Scituate." It was about the adventures of Togo the dog, and the people he met, including Walter Haynes and Christopher O'Neil. The article failed to mention that these two local characters were Inez's brother and her brother's father-in-law. On Saturday night, Togo would visit the Idle Hour motion picture theater and watch the film from in back.[122]

Besides the dog, the article's focus was on Peggotty Beach, curving between Second Cliff and Third Cliff. The dog, the beach, and summer residents appeared in illustrations for the article. Women strolled the beach with long dresses and hats or parasols. Cottages populated Third Cliff, in the distance. The article is one of the most evocative pictures of summer life in Scituate.[123]

Will's article described Peggotty Beach enticingly this way:

> Peggotty Beach of summers has an atmosphere all its own. It is a little half-moon-shaped strip of sand running without sudden drop into a surfless ocean. Above, the moss-houses fringe the rows of summer cottages; on the sand, groups of bathers, babies, and summer couples divide space with the dories and the beds of Irish moss, drying out from golden-brown to oyster-white; a safe and sociable beach, where one may loll with comfort and mild, innocent interest all day long.[124]

Will's article had beautiful illustrations by Henry J. Soulen of summer life in Scituate.

Peggotty Beach, illustration by Henry J. Soulen for Will Irwin's Togo article in *The American Magazine*, August 1914. View north with Humane Society station (upper left) and Second Cliff.

Peggotty Beach, illustration by Henry J. Soulen for Will Irwin's Togo article in *The American Magazine*, August 1914. View south with Irish mosser (right) and Third Cliff (in the distance).

In 1914, Will left this idyllic Scituate summer scene and went off to cover the war that had started in Europe.

Will had many adventures during the war, which he told in his autobiography. He tried to reach the fighting front, sometimes beyond it. Once, Germans surrounded Will and three other American correspondents. They surrendered, the first English-speaking prisoners of war taken by the German Army in World War I. America had not yet entered the war, and the Germans released the men. Will went back to the front. He was arrested temporarily in Maastricht, in the neutral Netherlands. Later, he was arrested temporarily by the British because certain people in England did not like his reporting on the battles at Ypres.[125]

On February 1, 1916, Inez and Will were married at Daisy's apartment in New York. His wedding present to her was two lots on Second Cliff in Scituate.[126] They left for Europe, honeymooning in Bordeaux. They lived in Europe for a while, reporting on World War I, which America entered in April 1917.[127]

During the war, Will was chief of the foreign department of the government's Committee on Public Information (CPI). This was America's propaganda ministry during the war, separate from the State Department. While there, he got work for Mary Heaton Vorse, and he worked with Vira Whitehouse, CPI's agent in Switzerland. Both women had been instrumental in the 1917 campaign that achieved suffrage for women in New York. Vira was a member of Heterodoxy with Will's wife Inez. All of them, along with the Irwins' Scituate summer neighbor Beatrice Forbes-Robertson Hale, moved from promoting votes for women to promoting the war effort.[128]

Because of their work in Europe, Inez and Will did not spend summers in Scituate in 1916 or 1917, so they missed key American suffragist activities. They returned to the United States by the summer of 1918, and had a short visit to Scituate in early August that year.[129]

Will was busy giving talks, including one in Scituate on August 5, 1918:

> Will Irwin, the well-known writer and war correspondent, gave a most interesting address in Idle Hour Hall last evening on personal reminiscences of the great world war. The proceeds went to the building fund for the new Methodist Church. Mr and Mrs Irwin, who are Summer residents of the Harbor, are on a brief visit for the first time in two years, at their home on Second Cliff.[130]

Will also spoke about his war experiences before a large crowd at the Marshfield Fair on August 23, 1918. (The widely attended fair is still held annually in Scituate's neighboring town of Marshfield.) The president of the fair was Scituate's wealthy Thomas W. Lawson. Before introducing Will, Lawson made a lengthy speech in which he announced he was running for US Senate, with his sole purpose being to defeat incumbent US Senator John W. Weeks. (Weeks, an opponent of woman suffrage, was defeated later that year by David I. Walsh.)[131]

After the war ended on November 11, 1918, Will and Inez lived in New York City, and spent summers in Scituate. Both were morning writers. One biographer describes the marriage as "profoundly satisfying; the couple shared a deep affection and many professional interests."[132]

Before the war, many came to Scituate and surrounded Inez and Will — the writers, the literary people, the composers, the illustrators, the playwrights, the theatrical agents, the theatrical people, the friends and friends of friends, the famous. After the war, most disappeared. Scituate was no longer a literary center. The scene in Scituate had changed. The town itself had changed, too. It was no longer the bucolic, isolated town with a Colonial-era air. It had entered the modern era, with cars, commuters, a new high school, a new country club, and burgeoning summer colonies.[133]

But Inez had her family connections for summers in Scituate. And she and Will continued to host their friends, some of whom had achieved fame. They included Charlotte Perkins Gilman. Gilman was a writer, feminist, and suffragist who was a member of Heterodoxy with Inez. They had much in common. Gilman's visit was probably for two weeks starting August 16, 1921, based on letters in Gilman's papers. Inez wrote to Gilman before the visit, saying:

> ... as I have said, there is a large family connection here. ... Beside our immediate family is my brother Walter, an ex-member of the Massachusetts legislature and present proprietor of the Scituate moving-picture house and the bowling alley; his wife Margaret [O'Neil], daughter of one of the Irish "mossers" here

> (of course you're wondering what a "mosser" is but that must wait), an Irish Catholic girl and very beautiful.[134]

Inez's Family and Life in Scituate

Inez had deep family ties to Scituate, as shown by her 1921 letter to Charlotte Gilman describing her large family. These ties were deeper than those of most other summer suffragists, or most other summer colonists.

Inez was one of ten children of Gideon Haynes and his second wife Emma Jane Hopkins Haynes.[135] As noted above, Inez and some of her many siblings spent summers in Scituate starting in 1901. Some eventually lived there year-round. Her brother Harry bought property on Second Cliff as early as 1907, and Inez bought property next to his. Harry, like Inez, lived in New York City when not summering in Scituate.

Inez's sister Daisy lived with Inez and Will Irwin in New York City, and spent summers with them in Scituate. Later, Daisy's daughter, also named Inez (nicknamed Ebie), joined them in New York. Daisy's "I Remember Scituate" mentioned Inez, Harry, and Maude, but identified only Maude Duganne as a sibling.[136]

Another sibling entered the Scituate picture. Inez said that her brother Gideon (named after their father) came from Chicago to visit and stay with her in Scituate. He brought his wife Christina ("Teenie") and her sister Elizabeth ("Lollie"). Inez's brother Harry, who was divorced, fell in love with Lollie and they were later married.[137]

Later in life, Daisy moved to Scituate. At the Meeting House Inn, she recorded her family history in a 40-page typed manuscript, "Inez and I." Inez was not the only writer in the family. Daisy's family history says that her great-grandfather married a Native American named Dorcas.[138]

Daisy's family history noted that Inez, then Daisy, then Walter, were born several years apart. They would play key roles in Scituate's history.

Walter Haynes (1876–1936), the younger brother of Inez, lived in Scituate year-round after he married Margaret J. (O'Neil) Haynes (1884–1965) of Scituate in 1912. She was a daughter of Jane and Christopher O'Neil, Sr. Her father Christopher was an Irish mosser and lifesaver, and he and his wife Jane lived on Gilson Road on Third Cliff. Walter and Margaret adopted a daughter named Rose. After Walter's death in 1936, the whole Haynes clan joined in conveying to Margaret the property on Hazel Avenue where Walter and Margaret had lived. In later life, Margaret lived at 125 Gilson Road with the O'Neil family.[139]

Walter and Margaret Haynes brought movie theaters and politics to the town. By 1918, they owned the Idle Hour theater, formerly named the Scituate Music Hall. It offered moving pictures on the second floor of the Richardson building on Front Street, opposite Beal Place. This was Scituate's first movie house. Margaret Cole Bonney's book *My Scituate* has delightful stories of going to the Idle Hour. Tickets were 10 cents for matinees and 15 cents for evening shows, which started at 7:00. The movies were accompanied by a pianist, the first one being Mrs. Fanny Merritt. Later, the Satuit Playhouse opened about 1921–1922 in a building set back from Front Street, opposite Otis Place, just a block north of the Idle Hour site. By 1926, Walter and Margaret Haynes owned the Satuit Playhouse.[140]

Walter Haynes ran for office in 1917 as a representative in the Massachusetts legislature. Politics was in the blood. Gideon Haynes, the father of Walter, Inez, and their siblings, served in the Massachusetts Senate in 1857–1858.[141]

A vegetable forecasted Walter's election:

> On exhibition in H. M. Macdonald's drug store, at Scituate Harbor, is a squash that forecasted the result of a contest in the election of representative to the state legislature in the South Shore district. On a squash, names were scratched in small letters. This was seven weeks ago, and the squash grew to show the inscription, "Walter Haynes, Representative 1917." Last week Mr. Haynes was elected.[142]

Walter served in the House of Representatives in 1917–1920, during the years of World War I and the governorship of Samuel McCall.[143] Walter gave a short address at the dedication of Scituate's Civil War monument in 1918, and his photo was in the printed program for the event.[144] Walter was one of those state representatives who voted on June 25, 1919, to ratify the 19th Amendment giving women the vote.[145] Walter died in 1936.[146]

Walter represented the same district that William Sturtevant Moore represented in 1909–1910. Moore died in 1914, leaving his suffragist wife Caro and his suffragist daughter Mary. They moved to Third Cliff for summers later in 1914, and they are covered in a later chapter.

Walter's accomplishments strengthened his sister Inez's bonds with Scituate. Inez and Will were fond of Scituate and its history.

Inez wrote a condensed history of the town for her autobiography. In 1936, when the town celebrated its 300th anniversary, Will wrote "The Story of Scituate" comprising most of an illustrated booklet of 48 pages. Inez wrote the legends for the accompanying map and program. At the end was a list of historic houses of Scituate. The town celebrated the anniversary with festivities including a speech by the first woman US cabinet member, Secretary of Labor Frances Perkins. Perkins was one of the speakers at the first feminist mass meeting in 1914 in New York City, along with Will Irwin. During her visit to Scituate, Inez and Will entertained her at their home on Second Cliff.[147]

In August 1937, Inez and Will fought a proposal to turn the historic house of Mary Ann Ford into a business. Mary was born in Scituate and taught school in Scituate and East Boston, where she was a friend of suffragist Judith Smith. (Judith is the subject of a later chapter.) Mary had been a trustee of the Scituate Historical Society from its beginning until her death in 1922.[148]

The use of Mary Ann Ford's historic house as a business required a zoning variance, and the zoning board of appeals held a hearing. Leading opponents appeared, including Will Irwin, Harry Haynes (Inez's brother), and Inez. The local paper reported:

Mrs Will Irwin spoke eloquently in opposition to any commercial use of the corner. Her testimony was given deep emphasis when she affirmed, in a voice touched by emotion, that she loved Scituate "most devotedly."[149]

The zoning board denied the variance, and the Ford building continued as a residence for a while. It is now the home of a dental office at 255 Chief Justice Cushing Highway (Route 3A) at its intersection with Cornet Stetson Road (Route 123).[150]

In July, that same summer of 1937, Inez and Will formed a club for summer residents, taking the old Humane Society lifesaving boathouse as the headquarters. A newspaper report does not say where this was, but it was undoubtedly the boathouse at Peggotty Beach. The Humane Society of Massachusetts was then disposing of its old boathouses.

Peggotty Beach, with Humane Society lifesaving station just left of center with peaked roof (in red in original), "Peggotty Beach and Second Cliff, Scituate, Mass.," postcard published by W. N. Seaver, early 1900s. Author's collection.

For Inez, summer life in Scituate inevitably changed over the years. When in her twenties, as she later told her friend Maud Wood Park, "I could have walked all day, played tennis two-thirds of the day, stayed in the water hours at a time."[151] In 1938, writing Maud at age 65, she contrasted her erratic days in New York with her leisurely days there in Scituate:

> There the days are very likely to be what I always seem to believe is what I want — a line of lucent beads on a string; work with my secretary in the morning; work in the garden early in the afternoon; the Garden Club twice a month; a little company now and then; some occasional cocktail parties, teas — very few evening parties; no formal dinners.[152]

Inez added, "You can think of me in a green world, for trees have emerged from the low bushes which covered Second Cliff, have grown to astonishing stature in twenty-seven years, and now are closing in about me."[153]

The Irwins' house on Second Cliff was called Broadwalls, according to a 1937 newspaper item. After Will Irwin's death in 1948, Inez retired to the Scituate house. Evidently, it was not winterized, since she and her sister Daisy moved from the Second Cliff home to Brook Street and the Meeting House Inn in Scituate for at least the winters of 1954–1955 and 1957–1958, respectively. In 1956, Inez opened the house for a tea to benefit the League of Women Voters. In 1959, she opened the house as part of a League of Women Voters house tour. The house no longer exists.[154]

Inez's older brother Harry Haynes died in 1958 at age 97. His obituary said that he and his wife made Scituate their summer home for 60 years, and they lived in Scituate for the previous seven years.[155]

Inez's sister Maude Duganne (1865–1967) was mentioned in Daisy's recollections of summer life on Second Cliff.[156] Maude's daughter Phyllis Duganne (1899–1976) was a favorite niece of Inez. She spent summers with Inez in Scituate, she was a suffragist, and she became a successful writer (like Inez) in her early twenties.[157] In 1920, a periodical said, "Phyllis Duganne is a niece of Inez Haynes Irwin and is the 'Janey' about whom Mrs. Irwin wrote in her girls' book [1911] of that title."[158] When Inez's sister Maude died in 1967, her ashes were buried in Scituate's Union Cemetery in the Haynes family lot.[159]

In later life, it appears Inez became more conservative, in the opinion of a historian who focused on her feminist activities and writings. The historian said that after Inez's book *Gideon* (1927), she produced little work of interest, and she stopped publishing completely after 1951, when she wrote her unpublished autobiography.[160]

Of the three bungalows in a row on Second Cliff, two remain. Inez's bungalow, which was at approximately 10 Crescent Avenue, has been replaced. Harry's house and the Futrelle house ("Stepping Stones") are still there, visible reminders of the age when artists and writers flocked to Scituate for summers.[161]

When Inez died in 1970, her remains were buried in Scituate's Union Cemetery in the Haynes family lot.[162] They are near Will Irwin's remains. His gravestone says "Beloved Husband of Inez Haynes Irwin. And Ever He Set His Steed Wherever the Press Was Thickest." Years before, Inez suggested the lines to him as an epitaph, and he said, "I like it."[163] Her gravestone has an excerpt from a 1657 poem by Henry King:

> Beloved Wife of Will Irwin. Wait for Me There, I Cannot Fail to Meet Thee in That Narrow Vale, Hark How My Heart, Like a Still Drum Beats My Approach, Tells Thee I Come, For However Long My March Be. I Shall at Length Lie Down by Thee.[164]

Inez Haynes Irwin was not just a summer visitor. She had deep ties to Scituate, to Second Cliff where she lived, to Third Cliff where her sister-in-law lived, and to both cliffs where her fellow suffragists summered. Scituate is where she retired after Will Irwin's death in 1948. Scituate can claim her as one of its major contributors to the woman suffrage movement.[165]

3

Caro Moore & Mary Moore Forrest

Scituate's Third Cliff was the summer home of Caro Moore and her stepdaughter Mary (or Marie) H. M. [Moore] Forrest, both of Washington, DC. Shortly before they moved there, both played key roles in the first suffragist procession in Washington, held on March 3, 1913. It was the day before the inauguration of Woodrow Wilson as US President.

Cover of 1913 suffrage procession official program, illustration by Benjamin Moran Dale. Original in color. Courtesy of Library of Congress.

Alice Paul, who organized the event, had only three months to prepare. It would have been difficult to draw participants from around the country. She drew from the District of Columbia to represent various states, and national and distant groups. This benefited locals Caro Moore and Mary Moore Forrest.[166]

Caro G. Moore (1860–1942) was Chairman of the procession's Homemakers Section. She was married in 1901 to Commodore (later Captain) William Sturtevant Moore (1846–1914), who was 14 years her senior. They had definite connections to Boston's South Shore.[167]

William Moore was a native of Duxbury, Massachusetts, south of Scituate along the coast. His father, Rev. Josiah Moore, had been pastor of the First Congregational (Unitarian) Church for many years starting in 1834. It was adjacent to Partridge Academy, an early high school that William attended. Rev. Moore married Rebecca W. Sturtevant in 1831. Tragically, she died in 1838. He evidently remarried, to Maria F. Doane of Cohasset, and they had children including William. Rev. Moore's church is where Sylvanus and Judith Smith were married in 1841, Scituate summer suffragists covered in another chapter. Rev. Moore likely officiated at their marriage.[168]

William Moore in 1910 MA state legislator "bird book." Courtesy of State Library of Massachusetts.

William Moore was a naval engineer. After Partridge Academy, he attended Harvard University and the US Naval Academy. He retired from the Navy in 1906, and Caro bought a summer home for them in Duxbury. It was William's old home, which had gone out of the family. It was the Capt. Gamaliel Bradford House at 942 Tremont Street.[169]

William Moore was a Massachusetts state representative in 1909 and 1910. He represented the district encompassing Duxbury, Marshfield, Norwell, Pembroke, and Scituate. He supported legislation to repair seawalls and breakwaters in Scituate, and he proposed legislation to prohibit pollution of the North River and tributaries in Pembroke and adjoining towns.[170]

Commodore Moore was one of the original members of the Massachusetts Men's League for Woman Suffrage in 1910. He was a prominent supporter of suffrage for women.[171]

His wife Caro Moore played a big role in the 1913 procession in Washington. Her biographical sketch, along with a photograph, appeared in the procession's official program. It was one of 59 such sketches. The program said:

> She has been interested many years in the suffrage movement but has only lately been an active worker. While carrying on mission work on the East Side of New York, she has come to appreciate the political as well as the material needs of toiling women and children.[172]

Photographs of Caro Moore in her parade costume appeared in newspapers across the country.[173]

The official program also included a biographical sketch and photograph of Caro Moore's stepdaughter, Mary H. [Henderson] Forrest (1873–1956):

> Mrs. Randolph Keith Forrest, whose maiden name was Marie Moore, has been chairman of the Office Hospitality Committee. She is the daughter of Commodore Moore of the Navy and was brought up

to believe in suffrage as a matter of course, but she has only joined a suffrage club since the opening of Suffrage Headquarters in this city.[174]

The official program for the procession listed members of the Advisory Council. They included US senators, Commodore and Mrs. Moore, and the noted poet Bliss Carman, who frequented Scituate in the late 1800s.[175]

Mrs. Caro G. Moore (left), and Mrs. Randolph Keith Forrest (stepdaughter of Caro Moore), from 1913 suffrage procession official program. Courtesy of Library of Congress.

With more than 5,000 marchers, this was the largest parade ever held in the nation's capital. Inez Milholland led the parade, dressed as a herald and riding a white horse. Next came sections representing countries with woman suffrage, American states, homemakers, nurses, college women, actresses, and other groups. A later chronicler called it "the monster procession." About half a million people watched the parade. Rowdy mobs mistreated the women by cursing, shoving, and tripping them, as the police stood by. Secretary of War Henry Stimson called out the cavalry from Fort Myers to protect the women. "Big Washington parade mauled by crowd" was how one period publication summarized it. Within days after the parade, Congress started hearings on the mistreatment of the marchers. The parade and resulting publicity were helpful for the suffrage movement.[176]

Some objected to the parade. Days later, anti-suffragists held a rally on Beacon Hill in Boston at the house of Mrs. William Austin Wadsworth. About 150 guests, all elegantly dressed, attended this "anti" rally. About one-third were men, including top political figures. The rally featured a speech by Frederick P. Fish, former president of American Telephone and Telegraph Company, and then a member of the State Board of Education. He told the rally:

> there is absolutely no excuse for women in Massachusetts wanting the ballot, since this is a representative government and the women are already represented by the men. ...there is a natural differenciation [sic] between men and women, [and] women should be the home makers and the home keepers, [and] by refraining from voting and working together they can so influence the men as to get anything they want that they ought to have.[177]

Frederick Fish had a Scituate connection. In 1880, he married Clara Livermore. (She was evidently not related to the noted suffragist Mary A. Livermore.) Her brothers Joseph (married to Agnes) and Henry both had summer places on Mann Hill in Scituate. These were in the Livermore family since about the 1870s. Both Livermore brothers were lawyers, as was Frederick Fish. Fish likely spent summers in Scituate with the Livermores, who were listed there in directories from 1915 and 1918. Fish was president of American Telephone and Telegraph from 1901 to 1907, and then he founded the leading intellectual property law firm Fish & Richardson in Boston. His wife Clara died in 1914, the year after Fish's speech opposing suffragism.[178]

In 1914, the year after the big suffragist parade, William and Caro Moore lived in Washington at 1221 K Street. In July, William Moore died at their summer home in Duxbury.[179]

In December, Caro sold the Duxbury home, and she and her stepdaughter Mary Forrest bought a summer place on Scituate's Third Cliff. We don't know why they chose Scituate, but perhaps the Duxbury home held too many memories. Their house on Third Cliff was "The Bijou" on Collier Road in Rivermoor, with an impressive view of the ocean and shoreline. In 1919, they bought an adjacent lot. That same year, Meyer Bloomfield (discussed in another chapter) bought the neighboring house. Bloomfield, like William Moore, was one of the original members of the Massachusetts Men's League for Woman Suffrage in 1910. One wonders how well they knew one another. In any event, after seven summers on Third Cliff, Caro and Mary sold their properties in 1921.[180]

During these years on Third Cliff, Mary Forrest was particularly active in the woman suffrage movement. She was considered one of the founders of the National Woman's Party in 1916. She was a member of the National Advisory Council of the NWP. The same council included Inez Haynes Irwin, who spent summers on Second Cliff. Mary said she was arrested for picketing the White House. Although this could not be verified, authorities arrested almost 500 women on suffrage picket lines between 1917 and 1919, and almost 170 of them went to jail. Mary Forrest was a member of the NWP's 1920 delegation to Sen. Warren Harding, then running for president. She also directed pageants for the party and other events.[181]

Mary Forrest and her husband owned a historic house in Washington, DC, later owned by nationally known journalist Rowland Evans, Jr. Documentation of the house describes Mary as a "well-known worker for women's rights," and "an advocate of women's rights and a founder of the National Woman's Party." The documentation says her pageants were "spectaculars" with up to 1,000 players, and she was a "large dynamic woman" with a large voice.[182]

No correspondence seems to survive between Inez Haynes Irwin and Caro Moore or Mary Forrest.[183] Undoubtedly, they knew one another and perhaps socialized during Scituate summers. One can imagine them even chatting while wading in the water at Peggotty Beach, which lay between the two cliffs where they lived.

In addition to Caro Moore and Mary Forrest, Third Cliff was the summer home for at least three other suffragists: Meyer Bloomfield, Margaret Colgate, and Mrs. Schuyler F. (Catherine W.) Herron.

Margaret Colgate of Rockland was an early resident of the Rivermoor summer colony on Third Cliff. In 1908, she bought lot 71 and part of lot 70 from George Welch, today's 20 Collier Road. A house was there by 1909, perhaps earlier. It was called "Campbell" after her middle name. She would own the property until 1928. (The house was demolished in late 2017.) During her tenure on Third Cliff, Margaret Colgate petitioned Congress in 1914 for woman suffrage legislation.[184]

Catherine Herron of Winchester spent at least the month of August 1918 on Third Cliff, where she rented or stayed with friends. Third Cliff was popular with Winchester residents. Catherine was married to Schuyler F. Herron, the Winchester Superintendent of Schools, who went to Europe in 1918 to work for the YMCA on the war effort after America entered World War I. Earlier, in 1917, Catherine had been president of the New England Home Economics Association, and the Massachusetts Woman Suffrage Association employed her in its food conservation work for the war. She spoke about food problems at the annual convention of MWSA's Third Middlesex Representative District.[185]

Catherine had a suffragist counterpart who was also working on food conservation for the war effort, Beatrice Forbes-Robertson Hale. Beatrice (who is featured in a later chapter) spent summers on Second Cliff, near where Catherine stayed on Third Cliff, including much of August 1918, when Catherine was there. Perhaps they knew each other.[186]

4

Meyer Bloomfield

One of the most prominent summer residents of Third Cliff was Meyer Bloomfield (1878–1938). He was a noted lawyer, social worker and industrial reformer. He and his wife Sylvia were early suffragists. This chapter covers his background, suffrage activity, professional career, and family life including summers on Third Cliff.

Meyer and Sylvia Bloomfield, probably wedding photograph (1902). Elmer Chickering studios, Boston. Courtesy of Bloomfield family.

Background

Meyer Bloomfield was born in Bucharest, Rumania, and moved to New York City with his parents at age four. He built a glittering resume, graduating from the College of the City of New York, Harvard University, and Boston University School of Law.[187]

Meyer became a national pioneer in the vocational guidance movement, which led to hiring guidance counselors in schools.[188] Later, he was a pioneer in the study of personnel management, which led to having human resources departments in corporations and large organizations. He was called the founder of the science of industrial relations.[189]

In his early years, Meyer served immigrants. In 1901, he founded the Civic Service House in Boston with the financial backing of Pauline Agassiz Shaw. He was the first director of the house, which settled and assimilated immigrants. (Another settlement worker about the same time was Alice Paul, in New York City, before her trailblazing work as a suffragist leader.) The Civic Service House opened October 26, 1901, in a new building on Salem Street in Boston's North End. It served primarily the Jewish and Italian immigrants who settled there.[190]

The Civic Service House was founded:

> when immigration reached its half-million mark. The following ten years the new immigration poured in at the phenomenal rate of a million a year. Boston was then the second largest port, and the North End, where the old immigration station is still [1917] located, was the great gateway, second only to Ellis Island.[191]

In 1901, while working at the Civic Service House, Meyer met volunteer Sylvia "Sadie" Palmer (1881–1949). She was an opera singer and graduate of Hunter College. In 1902, Meyer and Sylvia were married. They worked and lived at the Civic Service House.[192] Meyer remained director of the Civic Service House through 1909.[193]

What kinds of immigrants did the Civic Service House deal with in the early 1900s? A 1911 publication has this description:

> The North End dwellers of today are chiefly those whose work and necessities keep them there -- the Italians, on account of the vegetable, fruit and fish markets; the Jews, because of the many garment industries which supply not only the local market, but a large part of the big business district including some of the largest department stores.[194]

In addition to helping assimilate immigrants, the Civic Service House gave birth to the vocational guidance movement.[195]

The Vocation Bureau was founded there about 1908 by Prof. Frank Parsons, with the backing of Pauline Agassiz Shaw. He was the Bureau's first director. It offered vocational guidance counseling, and its example led to later having guidance counselors in public schools. After Parsons died, Bloomfield was named director in 1910. The Bureau moved its headquarters to 6 Beacon Street in Boston. It lasted there, with Bloomfield as director, until 1917, when it was taken over by Harvard University.[196]

It is interesting that 6 Beacon Street was also the home of suffrage activism, at least in 1909–1910, when the *Woman's Journal* was published there. One wonders if Bloomfield crossed paths at that place with Alice Stone Blackwell, the editor of the suffragist journal.[197]

Suffrage Activism

Meyer was an early and noted suffragist, in addition to his work at the Civic Service House. He was an original board member, the only man, of the Boston Equal Suffrage Association for Good Government (BESAGG), founded in 1901. Both the Civic Service House and BESAGG were bankrolled by a pioneering progressive woman, Pauline Agassiz Shaw (1841–1917).[198]

Pauline Shaw had access to wealth and used it to improve society. In 1860, she married Quincy Adams Shaw. He invested in the Calumet and Hecla Mining Company and, with Pauline's brother Alexander Agassiz, turned it into one of the world's largest copper mining companies. Pauline and Quincy had a handsome estate overlooking

Jamaica Pond in Boston's Jamaica Plain neighborhood. Quincy was one of New England's richest men. When he died in 1908, his estate was valued at $13,000,000. Considering inflation, that would be worth $365,000,000 today.[199]

BESAGG image (bookmark?), c. 1909–1915, in Maud Wood Park Papers, Woman's Rights Collection, #Pa-104, Schlesinger Library, Radcliffe Institute, Harvard University

Pauline backed a range of progressive activities. In 1877, Pauline boosted the young kindergarten movement, opening on her own two kindergartens that year and supporting 31 kindergartens in greater Boston by 1883. In 1881, she founded the Bennet Street Industrial School in Boston's North End, which gave classes in cooking, printing, metal working, and wood working. Pauline, who was born in Switzerland, had a special affinity for the needs of immigrants in the

North End. In 1901, she helped start the Civic Service House with Meyer Bloomfield, its first director. Pauline also contributed financial support to the *Woman's Journal*.[200]

Besides supporting that suffragist journal, Pauline was responsible for forming an organization that was significant for the woman suffrage movement. In 1901, the same year the Civic Service House started, Pauline, Maud Wood Park, Mary Hutcheson Page, and others formed BESAGG. Pauline served as president for the rest of her life, and Maud Wood Park served as executive secretary. Pauline hosted meetings of BESAGG at her building at 6 Marlborough Street in Boston from 1901 to about 1909. In those years, she also hosted the MWSA headquarters in her building. This was a large building just steps from the Boston Public Garden. She owned the property from 1882 until her death in 1917.[201]

BESAGG membership included major suffragists. Early members, along with Maud Wood Park, were Henry B. Blackwell and Alice Stone Blackwell. Meyer Bloomfield presided at one of its meetings in 1903. Then came Susan Walker FitzGerald, during an absence by Maud Wood Park. Susan graduated from Bryn Mawr College and worked in a New York City settlement house. She served as executive secretary of BESAGG in 1907–1908 and the MWSA in 1911. From 1911 to 1915, Susan was recording secretary of NAWSA. Back in 1908, when BESAGG's membership had grown to 351, Susan also served as secretary for the committee on equal suffrage lectures to women college students. This was a cause that Maud Wood Park and Inez Haynes Irwin started several years before. Susan later became one of the first two women members of the Massachusetts House of Representatives.[202]

In 1907, Meyer was one of eight persons, and the only man, chosen as a BESAGG delegate to the state suffrage convention. In 1909, BESAGG moved to 585 Boylston Street in Boston, along with many other suffrage organizations. That year, Meyer was one of those selected to give an address at a memorial meeting for Henry B. Blackwell. A famed suffragist, and an early member of BESAGG, Blackwell was the husband of Lucy Stone and the father of Alice Stone Blackwell.[203]

In addition to his involvement in BESAGG, Meyer was an original member of the Massachusetts Men's League for Woman Suffrage. It began in 1910 based on a similar league in New York. Massachusetts men's league members included Richard Y. FitzGerald, whose wife Susan worked with Meyer at BESAGG, and Blackwell family members. Descendants of the famous abolitionist William Lloyd Garrison also belonged to the Massachusetts men's league: sons William Lloyd Garrison, Jr., and Francis J. Garrison, and grandson Oswald Garrison Villard. Villard was also an officer of the New York Men's League for Woman Suffrage.[204]

Men's league members had ties to Boston's South Shore. A prominent vice president was John D. Long of Hingham. He was a former Massachusetts governor, congressman, and US Secretary of the Navy. William Lloyd Garrison, Jr., and Blackwell family members would have been well acquainted with Judith Smith at the MWSA. (Judith, who spent summers in Scituate, is covered in a later chapter.) Another early member was Commodore William S. Moore of Duxbury. His daughter and second wife would later spend summers on Third Cliff in Scituate.[205]

Meyer was one of those scheduled to join in marching with the men's league in the huge suffrage parade in Boston in 1914.[206]

In 1912, Meyer was one of the key speakers at a jubilee meeting sponsored by BESAGG to celebrate woman suffrage gains in the presidential election in Arizona, Kansas, Michigan, and Oregon.[207] He was probably still involved with BESAGG in 1914, when the association sponsored a rally in Boston's Post Office Square, with a talk by Judith Smith (covered in a later chapter).

In 1917, Meyer was an usher at the funeral of Pauline Shaw, the primary financial supporter and a founder of BESAGG and funder of the Civic Service House, organizations in which Meyer played leadership roles.[208]

Sylvia Bloomfield was involved to some degree in BESAGG. BESAGG sponsored the performance in 1913 of a morality play, "Everywoman's Road," to benefit the *Woman's Journal.* Sylvia was a patroness, along with many others, including Alice Stone Blackwell and

Scituate artist Alice Beckwith. In 1921, after BESAGG became the Boston League of Women Voters, the league appointed Sylvia to its conference committee. Perhaps in that role she met Judith Winsor Smith, another Scituate summer suffragist, who had been named as an honorary vice president.[209]

Professional Career; Industrial Reformer

The Civic Service House, where Bloomfield was director, had interesting connections with the garment industry, the trade union movement, and indirectly the woman suffrage movement.

When it started in 1901, the Civic Service House occupied the top three stories of a new tenement building in Boston's North End. The first story was the home of the Boston Wrapper Manufacturing Company, which made ladies' garments. The first story later held retail clothing dealers. In 1902, the Civic Service House fostered an early union of garment workers. In early 1903, the union went on strike against the Boston Wrapper Company, which occupied the first story of the Civic Service House building.[210]

The Civic Service House and Bloomfield himself were closely connected with a major department store chain in Boston that sold garments.

> Three teachers at the Civic Service House later became quite prominent: Therese Weil Filene, Max Perkins, and Walter Lippmann. Filene taught music at the Civic Service House. She was married to Lincoln Filene, who with his brother, Edward A. Filene, ran Filene's Department Store. [Therese Filene was also a cousin to Meyer Bloomfield.][211]

With these connections, plus Meyer's unionization experience and legal background, it was not surprising that Meyer played a key role in the "Great Revolt" of the New York garment workers in 1910. The clothing they produced would have been sold by Filene's, a major department store headquartered in Boston. According to historian Richard Greenwald, "Meyer Bloomfield, a prominent Boston social worker and industrial reformer, began another effort to end the strike on behalf of industrial democrat A. Lincoln Filene, owner of the Boston department store Filene's."[212]

The effort to end the New York garment workers' strike deeply involved Meyer and famed Boston attorney Louis Brandeis. Brandeis was hailed as a hero for creating a Protocol of Peace that settled the strike and established industrial self-government. By 1913, Brandeis's wife was an officer of suffragist organization BESAGG, of which Meyer was an original board member.[213]

The union movement was intertwined with the woman suffrage movement. For example,

- Alva Belmont poured her energy and wealth into the suffrage movement starting in 1908, and soon supported the New York shirtwaist strikers of 1909.
- Inez Milholland, who led the 1913 suffrage procession in Washington, was a lawyer representing union strikers in New York City.
- Mrs. William G. Stuart, who organized the Social Workers' section of the 1913 woman suffrage procession in Washington, DC, was a member of the National Women's Trade Union League, and she conducted an investigation of the shirtwaist (garment) trade. (She was also involved in immigrant settlement work, like Meyer and Sylvia Bloomfield and Alice Paul.)
- Before moving to New York about 1911, Inez Haynes Irwin worked as a reporter and speaker on labor issues in California, including strikes. Union use of pickets during strikes was an example for the NWP's later suffragist pickets of the White House.214

Meyer expanded his union work into the broader field of industrial relations. In 1919, along with his brother, Meyer established the journal *Industrial Relations: Bloomfield's Labor Digest*, published in Boston, with the masthead claiming: "Prompt, terse, accurate reports of labor events in the United States and other countries. Special industrial reports for busy executives. The first service of the kind in the world."[215]

In the early 1920s, Meyer moved from Boston to New York. There, he wrote many books, consulted on labor relations, and specialized in immigration law. Immigration had become a hot topic. As noted above, Meyer and his wife Sylvia helped assimilate immigrants in Boston's North End. After a 25-year period of progressive work to assimilate minority ethnic groups, the Immigration Act of 1924 restricted further immigration.[216]

Roger Babson put forward Meyer's name for US Secretary of Labor in 1930. Babson was a financial statistician and economist, and founder of Babson College. At the time, the incumbent Secretary of Labor, James J. Davis, was campaigning for the US Senate from Pennsylvania, and he eventually won that seat on November 4, 1930, so the Secretary position was open.[217] Meanwhile, Babson wrote that Meyer had a:

> unique practice of counsellor on employment stability problems to various corporations. That sort of service is needed in the Government. He has been the confidant of Presidents Harding and Coolidge, and I think he enjoys the confidence of President Hoover. Samuel Gompers, in his autobiography, speaks highly of Mr. Bloomfield. A lifetime of concentration on industrial stability problems, in terms of their human as well as economic meanings, fits one for the present emergency.[218]

President Hoover interviewed and considered Meyer, but eventually appointed William N. Doak on December 9, 1930.[219] Doak worked to cope with the Great Depression, retiring at the end of Hoover's administration on March 4, 1933.[220]

Doak oversaw intensive raids to single out immigrant aliens for deportation (many in the Mexican community), forcibly removing some 82,400 of them. But those methods were deemed unconstitutional in 1931. If Hoover had appointed Meyer — an immigrant who began his career by serving immigrants in Boston — how different might the immigrants' fates have been?[221]

Family Life on Third Cliff

Meyer and Sylvia Bloomfield had three children: Catherine Pauline, Joyce Therese, and Lincoln Palmer. Perhaps they chose "Pauline" to honor Pauline Agassiz Shaw, and "Therese" and "Lincoln" to honor Therese and Lincoln Filene.[222]

The Marguerite, Bloomfield summer home 1919–1944, unknown photographer, perhaps 1930s. Courtesy of Bloomfield family.

With a growing family, Meyer and Sylvia Bloomfield looked for a summer home. Their suffrage connections may have brought them to Scituate. They bought *The Marguerite* on Third Cliff in 1919. Suffragists Caro Moore and her stepdaughter Mary Forrest owned the house next door. Caro's late husband William Moore (discussed above) was an original member of the Massachusetts Men's League for Woman Suffrage, along with Meyer.[223]

Perhaps another advantage of the location was that by 1919, the nearby Mitton cottage was evidently no longer occupied by a member of the family that ran the Jordan Marsh department store. That was a rival of the Filene's stores owned by the Filene family that was so closely connected with the Bloomfields.

The Bloomfields must have enjoyed their summers in *The Marguerite.* It was a house built in 1909 with a big yard and a commanding view of the ocean from Third Cliff at 3 Driftway. This was one of George Welch's earliest houses in his Rivermoor summer colony, and it was typical of his later Colonial Revival houses in Rivermoor. It was a quiet respite from the family's life during the rest of the year in the heart of New York City. They lived at 412 West End Avenue, and later at nearby 315 Central Park West, an apartment building built in 1911–1912. By 1938, they moved to 490 West End Avenue in New York City. By then, their cottage on Third Cliff had a new name: "On the Cliff."[224]

Meyer died in 1938, and Sylvia continued to own the house on Third Cliff. In 1939, Sylvia was a patron of a local speech by a noted author, along with Inez and Will Irwin, Inez's sister Edith (Daisy), and others. Sylvia sold the house in 1944.[225]

The Marguerite was home to an important early suffragist, Meyer Bloomfield, one of America's most accomplished figures, and a family of accomplished figures. Meyer and Sylvia's grandson, Lincoln Bloomfield, Jr., created an excellent website that details their achievements. The house was torn down in late 2018.[226]

5

Beatrice Forbes-Robertson Hale & Swinburne Hale

Second Cliff, already home to Inez Haynes (Gillmore) Irwin, became a summer destination for two more nationally known suffragists, Beatrice and Swinburne Hale, starting in 1913. Beatrice Forbes-Robertson Hale (1883–1967) was one of the most prominent public speakers during the woman suffrage movement. By 1917, sources called her "one of the most sought after suffrage speakers in New York," and "one of the best known women orators of the world."[227]

Beatrice Forbes-Robertson, before marrying Swinburne Hale in 1910, postcard. Author's collection.

Beatrice came to Scituate through her friendship with Inez. Her husband Swinburne Hale (1884–1937) was an early, prominent suffragist in New York City. There, he was a trial lawyer who became a poet.[228]

History has overlooked Beatrice's many contributions to woman suffrage and the feminist movement. The Hale family's presence in Scituate, from 1913 to 1920, is practically unknown. Below, we explore these overlooked items, as well as the marital difficulties that led to her divorce from Swinburne, and his short marriage to a wealthy Massachusetts woman.

Early Years and Suffrage Work

Beatrice came from a family of stage actors and actresses. She was an actress and suffrage speaker in her native England and in America.[229] As Inez brought the literary world to the suffrage movement, and the "gilded suffragists" in New York City brought social prestige to the suffrage movement, Beatrice brought the theater to the suffrage movement. In 1910, her friend and future Scituate neighbor Inez Irwin said, "It's now fashionable among the actresses to be a suffragette -- Ethel Barrymore has come out for it and Beatrice Forbes-Robertson has even abandoned the stage to lecture upon it."[230]

In 1910, Beatrice received a copy of *The Yellow Wall Paper*, a classic feminist novel, signed ("With Love") by the book's author, Charlotte Perkins Gilman. Gilman was a leading feminist, and she would become a founding member of Heterodoxy in 1912 along with Beatrice and Inez Haynes Irwin.[231]

The book was likely a wedding present. In 1910, Beatrice married New York lawyer Swinburne Hale.[232]

Swinburne graduated from Harvard in 1905, where he was class poet, and from Harvard Law School in 1908. His mother, whose family name was Swinburne, was a graduate of Vassar College and a proponent of woman suffrage. In 1909, he was smitten with Beatrice when she spoke for woman suffrage, a movement Swinburne also supported.[233]

Swinburne Hale, senior photo, Harvard Class Album 1905. HUD 305.04 page 91. Courtesy of Harvard University Archives.

In 1910, besides getting married, Beatrice placed herself in the midst of the American woman suffrage campaign.

Beatrice and Harriot Stanton Blatch organized a matinee performance to benefit the Equality League of Self-Supporting Women (later named the Women's Political Union) on March 31, 1910, in New York City. The matinee had three suffrage plays, culminating in the suffrage drama *How the Vote Was Won.* A poem by Charlotte Perkins Gilman was also read. Performers included Johnston Forbes-Robertson (Beatrice's uncle and famous actor), Mrs. John E. Milholland (mother of suffragist Inez Milholland), Katherine Duer Mackay (socialite suffragist), and Harriott Stanton Blatch (New York suffrage leader). The matinee echoed the 1900 performance orchestrated by Inez Haynes Irwin and Maud Wood Park to benefit the College Equal Suffrage League.[234]

Also in 1910, Beatrice spoke at NAWSA's national convention, sharing the stage with Charlotte Perkins Gilman, among others.[235]

In June 1911, before the coronation of a new king, King George of England, Beatrice was reportedly going to participate in the Coronation Procession of the Women of Britain. The suffragist demonstration, not part of the official coronation ceremonies, stretched across the streets of London from Blackfriars Bridge to the Albert Hall. Perhaps this event partly inspired the great Washington procession of 1913 in advance of the inauguration of a new president.[236]

Beatrice was one of about 20 original members of the feminist group Heterodoxy. It started in New York City in 1912 and included Inez Haynes Irwin and her sister Daisy Thompson. Inez developed an early love of the theater, actors and actresses, and she even saw some English actresses perform. In addition, her father had been an actor and lived in England. Inez would have been excited to befriend Beatrice Hale.[237]

In addition, Beatrice, Swinburne, and Inez spoke at the same suffrage event at the Metropolitan Temple in New York City on March 11, 1912. It featured five-minute speeches by 25 eminent suffragists responding to anti-suffragist objections.[238]

"INDIRECT INFLUENCE IS ENOUGH"

By Beatrice Forbes-Robertson Hale

Mrs. Forbes-Robertson Hale

"THE INDIRECT INFLUENCE of women is enough" say the anti-suffragists, and conjure up a vision of the all-wise mother-wife, guiding her adoring men-folk by the light of her almost supernatural intuition up the foothills of the ideal.

How alluring are these flights of sentiment! How pathetic that we suffragists must apply the brakes to these starry aeroplanes and jolt them rudely to the earth! Yet it must be done, and can be, without broken bones or hearts. The sentimentalists must disembark and change wagons, if they desire indeed to be hitched to a star. We invite their inspection of an aeroplane of our own, built of reason and lofty purpose, and calculated—if properly driven—to carry us all to a region

"MEN WOULD CEASE TO LOVE US"

By Swinburne Hale

Mr. Hale

LADIES and Gentlemen, you will all cease to love each other as soon as you all have the vote. The anti-suffragists have said it! It has been proclaimed in the pamphlets of the League for the Useless Education of Women; it has resounded from the platforms of the National Association Opposed to Further Progress. Even the Committee for the Perpetuation of the Eighteenth Century has endorsed this great fundamental truth. When women vote, men will cease to love them. From which it follows that men will cease to marry them, will cease to have children by them, and will suffer the white nations to decline into sterility and emptiness, so that the invading Mongolian hordes of the year 2000 will find only deserted continents

Arguments countering objections to women voting. Excerpts from NAWSA booklet with speeches at meeting in New York City, March 11, 1912. Courtesy of Schlesinger Library (ref: 3x2, 32_002690_043_0001_0002_From_51_to_100-3).

Ten days after this meeting, Beatrice spoke at a dinner meeting held in New York City by the Men's League for Woman's Suffrage of the State of New York. Other speakers included Charlotte Perkins Gilman and Max Eastman, the secretary and a founder of the Men's League. Max was also editor of *The Masses*, where Inez was a fiction editor.[239]

By this time in 1912, Swinburne was on the executive committee of the Men's League, which began in 1909 or 1910, and he was active in its events.[240]

The Men's League participated in a series of suffrage parades in New York City in 1911 and 1912. Swinburne marched in the 1911 parade and the May 4, 1912, parade, carrying a banner for the League. Will Irwin also marched in the May 4 parade, and his report is described in another chapter. Even more importantly, Swinburne's wife Beatrice was in the parade on May 4, 1912.[241]

Beatrice was a conspicuous figure in the parade. She was in the cavalry brigade of 72 women horseback riders leading the parade up Fifth Avenue. Many of her fellow members of Heterodoxy also marched in the parade. About half a million people watched the parade. Beatrice later wrote a short item for the *Woman's Journal* entitled "Parade a Glorified Vision of Democracy."[242]

Women horseback riders leading the May 4, 1912, suffrage parade in New York City. Source: *Harper's Weekly*, May 11, 1912.

The May 4 parade was "the largest demonstration of its kind this country has witnessed," according to the *Literary Digest*, and "America's Greatest Suffrage Parade," according to the *Boston American*.[243]

The great success of the New York City parade on May 4 led to other parades all over the country, including one on May 8 in Kalamazoo, Michigan. There, Beatrice rode in one of the leading cars and later gave a speech.[244]

Beatrice was back in New York City on November 9, 1912, in the role of the Grand Marshal of a torchlight parade down Fifth Avenue. She rode a white horse and led the parade of more than 15,000 suffragists. Marchers carried Chinese lanterns and flaring torches. The parade celebrated the winning of four new suffrage states. A printed announcement for the parade had letterhead with Swinburne Hale as one of three representatives of the National Men's League for Woman Suffrage. Swinburne Hale and Will Irwin joined up to 2,000 men marching in the parade. Half a million people watched the parade. It was even larger than the great parade held in the same city just six months before.[245]

Suffragists parade up Fifth Avenue at East 23rd St., New York City, May 4, 1912. Photo by Paul Thompson. Courtesy of Wikimedia/National Archives (Identifier 593556/208-PR-14M-1).

Beatrice was active for many years promoting woman suffrage. Her name appears on up to 178 pages of the *Woman's Journal*, mostly from 1911 to 1913, when she was touring America. In 1911, she staged a suffrage comedy by Charlotte Perkins Gilman at the Broadway Theatre in New York, her hometown. Then, from 1911 to 1912, she went on tour to speak about suffrage in at least the following places, sometimes multiple times: Montclair, NJ; Kalamazoo, MI; Detroit; Baltimore; Connecticut; Pittsburgh; Chicago; Milwaukee; Cincinnati; Grand Rapids, MI; Williamsport, PA; Malden, MA (at the first suffrage meeting ever held in the city); and Chestnut Hill, MA.[246]

Busy, busy Bea.

In September 1913, Beatrice spoke in Scituate as the guest of Inez Haynes Gillmore (her married name at the time). More than 50 women attended the talk, which was held at Inez's summer home on Second Cliff. Beatrice was also spending the summer on Second Cliff.[247]

Beatrice was one of the speakers on the second evening of the "Feminist Mass Meetings" held in 1914 at Cooper Union in New York City. Her topic was "The Right of the Mother to Her Profession."[248]

Beatrice would continue to give talks on suffrage and other topics on women's issues all over America. Her touring days in 1914 and later are described in more detail later in this chapter.

In New York, Beatrice and Swinburne were friends with Rose O'Neill. She was perhaps the most famous illustrator in the country, and the originator of the Kewpie doll. In addition, she was "keen about the fight for woman suffrage and [she] walked in some parades, wore a placard, and made drawings [and made posters] for the cause." At Madison Square, she was asked to speak on a platform and "'hold the crowd' until the next speaker, Will Irwin, arrived." That was Rose's first and only suffrage speech. She would later create the frontispiece for Swinburne's book.[249]

Poster by Rose O'Neill, *Give Mother the Vote!*, 1915. Courtesy of Wikimedia/Missouri History Museum.

Beatrice kept in touch with other friends in New York. After returning from a speaking tour, in November 1916, Beatrice had lots of news for Swinburne, who was traveling to Paris.[250]

- Her old friend Mary Gawthorpe accepted enthusiastically their offer of Swinburne's old apartment on Jane Street.
- She would be dining at the Laidlaws. The Laidlaws were important figures in the woman suffrage movement. James Lees Laidlaw was president of the National Chapter of the Men's League for Women's Suffrage, where Swinburne was on its executive committee. His wife, Harriet Wright Burton Laidlaw, was an important suffragist who organized the 1912 torchlight parade, in which Beatrice was the Grand Marshal.[251]
- She was going to have lunch at the Colony Club with playwright Rachel Crothers, whose plays were noted for having feminist themes.[252]
- She "dropped in then to [Inez's sister] Daisy Thompson's shop, & found Inez, much to my delight, fresh from the boat. She was most interesting about the war of course."[253]

Like Inez, Beatrice wrote books. They included *What Women Want: An Interpretation of the Feminist Movement*, published in 1914. In the book she described her emotional reaction to witnessing a woman suffrage parade a short time before in "a great American city" – no doubt this was the procession in Washington, DC, in 1913.[254]

Beatrice's book heralded "the new man," such as those (like her husband) who marched in the suffrage parades in New York City under the banner of the Men's League for Woman Suffrage. Her book also critiqued the anti-suffragists:

> In America the anti-suffrage women are, I think, more numerous, and certainly more efficient, than in England. They are officered by wealthy women who have leisure to give to the work, and have as good a corps of paid and unpaid speakers as such a negative cause could readily produce. They were first organized among the conservatives of Boston, and have spread to many of the cities of the East and Middle West.[255]

In truth, plenty of wealthy women worked *for* woman suffrage, such as Pauline Agassiz Shaw in Boston, and Alva Vanderbilt Belmont in New York.[256] But Beatrice was accurate in saying the anti-suffragists were first organized by the Boston elite. Not so wealthy were the suffragists who summered in Scituate.

Hale Family in Scituate, An Overview

Beatrice and her family spent summers on Second Cliff in Scituate starting in 1913. She was almost certainly attracted by Inez's summer presence there. Beatrice would become a member of a "considerable literary colony" in Scituate that included Inez, according to a 1916 guidebook. The guidebook mentioned Beatrice as a "suffragette" – a British term.[257]

At first, the Hales rented the Tobin cottage, it seems, which had a view of Peggotty Beach. By 1916, they moved a short way up Peggotty Beach Road and stayed at the Barber cottage (perhaps a pair of cottages). The Tobin and Barber cottages are shown on the 1903 map, with the Barber cottage the fifth from the beach. This was a bit closer to the beach than Inez's house.[258]

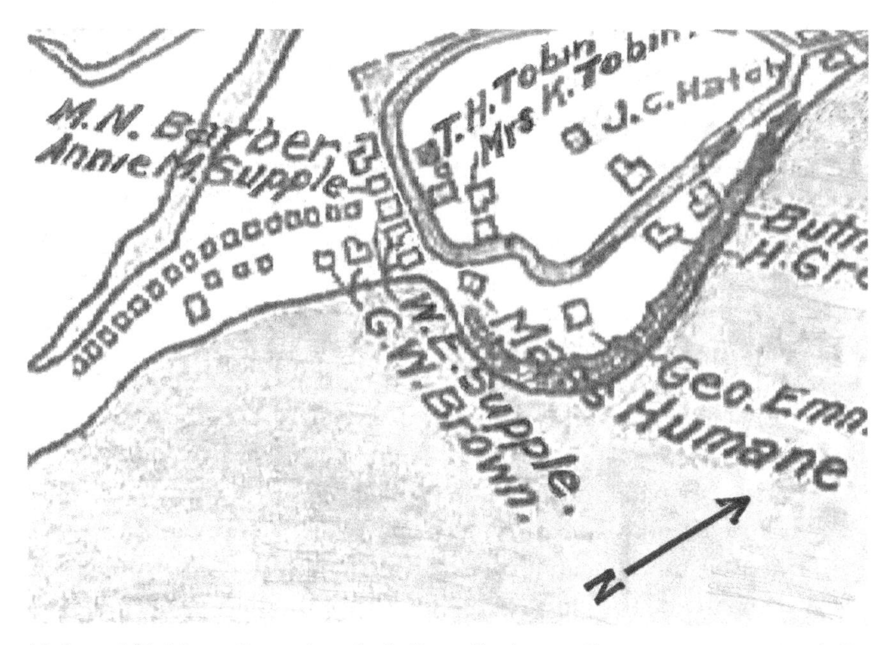

Hales at Tobin cottage (center), then Barber cottage, upper center left. Barber cottage is fifth cottage from Peggotty Beach and the ocean (bottom), in this author-modified detail of 1903 *Atlas of Plymouth County*. Courtesy of State Library of Massachusetts.

Beatrice's letters have survived, fortunately, since they give us a view of summer life in Scituate, her busy lecture tours, and her marital difficulties with Swinburne. Most of her letters were to Swinburne, and she wrote husband Swinburne frequently. She often wrote from Scituate, since he was busy practicing law in New York City. The letters are eloquent, and describe well what was going on in their lives. She almost always began with "Dearest Toodie." That was her nickname for him, unless she was upset, in which case she would call him "Bob," a name used by family and friends. She always said how much she loved and missed him. Her letters almost always ended with "Thy Beatrice."[259]

Beatrice's letters describe the family's arrival in Scituate in 1913. She listed many summer residents and a few locals that she met. The letters really capture what summer life was like in Scituate. Of course, these letters often mention Inez and her then-husband Rufus Gillmore, Inez's brother Harry Haynes, and Inez's future husband Will Irwin.

By definition, Beatrice's letters to Swinburne describe what happened when he was *not* there, and we don't have his own observations. But the letters we have show that he liked getting away to the cottage, he enjoyed being with his children there, and he generally treated Beatrice with affection. Spending the winter of 1917–1918 in the cottage inspired one of his poems, "Friends," later published in his book. Scituate had an impact on him. And Beatrice viewed it as a special, peaceful place.

The Hales spent summers there, and even some winters, from 1913 until at least early 1920. Swinburne bought the Barber cottage in 1919. In 1920, Beatrice and Swinburne divorced. Their time in Scituate is discussed in more detail below.

Beatrice Arrival in Scituate

Beatrice arrived in Scituate in July 1913, with "Baby" (Sanchia, born in 1911) and her nurse. This was probably her first visit to Scituate. Soon after arrival, she wrote Swinburne all about the journey there. She said Mr. Gillmore (Inez's husband) had kindly fetched their mail for them. She thought Swinburne would like it there.[260]

Her first impressions at the cottage on Peggotty Beach Road were:

> … poking ones head out of the window, one sees the water, a mere stone's throw away. There are wild roses & pleasant weeds round the house, & the cottages stand well apart from each other in a green lane with bushes & even small trees here & there, so that there is no feeling whatever of being in a "row". The larger cottages are on rising ground … the Gilmore's nearest, then the Haynes', while the Merwins are quite a quarter of a mile further back from the sea, in a little farm house with proper paint & wallpaper, meadows round them with the tide running up in channels, & a tree by the front door.
>
> … I like the cottage very much. [The cottage is noisy, and] little & clean & airy, so absolutely primitive, yet adequate, that it almost gives one the feeling of being in camp.
>
> … Mrs [Harry] Haynes has lent me a camp cot for baby …. The water from our fawcett is no good for drinking, but a neighbour's well supplies deficiencies.[261]

Beatrice said "the 'group' down here" consisted of:

> At the Gilmores —
>
> > The Gilmores [Rufus and Inez Haynes Gillmore]
> >
> > Mrs Dugan (housekeeper & older sister to Inez H. G.) [Maude Dugan/Duganne]
> >
> > Mrs. D's little daughter [Phyllis Duganne].
> >
> > Mr & Mrs. Gilliam Haynes, visitors from Chicago, [Inez's brother Gideon]
> >
> > Mr Will Irwin

> Mr "Al" Jennings (the convict, bandit, train robber, gunman, etc. & later lawyer & reform politician)

At the Haynes —

> The Harry Haynes (Mrs H. at present away) [Inez's brother]
>
> The Hales (Mother & step-father to the H. Haynes) [not related to Swinburne Hale]

The Merwin Family [Samuel Merwin, playwright and writer][262]

Some of them played tennis in the afternoon. Harry Haynes had a tennis court on his property. Beatrice watched. She did not play tennis. She preferred walks. The group gathered in the evening. Sam Merwin and Will Irwin were delightful, singing an opera they had acted in during that winter. Then,

> Al [Jennings] ex-convict, talked, telling about his prison experiences. He is marvelous. — "I don't believe there ain't no such critter." I hope to goodness he will be here when you arrive. Irwin tells me he is full of bullet holes, & has killed many men. [He was jailed, pardoned, and reformed, becoming a lawyer in Oklahoma and a politician.] He was in jail with O. Henry, & was his most intimate friend. He is an ardent woman suffragist, & tells me he is going to "take the matter up."[263]

Inez's sister Daisy Thompson said Al spent six weeks with them. "When the town heard that the Irwins were going to entertain a bank robber who had done time, all doors and windows were securely fastened but within a month Al Jennings had become a kind of hero."[264]

Al Jennings and Will Irwin soon wrote a book about Al's colorful exploits, published the following year, 1914.[265]

Many of the group came from New York City. They could easily take a boat (as Beatrice did) or train to Boston. From Boston, trains to Scituate were frequent, took a little over an hour, and cost only 60 cents.[266]

Two days after Beatrice arrived, the "group" was complete, with the arrival of the Boardman Robinsons, and Carl Ruggles and his wife. Boardman was a terrific cartoonist who worked for *The Masses*, a leftist magazine where Inez was fiction editor.[267]

Beatrice knew Inez, of course, and she had met Will Irwin and Harry Haynes, but not all the other members of the group. She commented on some of them in her letters to Swinburne. She described the Ruggles group as "a hideous little mad composer, — they say a genius, — & his rather charming wife, who gave up her career as a singer in order to nurse him along. ... he is, as Sam Merwin said, exactly like a gargoyle." In fact, Carl's later biographer described her first sight of him as a short man, and said, in profile, "his long pointed nose stood out like a beak."[268]

Beatrice reported,

> ... I find Will Irwin quite lacking in charm, which is odd, as the first time I met him I thought he had a little.
>
> Yesterday I went to Mrs Haynes' hen [woman] Tea-party. About 30 women were there, of all kinds. One of them, a Miss Beckington, a thorough lady of good sort. Has a barn here made into a cottage, is a miniature painter, & has a studio in Carnegie Hall. Not young, but an awfully nice woman. I am going to see her. I stayed at the Haynes' for supper. ...
>
> [Sam Merwin] has hired [a] row-boat to go through the channels in the marshes at high tide, and is going to take me out in it. I dare say we can borrow it from him when you come. By the way, apropos of bathing, there is no surf here at all, as we are in a little bay, & there are boats anchored that we can swim to, as well as a raft.[269]

A few weeks later, with Swinburne working on a long legal case in New York, Beatrice wrote,

> I read Mrs. Gilmore's serial [later a book] "Angel Island." I was really charmed with it. The writing is very well done, quite lovely in places, & the idea is excellent. ... Last night I read a mystery novel of Mr Gilmore's, but was disappointed to find the style completely undistinguished, & the characterization conventional. He tells me he was a complete beginner when it was written.[270]

The weather warmed up, and Beatrice finally got to swim at Peggotty Beach:

> I have had two good swims since writing last, on Saturday & Sunday afternoons. ... Yesterday I managed to get onto the raft, where Will Irwin & "Fuzz" [a dog] were sitting. Will I. & I plunged off, & Fuzz followed, landing with his stomach square on top of my head, & his hind paws scratching my arms! Irwin, who is only apparently accustomed to very poor woman swimmers, was quite alarmed lest I sink, or become panic-stricken, or what not! I some re-assured him![271]

That first summer of 1913, as she relaxed in the cottage in Scituate, Beatrice had a long letter from William Feakins, a prominent booking agent for lecturers. She called him "Feaks." He was already talking about the following spring. All sorts of offers were coming in for her to speak. This would continue and extend her prominent and extensive work for the suffrage movement.[272]

By the end of the year, she would give birth to twins to join baby Sanchia: Rosemary and Clemency, born December 1913. They would become known as the "suffrage twins" as Beatrice went out to tour America.[273]

Touring America, 1914–1919

For Beatrice, the lecture "circuit" would have been a misnomer. It was not an orderly movement in a circular track around various cities and towns. It was more like random train trips here and there, usually within somewhat the same region. Sometimes they covered great distances, going out as far as Colorado from her home base in New York. There were plans, engagements, itineraries, and schedules, but they changed at a moment's notice. The notice came from her booking agent, William Feakins, by mail and sometimes by telegram. "Feaks" was as much a taskmaster as an agent.

Much of the time on tour, Beatrice was tired and did not get enough sleep. Few of the hotels engaged for her were restful and pleasant. She did not like many of the places she went, complaining of "these mean and ugly little towns with their houses lacking all taste and beauty, and their inmates utterly ignorant of cultivation or grace." She was often unimpressed with the people she met. "I stay with many women & meet many hens, — house succeeds house & hostess hostess, all middle-class, & all alike. They make very little impression on the brain one way or the other." She was rarely with friends.[274]

There was little glamor and prestige in this suffrage work, despite the publicity surrounding her talks. Beatrice's suffrage tours meant grinding it out, one meeting at a time, city by city, town by town. Perhaps this is how the suffrage movement should be remembered, rather than by the hoopla of the great parades.

1914

Beatrice's tour in May 1914 included Ottawa and Pittsburgh. Then it was on to Oswego and Rochester, NY, then back to their home in Forest Hills on Long Island, NY, for a brief rest.[275]

Then she was on to West Virginia. On June 2, she stayed at The Waldo hotel in Clarksburg, WV. It was an elegant hotel. But she reported, "The people here are nuts, & put me in this hotel surrounded by car and train tracks so that sleep wasn't easy."[276]

Waldo Hotel, Clarksburg, WV, postcard posted 1909. Author's collection.

In a break from the tour, Beatrice traveled to England in July 1914, just before England declared war on Germany. On her return, she was able to relax in Scituate until late September. Then she was back on tour: Pittsburgh and nearby Connellsville and Greensburg, then on to Vermont. There, she earned a check "honestly earned, because they (a large roomful of men and women) ate up my dramatic hot air with avidity, enjoyed themselves hugely, and paid me many fat compliments at the end. Joy!" When she arrived back at Grand Central Station, her agent Feakins met her "in a grand sweat because he had received no cheque from me." She assured him she had paid him "$50 for his 10% — the two Penna. weeks, and $18.75 for his Pittsburg & Huntingdon 25% — making $68.75 in all."[277]

1915

On February 23, 1915, Beatrice spoke in Baltimore to a group of 200 people at a dinner of the Woman's Suffrage Party of Maryland. Her speech was the big feature of the evening. The *Maryland Suffrage News* called her speech convincing and brilliant, and said it was warmly applauded. The *Baltimore Sun* reported that some of the anti-suffragists in attendance were unconvinced.[278]

In June, Beatrice came under attack by the anti-suffragists. In a letter to the *Boston Evening Record*, George B. Conroy criticized Beatrice's book *What Women Want* for a number of reasons, inferring that she favored unmarried motherhood, which was incorrect. The *Woman's Journal* pointed out his inaccuracies and said:

> Mr. Conroy is one of the publicity men employed by the anti-suffragists. He and officers of the "anti" association are scattering these attacks continually in the press and in public addresses. The systematic use of poisonous falsehood and slander in a campaign is on a level with the use of poisonous gases as a weapon in war.[279]

In September 1915, Beatrice spoke at Alexander Hall in Princeton University, saying, "Men and women are not equal, and as individuals never can become equal, but we do believe that they should have equality of opportunity."[280]

Beatrice Hale gave many talks in 1915 in Massachusetts, as the campaign heated up for the state's suffrage referendum. In June, she spoke at the Waltham Equal Suffrage League. On August 12, she gave a reading at the Scituate Woman's Club. She was joined by Will Irwin, back from reporting in Europe on the World War, who gave a talk on his experiences at the war front. The matrons were Mrs. E. R. Bacon, Miss Annie Kelly, Mrs. H. Warren Cushing, Mrs. N. J. Neall, Mrs. Roger S. Dix, and Mrs. George C. Warren. In September, Beatrice spoke in Manchester-by-the-Sea, and in Jamaica Plain, where 800 persons attended. On October 31, Beatrice Hale closed the campaign for suffrage in Massachusetts at Springfield, with an audience of 1,000 persons.[281]

Despite Beatrice's best efforts, and those of many other suffragists, Massachusetts defeated the suffrage referendum.

About the same time, New York also defeated a suffrage referendum. But suffrage leaders there did not give up. They held a meeting at Cooper Union and raised $100,000 to continue the fight for suffrage. Speakers at the meeting included Carrie Chapman Catt, Dr. Anna Howard Shaw (president of NWSA), and Beatrice Forbes-Robertson

Hale. Beatrice was clearly considered a key figure in the movement, and enjoyed distinguished company.[282]

1916

In January 1916, Beatrice spoke in favor of woman suffrage before a joint session of the House and Senate in Kentucky. Later, she gave talks in Memphis, TN, and Kenwood (near Oneida), NY. She wrote Swinburne, "This tour is purgatorial, and the worst is yet to come, for so far, I have been with friends." [283]

After a summer in Scituate, Beatrice was back on the suffrage road in October, to West Virginia again, and Ohio.[284]

During her tour, anti-suffragists accused Beatrice of advocating free love. The *Woman's Journal* came to her defense in articles written by Alice Stone Blackwell, rebutting the accusation:

> In her book, "What Women Want," Mrs. Hale, in her chapter on "Love," says (page 270): "Faithful monogamy must ever be woman's standard in love, because only in its still certainty can she fitly prepare and keep the place for her child."[285]
>
> ... the opponents of equal rights ... are circulating a leaflet [saying Mrs. Hale believes in easy divorce]. This is a dastardly slander. Mrs. Hale advocates nothing of the sort .... In her book she argues at length against unmarried motherhood, trial marriages and "the fallacy of free love."[286]

These themes reappeared in a lengthy interview published in the *Boston Globe* in late 1916. Beatrice described the ideal woman for a successful marriage:

> The "mate-woman" ... is the woman who believes that she does not possess in herself all the qualities and attributes, but that only when she is united with the right man do the two become a human being. When both husband and wife feel that, separated, they are as

> the broken halves of a coin; that together they form a complete, efficient unit – then you have the real marriage.
>
> ... I believe in marriage, spiritually, physically, eugenically. ... It is the most beautiful ideal of human relationship that the human mind has conceived.[287]

These ideals contrasted incongruously with Beatrice's private problems in her marriage to Swinburne, who had affairs with other women, as discussed later in this chapter.

1917

Beatrice's busy 1917 began with the following notice in the *Woman's Journal.* "A suffrage training school is to be conducted during January and February by the educational section of the New York State Woman Suffrage Party." Subjects would include "organization and suffrage activities, by Mrs. James Lees Laidlaw and other organizers, and public speaking, by Mrs. Beatrice Forbes-Robertson Hale."[288]

In January, Beatrice addressed the annual mid-winter convention of the Massachusetts Woman Suffrage Association (MWSA).[289]

An early stop in her next tour was Charleston, SC, where she stayed with some "really nice women," who were all staying at their bungalow on an island in the bay. Beatrice reported, "My meeting last night was really splendid, about 4 hundred people, a collection of over $50, and actually a smiling, laughing audience."[290]

Then it was on to Savannah, GA, Daytona, FL, Chicago, Tennessee, Peoria, Minneapolis, Kansas City, MO, and New Orleans.[291]

By May 1917, Beatrice was back in Scituate for part of the summer.[292]

Then she had an important engagement on Friday, August 10, at Chautauqua, NY. This was the famous educational and cultural center founded in the 1870s. It featured about 100 lectures during a nine-week season by some of America's leading figures. Beatrice gave the key address on August 10, Suffrage Day. She spoke on "Women in the Great War."[293]

The Chautauqua journal published a transcript of her speech the next day. She had an interesting view of the militant suffragists then picketing the White House.

> I have been asked what I think of the militants picketing the White House. Personally, I don't care what they do but as a member of the suffrage organization, I do care because we are engaged in bringing the war to an end. Anyone who makes rude faces at Congress will have rude faces made at him by the people, and this is merely hindering. Congress is not going to pass the Suffrage Bill now because they are too exclusively occupied with other matters. But if they were to pass it, one way not to make them do it would be to "pull" faces at them. If they are snarled at, they will stand back and snarl too. If militancy didn't succeed in England how can it succeed in the United States where it is only copy-catting? … The great masses move by instinct, and if you get them to feel right they will not make the militant an excuse to vote against suffrage. Show them the whole picture, so big that they can't see the little spots that blemish it.[294]

With these words, Beatrice was on record against the militant approach taken by the National Woman's Party, of which her friend Inez was a leader. When Beatrice spoke, suffragist picketers had already been arrested in June. Still to come, in November, was the "Night of Terror," when picketers were jailed and brutally beaten.[295]

Beatrice was happy with her Chautauqua speech, which had one of her largest audiences. A few days later, on Sunday, August 12, she wrote Swinburne, "I had a great success (you will be glad to hear) on Friday with my speech. I spoke before several thousand people, in a roofed-over open air amphitheatre which has the most perfect acoustics. People said it was the best speech they had had this year, & similar remarks."[296]

The occasion also gave Beatrice a chance to visit with her good friend Mary Gawthorpe (1881–1973), a British suffragist who moved to the US in 1916. "We had an informal suffrage meeting in the evening, with a supper before it. Mary Gawthorpe was there, & with me all the afternoon (after my speech) and in the evening. My hostess here invited her to luncheon yesterday, so that I had a good chance to see her, & enjoyed it immensely."[297]

Then Beatrice traveled to Bay View, MI, a resort town in far north Michigan. The Bay View Assembly there, where Beatrice was to speak, seemed to be a junior version of Chautauqua. She met with Trumbull White (1868–1941), who was a noted editor, prolific author, and war correspondent. He was also director of the Bay View Assembly in 1916–1917. Beatrice said he was a "man who has read & likes both my books, & spoke about them glowingly in introducing me – which warmed my heart to him. His wife & young sons are also here."[298]

In September, Beatrice returned to upstate New York. She said, "Made a speech at the state fair yesterday [in Syracuse] between a horse race & the auctioning of a pig for the Red X [Red Cross] fund. The pig applauded my remarks by beating a tattoo [drumroll] with his hoofs." She stayed in Poughkeepsie with two women Vassar professors.[299]

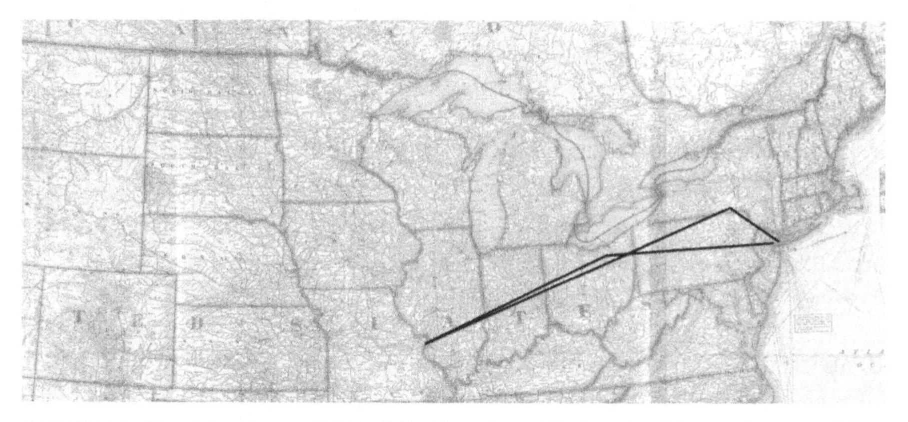

1917 Oct. Beatrice tour: NYC, Binghamton, St. Louis, Akron, Jersey City. Source: National Railway Pub. Co. 1918 map, Library of Congress.

In October, Beatrice traveled to Binghamton, NY, St. Louis, Akron, and Jersey City. It was "incessant travelling" by train and "pretty much of a grind," according to Beatrice.[300]

The tour included Owego, NY, where a local newspaper report called Beatrice "one of the most sought after suffrage speakers in New York." She spoke on "Woman's Work in War Time," as America had entered World War I.[301]

Later on the tour, Beatrice stayed with the Seiberling family at their fabulous estate in Akron, Ohio. Stan Hywet Hall was built between 1912 and 1915 for F. A. Seiberling, co-founder of Goodyear Tire, and his wife Gertrude, an accomplished artist and patron of the arts who attended Lasell Seminary in Auburndale, MA. It included a magnificent Tudor Revival manor house and service buildings.[302]

Beatrice was impressed with this place.

> I find myself in halls of incredible splendor – the result of a 10-year boom in Goodyear tyres. The grounds are 8 or 9 hundred rolling & wooded acres close to the town, the house, Tudor, the furniture, mostly genuine English Jacobean, Elizabethan, Hepplewhite, etc. — No mahogany except the Hepplewhite. The hall soars to a gothic roof — the drawing room (of mythic size) conceals a pipe-organ played by electricity. Below it, is a gymnasium. There is a huge & deep swimming pool in which I have just swum; the bathrooms are countless, every bedstead is a hundred years old at least; there are terraces, pools, fountains, a little lake, canoes, saddle horses, a chef, housekeeper (the only lady in the house), a separate kitchen for the breakfast room, a servants' dining room far finer than most masters', & I know not what.[303]

On her way back from Akron, Beatrice had a speaking engagement in Ithaca, NY, where Swinburne was born. She visited his old house, and described to him how it looked. In addition, she "had an hour's wait at Buffalo, & little Mary Gawthorpe [her suffragist friend from Britain] came down to the station & lunched with me – that was very nice. … Mary was delighted you have left the law." Swinburne had decided to become a poet.[304]

After a few days rest in New York City, Beatrice was back on the road. She stayed in Penn Yan, NY, in the Finger Lakes area, not far from Ithaca. As she wrote Swinburne,

> Have I ever heard of Penn Yan before? No! Do I ever want to hear of it again? Ditto! It is the kind of place I think you have never seen in which the best hotel has no bathrooms, the steam-heat smells to heaven, & each bedroom enjoys at least two varieties of wall paper. The inhabitants are agricultural & stolid, & only 54 of them were alive enough to venture forth into the dangers of a suffrage meeting![305]

Late in 1917, now quartered in Scituate, Beatrice was off on another tour, this time to St. Louis (again), Kansas City, Chicago, and Madison.[306]

1918

In early 1918, Beatrice was again on tour, speaking in Cleveland and Savannah on "Women in the War." When she reached the Washington, DC, train station, she "bumped into Ida Proper, an old member of Heterodoxy, who is now working in the War Office. She took me to her rooms, we had lunch together & she told me interesting things about Washington."[307]

Washington represented a turn that many suffragists and feminists took at this time, toward war work. Beatrice met with Mrs. Mina C. Van Winkle, who formed and had been president of the Woman's Political Union of New Jersey, affiliated with the NJ Woman Suffrage Association. She had also been a friend of suffragist Harriot Stanton Blatch. Now she was head of the Lecture Bureau at the US Food Administration.[308]

The Food Administration's slogan was "Food will win the war — don't waste it!" The agency was responsible for providing food to the US Army and US allies, stabilizing food prices and supplies in the US, reducing domestic consumption, and increasing home production of food. Wheat, meat, and sugar needed to be saved, not wasted.[309]

Mrs. Mina Van Winkle in uniform of US Food Administration, 1917–1918, lecturing on Victory gardening in World War I. Courtesy of Library of Congress.

food – don't waste it

1 – use less wheat and meat
2 – buy local foods
3 – serve just enough
4 – use what is left

United States Food Administration

US Food Administration poster [PR 055-07, Folder 29], 1917–1918. Courtesy of New-York Historical Society.

The agency was hiring speakers to go out in America and promote its goals. According to Beatrice, Mrs. Van Winkle (whom she had met before) had "great difficulty holding her job & engaging women speakers because of the 'Male' attitude of the Administration." She was going to try to have Beatrice meet Herbert Hoover, head of the Administration.[310]

Probably because of Mrs. Van Winkle, Beatrice shortly became a speaker for the Food Administration. Some agency speakers were said to have "stirred crowds to such a pitch that in rural communities farmers arose to say that henceforth their 'hogs belonged to Hoover.'"[311] Beatrice said, "I intend to show them how a Food speech should be made — I hear most of the men they use are dull."[312]

Her scheduler now, instead of William Feakins, was W. A. Milne, head of the Food Administration's Speaking Division. Beatrice would travel even further around America than before, all the way out to Colorado. In six weeks in February and March 1918, she visited Cleveland, Ypsilanti, Chicago, Louisville, Maryville (MO), Kansas City, Colorado cities (Denver, Idaho Springs, Pueblo, and Colorado Springs), and Little Rock, AR, her furthest point south.[313]

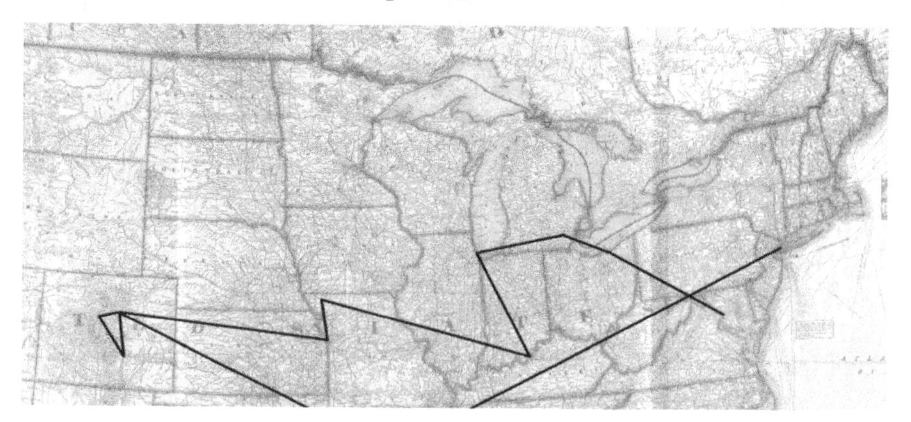

1918 Feb.–March Beatrice tour out to Colorado & Arkansas for US Food Administration. Train lines were not as straight as shown here. Source: National Railway Publication Company 1918 map, Library of Congress.

Unlike before, Beatrice was having a "ripping time."

> I've never before had a trip on which I have been so well looked after, & travelling always with one or two friends is a very different thing from the loneliness of my usual tours. Everywhere we are met by minions of

> the Food Ad., — I have not carried my own bags once, I think, since we left Minnesota.
>
> Mr Trefz [a key Food Administration official and lecturer on the tour] & I have become very good friends. He is really a fine chap, and is – in spite of being a regular man's man, fundamentally good, I believe – just the kind of friend I can enjoy. He is a Princeton man, but has even more than the Will Irwin westerner's lack of polish. Marcus Simpson hinted to Trefz that I might correct some of his French pronunciations. He replied "she is already correcting not only my French, but my English!"[314]

By May 1918, Swinburne joined the Army's Military Intelligence branch, working out of Washington, DC. Beatrice began addressing her letters to him as Captain Swinburne Hale. In one, she wrote about her great success on tour for the Food Administration:

> You will be glad to hear that I have had a great success with my first 2 big meetings. The state Administrator Mr. Spaulding has telegraphed Washington to that effect, & I have already had congratulations from Milne! A man rang up my hostess this morning, & asked her to tell me that the result of my speech on him was that he should buy $2000 more Liberty bonds, sow 2 acres more potatoes, & eat no sugar till the end of the war! Rather touching?[315]

In May, Beatrice was getting many compliments, a service pin, and roses. Later that month, she reported,

> The tour, on the professional side, is going very well. I had over 1000 people both last night and Monday, & besides that, spoke in 2 high schools & a factory yesterday, & am to speak in another high school in twenty minutes from now. But I am alone this time – no company in manager or other official is travelling with me; I have no friends in any of the towns I am to

> be in this week; the hotels are empty & strange, and I am bored.[316]

Her tour in May took her to Manchester, NH, Bangor, ME, Portsmouth, NH, Barre, VT, Hanover, NH, and Concord (near Buffalo), NY. She was so busy that she did not have much of a chance to visit her children in Scituate or see Swinburne in Washington. Now in the spring, she wrote him about their winter together in Scituate, "I enjoyed our 6 months at Scituate so much — I shall remember them very long, dearest."[317]

But they had marital troubles during this time, discussed later in this chapter.

Her July 1918 tour took her to upstate New York: Rochester, Waverly, Cortland, Oswego, Clarke's Mills, Little Falls, Oneonta, Utica, Seneca Falls, Geneva, Ithaca, and Tarrytown. On July 12, she said, "I had a wonderful meeting at Oswego, in the armory. 2,500 people, a brass band, soldiers, — all for me! Very fine! But I am tired and long for Scituate."[318]

In August, Beatrice returned to Chautauqua as one of the speakers for Food Administration Day. She spoke on "Winning the War." Mr. Picard later described the speech:

> In the evening, Mrs. Beatrice Forbes-Robertson Hale, one of the best known women orators of the world, delivered an address to a large audience. Mrs. Hale, during the existence of the Food Administration, rendered splendid service throughout the country by her eloquent appeals in support of the great cause.[319]

When Beatrice got back to Scituate, she said it was "a vastly successful time at Chautauqua. I addressed 5,000 on Friday night; & Mr. Picard, who had written that 'blurb' about me on the strength of my two speeches in his county in July, said that 'without detriment to these two, this speech was 100% better.' So I made good, & I was glad, for it was really a marvelous audience to talk to."[320]

By October 1918, the influenza pandemic swept into Boston, with severe results.[321] In Scituate, Beatrice reported on October 17,

> The admirable Bostonians are not yet influenza-freed enough for evening meetings, so I bought a strip-ticket, & am commuting daily for noon meetings. Today I made 2 short speeches to the first 3 second sittings of a cafeteria for the hands of Chase & Co, government contracts for soldiers equipment (belts, haversacks, horse blankets, etc) at Watertown, just beyond Cambridge.[322]

The next day, October 18, Beatrice was the featured speaker at a mass meeting organized by the Woman's Liberty Loan Committee of Massachusetts. It was in the final days of a campaign promoting the purchase of the fourth series of Liberty Loans. They were essentially the same as the earlier Liberty Bonds, all serving the country's war effort. The mass meeting was scheduled for the Boston Common, but because of bad weather, it was moved to Tremont Temple. Public health authorities had to give permission for the move, because of concerns about mass meetings during the influenza pandemic. The mass meeting and the committee's out-of-door booths on Boston Common helped raise $3,524,000 in the committee's campaign.[323]

A few days later, on October 22, Beatrice said, "I imagine the ban on Food Meetings will begin to lift soon now, since all theatres, etc. have opened again in Mass."[324]

World War I ended on November 11, 1918. Soon, Beatrice was off to Chicago, where she could be with her children and Swinburne's parents. In Chicago, she gave a talk, reported in the *Chicago Commerce* journal:

> My excuse for being here is that Mr. Hoover [Herbert Hoover, then chief of the Federal Food Administration] sent out last week throughout the United States thirteen or fourteen members of the administration to bring the message of the new work of food conservation for this harvest year to the

> organization of the food administrators throughout the country.[325]

She gave talks in Illinois towns, but then she was recalled to Chicago when two dates were canceled due to the recurrence of influenza.[326]

1919

Beatrice continued touring, perhaps now back on suffrage and feminist topics. In early February 1919, she could be reached c/o Mrs. R. G. Shaw, 1101 Beacon St, Brookline, MA. She was the wife of Robert Gould Shaw II, the son of Pauline Agassiz Shaw, who was so important in the life of Maud Wood Park and Scituate summer suffragist Meyer Bloomfield.[327]

Beatrice knew Mrs. Shaw from a previous tour in 1915, when she gave a talk in Manchester-by-the-Sea on Equal Suffrage. The *Boston Globe* reported then:

> This will be one of the early Autumn events on the North Shore and perhaps the only opportunity there to hear and meet "the beautiful Beatrice Forbes-Robertson," who is now Mrs Swinburne Hale of New York. Mrs Robert Gould Shaw, chairman of the Equal Franchise Committee, will bring Mrs Hale to Manchester in her motor car.[328]

By October 1919, Beatrice was back with the Feakins agency and on tour, to Chicago, Toledo, and Pittsburgh. She said, "These tours are unspeakably boring, being almost wholly for women's clubs." Yet she would continue public speaking for many years afterwards.[329]

Later Times in Scituate

With all this touring, Beatrice looked to Scituate for peaceful relaxation. But summers in Scituate were not always peaceful, as shown by the "suffrage twins" incidents.

The Hales had three daughters, Sanchia (born in May 1911) and twins Rosemary and Clemency (born in December 1913). After her "suffrage twins" were born, Beatrice returned to her lectures, in the midst of the battle for woman suffrage. In a national controversy, the "antis" were outraged by that "brazen Mrs. Hale," presumably for going back to work as a new mother. It would not be their only attacks on her.[330]

In August 1915, when her "suffrage twins" were 18 or 19 months old, they were taken to the beach in Scituate, almost certainly Peggotty Beach. The wife of state representative Peter F. Tague was there. The Tagues owned the former Tobin house overlooking Peggotty Beach, evidently the one that the Hales had rented before. Inez and Will Irwin were acquainted with the Tagues. Mrs. Tague threatened to call the police because the twins bathed naked. Beatrice Hale responded:

> I am engaged in writing every morning, so that I am not on the beach with my children, who during these hours are in charge of either my mother or of a nurse. I have no theories whatever on the subject of unclothed bathing for infants.
>
> I understand that on two or three mornings my mother slipped off their suits at the edge of the water and carried the babies in without them, as the babies were playing in their suits and she wished to have them dry to put on immediately after the dip.
>
> On one such occasion I joined my mother. About that time my mother informed me that a neighbor, personally unknown to us, had objected to the proceeding, since when it has not been repeated. That is the whole matter.[331]

The whole incident was reported in the *New York Times* and other newspapers around the country, with headlines like "Suffrage Twins in Nude Give Shock." This incident, along with the earlier controversy when Beatrice went on tour for suffrage just after the twins were born, meant that the twins made national news twice before they were two years old.[332]

The kerfuffle did not keep Beatrice and the girls from going back to Scituate. On June 21, 1916, Beatrice wrote, "The day was perfect when we arrived. A young blue sky, a full tide in the marshes, and everything looking divinely green."[333]

The Suffrage Twins (clothed), Rosemary (left) and Clemency Hale. *Boston Globe*, August 15, 1915.

That year the Hales were renting Mr. Barber's cottage, about the fifth cottage from Peggotty Beach. (It is shown on the 1903 map detail above.) When they arrived, the furniture and beds they ordered from Leavens' store in Boston had not yet arrived as promised. Nanny and the babies had to stay at the Kent, a hotel on Front Street in Scituate Harbor. Mattresses were fortunately at the cottage, since they came from Welch's store in Scituate Harbor. The servants — Charles, and Louise the cook — slept on the mattresses in their own bedroom. Beatrice stayed with Maude Dugan, Inez's sister, until the furniture finally arrived and was set up.[334]

Beatrice told Swinburne about the people at Second Cliff, including the Pipers, the Futrelles, the Miners, and the Renaults. She added,

> Phyllis Dugan is a sweet little thing with a maiden's budding figure. Sanchia adores her already. Maude was apparently delighted to see me & has been most kind. ... The village enquires respectfully after you, & is duly impressed that you go to England on legal business. Howard Frye leaves on Saturday for camp, with his regiment of militia! Even here, rumours of war! Inez & Will alas, will not be back until the autumn; of the old jolly group there will be none.[335]

Howard Frye, about age 29 at the time, was a son of Charles Frye, the owner of a general store and postmaster on Front Street. Inez and Will were away, covering the war in Europe.[336]

Beatrice said the Barber cottage "is immeasurably better than Tobin's." The Hale babies were "in the wildest spirits — saw 3 men in a boat on the marshes, and nearly fell off the porch in their excitement. They will adore it here."[337]

Beatrice was often concerned about finances, through all the years of her letters. For example, on June 28, 1916, she wrote Swinburne,

> This is just to tell you ... that I shall need at least $500 a month during the summer. I had forgotten in speaking of it to you that the May food bills are unpaid, & that as those for Scituate should be paid before we leave here, five months of tradesmen's bills have to be attended to. In addition there is the furniture here to be paid for, & a payment to Barber [owner of cottage] in September.[338]

Later that year, she said she earned $75 one morning speaking on feminism. "Financially it looks as though we shall pull through December by the skin of our eye-teeth." She paid some Macy's and Gimbel's bills, but the October bills would have to wait until the next year.[339]

It is not clear why finances would have been a problem with their two incomes. However, finances were particularly important at this time. They were in the midst of a separation, discussed in more detail elsewhere. Swinburne came up to Scituate for a visit in late August, and that brought her joy and solace. But finances were a problem. They considered renting out their house in Forest Hills and finding a flat (apartment), or maybe two, in New York City.[340]

Beatrice was laying in supplies in case of a national railroad strike threatened at the end of August 1916 by railroad workers. She understood that milk and mail trains would continue to run. Fish and vegetables were available locally. Evidently, the strike was called off, and Beatrice was able to travel to visit Swinburne in September.[341]

On her return to Scituate, Beatrice found that "the place looks very sweet — the weather is perfect, & the air divinely fresh. But — they caught an 8 ft shark off Pegotty [sic] this morning, which does not encourage one to go bathing! I shall go down to the beach to see it." It was big news. The *Boston Globe* reported that William Flynn of Third Cliff caught the shark in his net, and "landed the fish at the bathing beach at Peggotty." It was eight feet long and weighed about 700 pounds. The *Globe* commented, "it was mighty nice of him [the shark] to wait until the end of the bathing season before making his appearance in these waters.[342]

The following summer, Beatrice was back in Scituate by May 21, 1917, and Swinburne was planning to come up from New York City for a visit. She visited Maude Dugan's place on Second Cliff, saw Maude's daughter Phyllis, and saw John Futrelle, who was the son of the famous novelist who died on the *Titanic*. John had just been appointed to the US Naval Academy at Annapolis.[343]

After speaking in Chautauqua, NY, and Bay View, MI, Beatrice returned to Scituate. Swinburne spent time there with the family until returning to New York in early September. The children "rifled the Haynes garden for hydrangeas & golden rod for her & for the dining-room." She was just finishing up another book, with her manuscript already in the hands of her New York publisher, the Frederick A. Stokes Company.[344]

At the end of the summer, Swinburne had decided to leave the law and to write poetry. Beatrice supported his drastic decision, saying, "Bravo my darling, I'm so happy about the poem. It is indeed joyful, and makes up for all the struggle, to know that you feel so happy and in tune with yourself. You shan't go back to the law dearest — even temporarily — I feel sure we can manage somehow — Inward harmony is too valuable a thing to lose for the sake of mere money."[345]

To save money, the Hales decided to spend the winter of 1917–1918 in the Scituate cottage, while renting out their Forest Hills house. The cottage would be cheaper and it would be a peaceful place for Swinburne to write. He settled in to the cottage by October. They were now winter suffragists in Scituate.[346]

Beatrice, on tour again, wrote to him at the cottage, "I'm so pleased you took Sanchia to the movies, & long to hear all about it. It does my heart good to think of you & her having a chance, for the first time, to become real friends." She advised Swinburne "to give Stenbeck (butcher) a check for $200. He has not had a cent the whole season, & his bill must be — well! The milk bill — Whitings — should also be paid." She added, "Before, I always felt I was working only to help keep a machine going which was wearisome to you. Now, I know I am working for your happiness, your freedom. What a difference! And how I shall enjoy writing with you, & our 'mutual criticism & co-operation society!'"[347]

Beatrice finally got back to Scituate in November 1917, after a month of touring St. Louis, Akron, and upstate New York towns of Penn Yan, Niagara Falls, Geneseo, Binghamton, and Hancock.[348]

Beatrice then had the task of getting the cottage ready for winter, as Swinburne was visiting New York. Fortunately, the Welch Company in Scituate Harbor was able to supply nearly everything for a house. On November 27, she reported,

> Welch's men are now setting up a little wood stove (there was no medium size) in the sp. room, & will — if I can finish it in time — take this [letter] in for me. … It was bitter last night, owing to the wind, but today, though it is freezing, the wind has gone, so one does not mind. Water standing 1 yard from the stove froze in the night last evening. … Hence the new stove today to be on the safe side![349]

The next day, snow came and then turned to slush. Beatrice reported,

> Walter [Haynes, probably] & Mr. Ward tell me that the night you left — in its combination of low temperature & high wind — was as bad as anything we are likely to get here. My stove is still alight, & my bedroom quarters arranged most agreeably next door. I shall sample them tonight with pleasure. The children have been quite excited over the snow, & Gyp [their dog, evidently] has only tracked modest amounts of it into the house.[350]

Beatrice went to a movie and spent time working on a play. She was concerned about their finances, and wondered if Swinburne could raise money by selling some furniture. "Burke's little store has sent me in a bill for $25 with a civil line asking if they can have it by Dec. 1st, as they have heavy bills to meet, etc. I don't see what I can do but – give it – we can't have our credit here questioned." Burke's was a variety store on Front Street at Otis Place.[351]

There was a dramatic incident involving Gyp, evidently their dog.

> The babes took Gyp to the village with them this p.m. & lost her. When they returned she had not arrived, & they were a little anxious. But 10 minutes later I heard a snuffling under my door, & when I opened it she tore in, almost knocking the whole room down in a perfect transport of joy — she had evidently been a little anxious herself, as it was dark, & she did not quite know where I was.[352]

The snow must have stayed around for several days. On November 30, Beatrice said, "I met Mrs. Walter Haynes in the village yesterday on skis, which she says they both use a lot in the winter, & infinitely prefer to snowshoes." Beatrice added, "This morning I had my breakfast in bed, & all 3 children insisted on getting in with me, which — as the bed is only 3 ft wide — was 'some' tight fit!"[353]

By December 3, 1917, Beatrice was ready to return to New York for a visit, to escape boredom, and for warmth, a hot bath, and dinner with

"Johnston" before he sailed. Sir Johnston Forbes-Robertson was her uncle (her father's brother), and a famous actor whose American farewell tour in 1916 concluded with three performances of *Hamlet* at Sanders Theatre, Harvard University.[354]

In December, Swinburne returned to Scituate to be with the children, while Beatrice was off on another tour, this time to St. Louis (again), Kansas City, Chicago, and Madison.[355]

Spending winter in the cottage in Scituate inspired Swinburne's poem, "Friends." It was one of Beatrice's favorites, and it was later published in his book.[356]

In 1918, Beatrice worked for the US Food Administration, again touring the country to give talks. She returned to Scituate whenever she could. In August, she came back from Chautauqua. She adored being with the children. She made a doll for Rosemary. Will and Inez Irwin were there, and they got together for supper. She went to the movies. Mr. Wagner was still delivering milk to the cottage, but no other tradesmen delivered. She still loved the "Helena," the cottage they were renting from Mr. Barber. She said, "the Helena is chaste and fair … thy ghost [Swinburne's] still haunts the Helena."[357]

The "Helena" was one of two cottages that Barber rented to the Hales. It was probably named for the ship that wrecked at Fourth Cliff in Scituate in 1909. The US Life-Saving Service crew there rescued all eight men aboard. One of the lifesavers was Marcus Barber, who had a 30-year career with the lifesaving service.[358]

The war haunted Scituate. In 1918, it became home to the new Proving Ground, which test fired howitzer carriages and tested related material. Beatrice was worried, and wrote Swinburne,

> It appears that all cottage owners here are preparing to profiteer, in view of the Proving Ground bringing so many war-workers to Scituate. Rumour is so rife as to the intentions of Barber, that I am certain he would not rent again to us save at a heavy increase. This being so, & in view of the filth & general demoralization here, I feel (with your agreement) we had better give up

> Scituate. Unless I hear from you to the contrary therefor, I shall begin demobilization here.[359]

Beatrice planned to offer the furniture to Barber, send the children off to the grandparents in Chicago, and advertise their remaining belongings "by hand-drawn bills in the village stores. I shall be my own auctioneer, & shall serve tea. Rather amusing!" She believed their tenancy ended the following spring.[360]

But when Barber met with her, she learned the lease ran beyond the spring, to June 1, 1919. She reported to Swinburne,

> Barber has no intention (village gossip to the contrary) of turning us out, save that he is very anxious to sell. I told him I should not dream of standing in the way of a sale, but that if he did not find a purchaser, I might ask to rent the Helena only for one more summer .... He was most nice, & said he was certainly not going to turn us out for any other tenants. He also said, if no purchaser turns up, he might be glad to buy our furniture of us, so as to rent the cottage, or cottages, furnished for the summer.
>
> In view of all this, but particularly in view of the fact that we have still 7 months of the lease to run, I have decided to give up all idea of selling off the furniture here until next year. We don't want to pay for an empty house for so long, which, if furnished, might be a convenience to us in the spring. I might find it a blessing to have this place to come to for a rest in April or May, or you might – one never knows what may happen. Also, I can dispose of the furniture much better in the spring, when the "Summer People" have arrived.[361]

The financial situation was precarious, since they owed money to various family members, and they were not able to rent their house in Forest Hills. Beatrice thought they must sell their house in the spring. In the meantime, she packed the children off to the grandparents in Chicago. In early December, Swinburne reported that he had an agreement to sell their house. With this and other financial transactions, Beatrice could see the way to get entirely out of debt.[362]

Swinburne used the cottage in March 1919. When the lease ended on June 1, Swinburne bought the cottage. He must have been able to buy it using funds from selling their house in Forest Hills.[363]

Beatrice traveled to England in July 1919, and she was looking to buy a cottage there. But she was also looking forward to "the peace of the Scituate summer." She spent August and October in Scituate, it seems with her children. She thought Scituate was dull, but pleasant. On her return from speaking in Chicago, Toledo, and Pittsburgh, she "slept like a dormouse in the good air last night, after ten nights of semi-vigil."[364]

Beatrice had the cottage prepared for another winter in Scituate, 1919–1920, and Swinburne visited after she left on tour to Cleveland and Detroit.

> It seems certain the water is to remain on this winter, so I am seeing about the pipes being sunk to the house, & heavily wrapped in the coal-cellar. Thus we could have water in the kitchen, even if not elsewhere.
>
> The children seem to get dearer & more interesting each time I return to them. Their manners are improving now that the beach-brigade has left.[365]

That winter, it seems, was their last time in Scituate. Beatrice and the children moved to England. Swinburne and Beatrice divorced in 1920. He married Marie Tudor Garland in 1921. By March 1925, he had sold his property in Scituate.[366]

Marital Problems

They were a promising couple. Swinburne was handsome, well-educated, and a talented lawyer. Beatrice was beautiful, accomplished, and a talented lecturer. Both came from good families. Both were deeply involved in the woman suffrage movement in the early years of their marriage. They could have been the models of the "new woman" and the "new man" that she heralded in her 1914 book, or for Rose O'Neill's poster "Together for Home and Family." They had beautiful children: Sanchia (born May 30, 1911) and twins Rosemary and Clemency (born in December 1913).[367]

Poster by Rose O'Neill, *Together for Home and Family*, 1915. Courtesy of David O'Neill and New-York Historical Society.

So what happened with their marriage?

Most of what we know comes from letters by Beatrice. Allowances must be made. But she often described the positions Swinburne took in his letters to her, so we have some sense of his views as well.

While Beatrice always wrote her "Toodie" lovingly, and almost always treasured her time with him, Swinburne could at times be difficult. In addition, he was unfaithful. It started early in their marriage, with episodes reported in her letters.

On May 20, 1914, writing from Pennsylvania where she was on a lecture tour, Beatrice's anguished letter strongly hints at his affairs. She wrote Swinburne,

> One thing at least the disclosures of last Saturday revealed anew to me, & that is the vital quality of my love for you. … I dread the repetition of the misery I felt on Saturday, the pain of it, …. And I know it will come again, that's the worst of it. Nor can I see how you can help it coming, being the kind of man you are. We must just try to help & understand each other through these crises as best we can dear. God knows I would give everything in the world to be able to be to you all that your nature craves. That is the bitterest thing in my life to me, that I cannot satisfy you, though loving you a thousand times more than those who, apparently, can. …
>
> Forgive me for all this stuff, it eases my mind, which revolves in the same lost circles it followed night and day two years ago [1912].[368]

Soon after, on May 24, she wrote Swinburne that she had an ache in her heart and throat, could not separate the physical and spiritual as he could, and was in agony "to think that that body of yours, every inch of which seems part of me … may have to be shared again with some stranger to whom my sacrament is only a voluptuary adventure."[369]

Almost two years later, in February 1916, Beatrice stayed in Chicago with "Mamma and Papa," Swinburne's parents. In a cryptic letter to Swinburne, she told him she had a confidential talk with them, evidently about Swinburne's unfaithfulness. She got from them "an expression of opinion as to what, under certain circumstances, they would wish me to do, and what they would or would not believe me justified in doing."[370]

It seems they separated by the middle of 1916. After Beatrice wrote to tell him about her arrival in Scituate, Swinburne wrote an astonishing letter June 26, but he did not send it. It reveals a lot about his state of mind:

My dear: I have not answered your letter because I found it hard to write.

It was very sweet of you to write me so kindly, so lovingly, but a twelve page letter all about the babies, & concluding with messages of love such as would have been natural some years ago, does not make the separation seem very separative! I want to put you out of my mind & clear it completely for whatever the future holds, whether of coming together or growing farther apart. I would much rather write to you – if you should wish it — than have you write to me — at least anything beyond the merest news. I do not wish to enter into your life or that of the children until I am perfectly certain that some hope of happiness lies that way. I am determined never to resume the common life in this country, or entirely in this city, & until something else offers itself — if then — I wish to forget that the common life ever existed. When you left, after the strain of this last year, it was an instant lightening of everything to me; I walked on air until your letters came; I was immeasurably cheerful, soon my cough didn't last an hour — when the letter depressed me to the earth. I felt as if I could never escape, as if your love had a strangle hold on me, as if your forgivingness were so relentless that nothing could save me from it. This letter is a result; I simply must finally say these things to recover myself, to face life at all. All these last days I have been fighting against that letter, & against all the power of association & long piled-up time that it meant. You have got to let me go for the present; this must be a real separation, not one of space alone; I absolutely demand to be relinquished.

... Do let this be a real separation, mental as well as physical. Pull down the asbestos curtain. I cannot stand any more suffering, I am simply used up with it & I must be happy my own way.[371]

Although Swinburne did not send the letter, he must have communicated its essence to Beatrice. On June 28, she responded:

> Your suggestion about correspondence is noted. I had not, of course, the faintest idea of carrying one on. But it suited my mood to write you that one letter of affection and goodwill on my arrival here, and I do not regret having done so. You will have a purely business letter from me either in London or Paris with reference to the house, but I will not bother you with my plans during your last busy days at the office. Bon voyage, B.[372]

They saw each other later in 1916. On November 16, she wrote him in response to his letter, including:

> ... my dear, you have given my pride and my love (transpose their order) such staggering blows that they could not have suffered up again to make the first advance. The things you have said to me, even now, make my flesh shiver to remember — for I do remember them, that is the pity of it. To you, they are the mood of a moment, to me, a lasting and open wound. Not for any considerations would I go back to a condition of life in which I was again open to these shafts, and it is only because I believe your scheme will not bare me to them that I am ready to accept it.[373]

He had criticized her as being too talkative. She said that was from being unhappy.

> I erect a rampart of cheerful speech about the bleeding garrison of my heart. I don't think I have ever been consciously insincere with you, but for very long now I have never been at ease in your presence — my talking has been the signal — not so much of instability as of nervous apprehension.[374]

Beatrice addressed another complaint:

> You write of having thought in moments of bitterness that I only loved you as part of the "institution." There you are all wrong dear, and I have to make you see just how entirely wrong you are. You think of my life, my character, as something entirely architectural, and so, in externally, it is, and the responsibilities which our marriage has forced upon me of housekeeping, children and the rest, have perforce thrust this side of my mature forward. But — I came of a family of artists, am one myself in my small way — spent my youth largely among unconventional people — loved beauty, poetry, and romance — never even knew people who lived suburban existences. Do you suppose it has been easy for me to give up England and all the thrilling people I used to know, and settle down as a middle-class American wife and mother, with little duties, petty and unlovely obligations, bourgeoise acquaintances, and the rest? It hasn't been easy, it has meant a definite loss and sacrifice, which even the stimulations of my work has never enabled me to forget. One thing, and one thing only, has outweighed the loss and made it gain, and that was you.[375]

She complained about his "variable uncertain temperament," and she said his "dissatisfied complaining mood" wears her out. She said, "what hurt me so bitterly and led to my willingness to have a separation was that you had for a year and more [since before mid-1915] been offering me all the dust and none of the gold." She closed by saying she wanted to forget the wounds and "to begin again, with a fair start. … Thy own Beatrice. P.S. We will not even think the word parting again, unless this plan should fail – not even think it dear!"[376]

They seem to have reconciled for a while, but that was in flux by March 1917. Beatrice, on tour, wrote Swinburne in response to his letter:

> We have come to a point dear when our future relations lie entirely in your hands. Take your time, and be sure of yourself. I do not want to see you, at present, (unless business makes it necessary), for I am too

> acutely conscious of what is now again happening in your life to take pleasure in our meeting. … I can never come back to the precise scale of values you have been developing in the last months. You are still my dearest, but I know now that there is a Something, beyond even love, which I must be faithful to, or perish.[377]

But in the summer of 1917, they were spending time together in Scituate. Swinburne had decided to leave his law practice and become a poet. He returned to New York in early September, and Beatrice wrote him, "You have been so dear to me all this summer, beloved, and really made me feel that you love me more than you used to (not speaking of being "in love"). That is a great solace to me, & I am very grateful to you and fate for it."[378]

They spent the winter of 1917–1918 living in the small cottage in Scituate. He was writing poetry. They seemed to have had a happy time together. After this, in May, Beatrice wrote, "I enjoyed our 6 months at Scituate so much — I shall remember them very long, dearest." Beatrice was then on a speaking tour for the US Food Administration, and Swinburne had joined the Army and was working in Washington, DC.[379]

This separation, along with Swinburne's increasing irritability, was not good for the marriage. By June, when they spent time together at his apartment in Washington, she left a letter for him there:

> Ever since my return from my second New England trip, on June 1st, you have been wounding me very deeply, my dear, waking again old miseries & humiliations which I thought we had buried together forever, two years ago — Not [wholly] your fault perhaps, since your nerves are in such bad shape — but the fact remains. Now I want a little rest; I am tired, & my heart is very heavy. If I see you, it upsets me – makes me feel the irony of my position — makes me wonder, with an acheing sense of loss, where my friend & comrade is of other days, & why love dies so young in some hearts. If I have the comrade, he can assuage

> me somewhat for the loss of my life's love — but when he too, goes away, it hurts me to see the vessel that has contained him.
>
> … Don't be cross, dear Toodie. I don't want to see you again until you have passed through the mood in which everything I say and do irritates you. Go your way with as little fatigue and nervous strain to yourself as you can, & let me go mine. Under other circumstances, we may be good pals again — let us wait till those circumstances, or that time, arrives. … I want peace, Toodie dear, & to be free from the burden of unrequited affection. — I've got to have it. The day will come when you can be kind to me again, and then I will gladly see you.[380]

She left another letter for him on June 18,

> Good-bye, my darling. I'm doing the only thing I can think of to help you — going away. It hurts a little, but I am sure it will be best for us both. You won't see me again until such time as you might need or want me.
>
> My address is the Food Adm. at present; when I go to Scituate, or on tour, I will send you my new address, for emergencies. …
>
> There is nothing heroic or dramatic about this departure of mine dearest — it just seems the kindest & best thing to do. I only waited long enough to hear from you if I could give you anything at all, or do anything but this to help you, these days.
>
> Good-bye, my heart's beloved.
>
> Your
>
> Beatrice.
>
> P.S. You will, of course, simply say I am on tour, if any of your friends should ask after me.[381]

But they kept in touch, even getting back together enough for Swinburne to see her off in July at the train station in Washington and to arrange for her to have a dinner on her train trip:

> Thank you dearest, for the excellent dinner — you certainly saved me from starvation. Your man appeared as soon as the train drew in to Baltimore, with a neat little card-board box, containing two admirable chicken sandwiches (he explained apologetically that it was a "beefless day") — salt, pepper, two bananas, & a pint of milk. — All for only 55 cents. I made a really excellent dinner, & turned in, much refreshed, for a long night's sleep. You managed it in your usual excellently efficient way darling; — how lucky for B that He saw her off![382]

A month later, the off-and-on-again relationship was again in tatters. Beatrice responded to a letter from Swinburne, who awaited a possible assignment in France,

> I am really distressed to learn that my two letters "disturbed" you with romantic "yearnings." — Also surprised. — I had thought them merely affectionate & rather maternal. My understanding is that our relations are now & henceforth based only on mutual obligations, friendship & affection. This has been perfectly clear in my mind ever since our talks – the week-end we moved from 18th St [probably late June, in a move to 1306 I Street], and I have had no idea of not living up to it. I did not understand however that loving or affectionate phrases were to be barred, though I can quite understand they may bore.
>
> I can appreciate, too, your desire to be let alone. It was the one thing I prayed for when I came up here [to Scituate].[383]

By early December 1918, the children were staying with Swinburne's parents in Chicago, and Beatrice was also staying with them while her speaking engagements were around Chicago. Swinburne had reached an agreement to sell their house in Forest Hills. Beatrice wrote him with family and financial considerations. She added,

> I find I am entirely uninterested in a divorce (after quiet reflection,) so that must be as you prefer. For my part, I shrink from the emotional strain & probably disappointment of a second marriage, & I shrink greatly from inflicting so deep a wound upon your parents as a divorce would entail. Besides, the proceedings are ugly, public, & expensive. Frankly, I don't concern myself with the idea. It could be done at any time, should the need arise. Further, I don't care much for the moral responsibility of putting such a barrier between you & your children as divorce would erect. I am neutral; it's "up to you", my dear, & I shan't bother myself further in the matter.[384]

But later that day, Beatrice *would* be bothered. She had just read Swinburne's letter to her, saying he had fallen in love with a woman named Evelyn, and he wanted to marry her.

Swinburne's Other Women

In early December 1918, Swinburne wrote Beatrice that he had fallen in love with a woman named Evelyn, and he wanted to marry her. (Her last name does not appear in records reviewed.) Evelyn came down from New York City and spent a few days with Swinburne in his apartment in Washington, DC, where he was just about to complete his tour of duty as a Captain in Army Intelligence. World War I had just ended.[385]

Swinburne's affair with Evelyn and desire to marry her prompted what seemed to be the final rupture of his marriage to Beatrice. She told Swinburne in a letter of December 9, 1918:

> It is difficult for me to understand how you can feel so sure of your love, with less than two weeks' knowledge of the lady. I am sure she is all that you say of her, but

> I think I too was always "kind" to you till you tried me, these last weeks, past bearing; and I think I, too, have always loved and appreciated your art. The one test (it seems to me) is not whether she is kind or well-to-do or distinguished (several of us, including myself, are the last) – but whether you feel for her such a deep & all-consuming love that life without her would be unthinkable. …
>
> You write of your happiness my dear. I trust you may find it. For my part it is unthinkable that happiness of the lasting kind can be obtained through the burnt-sacrifice of all those nearest to one by blood, — who love one best; & by the evasion of one's parental responsibilities. The loss of this father by the children will be irreparable, and your parents will never recover from this blow.[386]

A week later, Beatrice wrote,

> I can only say that I have never felt so humiliated & revolted in my life as I did over that last affair of yours (I mean the circumstances of course not merely the affair) …. Consequently, I had become entirely numb, & had only one impulse — to escape from ignominy. — I thought I could not suffer any more than I had ….[387]

It was not clear which affair she was referring to or when it occurred, although it seemed to have been recent.

Swinburne's affair with Evelyn did not last long. Swinburne wrote devoted love letters to Evelyn, and sent her poems he wrote that she had inspired. At first, he said how much joy she brought him, and how he would go soon to New York to get the divorce proceedings started. He missed his children, whom he had not seen in nine months. His letters gradually disclosed that he had difficulty getting Beatrice to agree on a quick divorce, and that he and Beatrice had separated in 1914 and 1916. (He did not disclose that the separations were due to his affairs with other women.) Evelyn must have cooled, asking for some time apart, and she disappeared from his life by early January 1919.[388]

An air of desperation crept into Swinburne's beautifully written letters to Evelyn. "I can't conceive of the misery this life would have been these last four weeks, & the misery I should be looking forward to now, had it not been for you," he said. "I doubt if I should have lived more than another year if I had not met you." But the affair ended, and one would think doom was next for Swinburne. However, things turned around quickly. By mid-January 1919, he moved to Buzzards Bay, MA, at the farm-estate of Marie Tudor Garland, who would become his second wife.[389]

Beatrice was, at first, glad to see Swinburne moving to "the country" instead of growing despondent in New York. Her letters were always supportive, apart from her distress with his affairs, but she began to realize his relationship with Marie was growing more serious. At first, her letters to him in New York were forwarded to Buzzards Bay. By August, she wrote directly to him at Buzzards Bay. Her letter of August 14 said she did *not* want to see him while he was living at "B. B." [Buzzards Bay], and she discussed his desire for a divorce. She said, "I am not used, & never could be, to your establishing yourself as a recognized inhabitant of your mistresses house." She continued, "a divorce would have to [be] absolute & perpetual. There could be no friendship, no letters, no messages through friends. You would be dead to me, & this not because of theories, but because it is the only way I could do it & still live."[390]

Swinburne, meanwhile, had moved from despondency to a fairy tale life. Marie Tudor Garland (1870–1949) was attractive and wealthy. She owned large estates, including her Bay End Farm at Buzzards Bay.[391] It was only about an hour south of Scituate, but a world apart. A member of Marie's domestic staff described the estate this way:

> We have spent three days in over opulence at large country house where millionaires go barefoot .... Mrs Garland's estate is enormous and each member of the family has his or her own little cottage tucked somewhere in the woods. There are several tiny lakes

and from all most all the verandas one has some sort of glimpse of black pine trunks against blue water.[392]

The cottages were for artists as well as family members. About 1916, Marie established an artist colony at the farm, and had various cottages constructed. In 1918, she invited a young writer, Kahlil Gibran, to her farm, and there he wrote much of *The Prophet*, a book that later proved popular. In early 1919, Swinburne the poet found his way to this place.[393]

Marie was able to afford this splendorous place through inheritance and marriage. She was the granddaughter of Frederic Tudor, Boston's "Ice King," who built a fortune shipping ice from Massachusetts to the Caribbean, and later to India. His son Frederick Tudor, Marie's father, built a family retreat at Buzzards Bay in 1880 called Tudor Haven. He sold it in 1890 to President Grover Cleveland, who renamed it Gray Gables. It was his summer White House from 1893 to 1896.[394]

Her wealth enabled Marie to establish another Tudor family haven not far from Gray Gables in 1908. This was Bay End Farm. It was in Bourne, at Buttermilk Bay, at the very upper end of Buzzards Bay, and close to the Cape Cod canal. It was at the intersection of End of Bay Road and Old End of Bay Road. It comprised 250 acres of land and ponds, eventually growing to 900 acres or more. It included Grazing Fields Farm with its 1785 farmhouse and multiple cottages.[395]

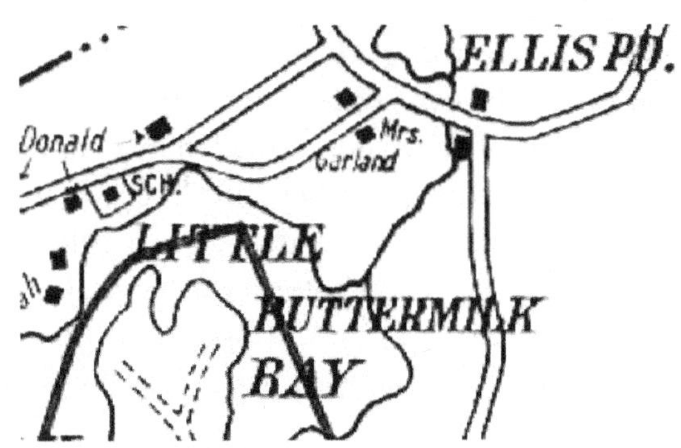

Garland estate at Buzzards Bay (upper center). Walker 1910 *Atlas of Barnstable County*, detail. Courtesy of State Library of Massachusetts.

Marie, who had lived variously in Portsmouth, RI, and New York City, would also come to own a cottage at Cornish in the mountains of New Hampshire. She bought it from Maud Howe, the daughter of suffragist Julia Ward Howe.[396]

Marie contributed to the local life of Bourne. She had a clubroom built in 1911 for the Old Colony Union (later the Old Colony Union Women's Club), which helped women earn money with crafts and sewing. On August 4, 1916, Marie opened up her farm for a large celebration to benefit the Society for the Prevention of Cruelty to Children.[397]

Marie was "an international suffragette." She gave a talk in January 1918 on "The Problem of the Woman at the Cape," in which she said, "The woman should be free to earn her share of the family funds, either in the home or out of it — free to go out into the world when possible and fill the place of some man who has been called to the colors." This sounded like a speech by Beatrice.[398]

Marie had a history of marriages. In 1893, she married wealthy James A. Garland. They divorced after six years of marriage based on her alleged infidelities, but they later remarried. James Garland died in 1906. In 1912, Marie married her MIT-educated gardener and estate manager, Francis Cushing Green, at Bay End Farm. By marrying him, she forfeited the income from the Garland estate's $10 million fortune. Then she wound up divorcing Green in 1915.[399]

Swinburne gained many seeming advantages by living in Buzzards Bay with Marie, who was 14 years older than him. He lived in a large country house with multiple cottages, rather than a cramped apartment in New York or the tiny cottage in Scituate. He was free to work on his poetry, uninterrupted by his children. He could spend time at isolated estates, rather than in crowded New York. He had wealth at his disposal, in contrast to Beatrice's continual worries about family finances. Marie had a fortune, Beatrice had to lecture for a living.

In early 1920, Beatrice sued Swinburne for divorce, which presumably was granted.[400]

In early March 1921, Swinburne married Marie in Paris. With this marriage, in addition to the other advantages mentioned above, Swinburne improved his social standing, and made it into the *Social Register*.[401]

Swinburne and Marie, Divorce, and Demons

After marrying in 1921, Marie and Swinburne spent much of that year at Buzzards Bay. Then they escaped the New England winter weather, and went to their large estate in Somerset, Bermuda. There, in early 1922, a member of Garland's domestic staff observed, "Swinburne has been ill — had a curious partial paralysis of the face, they [Swinburne and Marie] were both very nervous and full of domestic complexes."[402]

Swinburne and Marie had decided to part by the second winter in Bermuda, 1922–1923. They were living apart in separate lodgings at the Bermuda estate, he in Ely's Lodge, and she at Parapet.[403]

In October 1923, Swinburne turned to his close friend and law partner, Walter Nelles, for advice about divorcing Marie. Walter and Swinburne had been through a lot together, and they had developed a national reputation for defending socialists and Communists. Looking back at their relationship and work, we see:

- Walter was Swinburne's classmate at Harvard, and followed him at Harvard Law School.[404]
- As early as 1913, Swinburne may have been defending anarchists.[405]
- They were partners in the New York City law firm of Hale, Nelles & Shorr, which operated under that name from about 1917 to at least 1924.[406]
- Both were dedicated to protecting the civil rights of unpopular socialists and Communists (sometimes called radicals or anarchists). Their clients opposed war, and they fought the government's use of the Espionage Act to suppress their constitutional freedom of expression.
- Walter was a defense attorney in the second trial, October 1918, of the government's criminal action under the Espionage Act against writers and publishers of *The Masses* magazine,

including Max Eastman. There were deep connections with Scituate's summer suffragists. Inez Haynes Irwin had worked with Max on *The Masses*. She was also a member of Heterodoxy along with Max's activist sister Crystal Eastman and Swinburne's wife Beatrice. Swinburne was an early officer of the Men's League for Woman's Suffrage, founded by Max. In addition, another summer resident of Scituate, Boardman Robinson, was on the editorial staff of *The Masses*, although not charged in the case, United States v. Eastman, et al. Neither of the two trials resulted in convictions.[407]

- In October 1919, Swinburne was defense counsel in a criminal anarchy trial that the government won.[408]
- In January 1920, Swinburne represented Englebert Preis, an alien facing deportation for being a member of the Communist party. The deportation hearing grew out of the so-called "Palmer raids" of aliens and Communists. J. Edgar Hoover organized the raids. He was then head of the General Intelligence Division of the Bureau of Investigation under Attorney General A. Mitchell Palmer, and later head of the FBI. Hoover represented the government at the hearing. After the hearing, the government deported Preis. But Hoover was infuriated by Swinburne's behavior at the hearing, and asked Military Intelligence for any derogatory information about Swinburne, who had been a Captain in Military Intelligence during the war.[409]
- Swinburne was the main editor of a report condemning the Palmer raids as a violation of the law and the Constitution. The *Report Upon the Illegal Practices of the United States Department of Justice* was based on investigations cosponsored by the ACLU and was issued in late May 1920. Swinburne and some of America's most illustrious lawyers, including Roscoe Pound and Felix Frankfurter, signed the report. Hoover conducted an investigation of the signers.[410]
- In September 1920, Swinburne wrote about his firm's work, "We are in a hot bed of repression here, with only a very few lawyers who are willing and able to handle the situation, and who are hopelessly overworked."[411]

- The work by Walter and Swinburne led to Walter's founding of the American Civil Liberties Union (ACLU) in 1920, along with fellow Harvard graduate and Bostonian Roger Baldwin and Massachusetts-born Crystal Eastman.[412]

It is hard to imagine how Swinburne had accomplished all this during the turbulence of his divorce from Beatrice and courtship of Marie.

Now, in 1923, as a divorce from Marie seemed imminent, Walter gave advice to Swinburne. He was not sure a divorce would be worth anything. He told Swinburne, "You're my oldest and dearest friend, and I have both admiration and affection for Marie, and I don't want to be in a position of being agent for either of you in hurting the other for ends of which I doubt the value."[413]

Walter was not happy with Swinburne's position. "It's in part because [Marie's] money gives you so soft a pillow that you're kept bed-ridden. You can't, except speciously, elect to treat the money as a compensation for your suffering." He proposed a number of ways for Swinburne to get his finances in order, including a trust for his children, all four of them. (This is a big surprise since no other documents reviewed mention children besides the three he had with Beatrice.) Walter cautioned Swinburne against "a life of torpid philandering with intentions of playing for kicks instead of results."[414]

Swinburne and Marie divorced in 1924.[415] Early the following year, Swinburne sold the summer property in Scituate.[416]

Meanwhile, Swinburne had moved on to Taos, NM, where he spent most of 1922–1924. Taos is where his sister Margaret (Margué) lived with her husband, print artist Ralph M. Pearson, and their daughter Pavli. By 1923, Pearson left his wife, child, and Taos, moving to California. In Taos, Swinburne developed an intimate relationship with Greta Hercz, a young art student. In addition, he became acquainted with other writers in Taos, notably D. H. Lawrence.[417]

Swinburne was a writer, too. He had been class poet at Harvard, and was working on a book of poetry since 1917, when Beatrice critiqued and promoted early drafts. He finally finished it, his only book, and it was published in 1923 — *The Demon's Notebook—Verse and Perverse*

(New York: Nicholas L. Brown, 1923). The poetry contained much sympathy for the demon, with opening lines, "Let the Demon work in you! / Do not cast him out!" The frontispiece for the book was by Rose O'Neill, the famous illustrator and originator of the Kewpie doll. One of the book's poems was dedicated to her. The book was reviewed favorably in the *New York Times*.[418]

Illustration by Rose O'Neill for
Demon's Notebook (1923)

The title of his book is interesting, because Swinburne had his own demons. He had a history of nervous problems. They were not diminished by the advantages of marriage, whether to Beatrice or to Marie. In 1916, a frustrated Beatrice criticized his "variable uncertain temperament" and "dissatisfied complaining mood." She said, "When you are alight, & not a banked fire, you blaze away so contagiously." In 1917, Beatrice wrote him, "I think it was this demon of yours, working in you, who really brought about the fortunate seeming-disasters of last winter!"[419]

And in June 1918, when they were having another period of marital difficulties, Beatrice left a letter in their apartment for Swinburne, saying, "I don't want to see you again until you have passed through the mood in which everything I say and do irritates you. Go your way with as little fatigue and nervous strain to yourself as you can, & let me go mine."[420]

Moodiness was one thing, but late in 1918, Swinburne made at least one short visit to a sanitarium. About the same time, he warned Evelyn, "if you care for me, you mustn't expect me to be always the same, for I never am. You must discount both my excitations & my depressions. I go up & I go down."[421]

Looking back, it seems Swinburne might have had bipolar disorder, the current name for manic-depression, a term first formally used in the early 20th century. It is a serious mental illness that can cause dramatic mood swings, lapses in judgment, and episodes of psychosis. At the time, there was no medicine to treat the illness.[422]

Swinburne suffered a major breakdown in 1925 and was admitted to the Westport Sanitarium in Westport, Connecticut. He died there in 1937 at the age of 53.[423]

Meanwhile, Marie continued to lead an unconventional life. She was "a life-long hell-raiser" according to the biographer of her son Charles. Charles became infamous in the 1920s for operating a "free love" farm commune. Swinburne would have known Charles at Bay End Farm. Marie, like Swinburne, moved to New Mexico. She had a dude ranch in Alcalde and was a friend of Georgia O'Keefe. A grandniece later reported that Marie held wild parties in Santa Fe in the Roaring '20s, and she was "a not-so-proper Bostonian who married seven times (once to a Polish count) and was murdered at age 75 by a jealous lover." Her grandchildren say the last man in her life murdered her in a tub in an El Paso hotel. News reports say she died from injuries in a fall in 1949, at age 79. She had been a prominent resident of Española, NM, about 25 miles north of Santa Fe and about 40 miles from Taos, where Swinburne lived after they divorced.[424]

Epilogue

For her divorce, Beatrice got no sympathy from the anti-suffragists. She became a target of their *Woman Patriot* magazine. The magazine's banner headline motto was "Dedicated to the Defense of

Womanhood, Motherhood, The Family and the State AGAINST Suffragism, Feminism and Socialism." Its issue of March 20, 1920, announced Beatrice's divorce, recounted her twins' nude bathing episode of 1915, and quoted disapprovingly from her 1914 book *What Women Want.*[425]

At the *Woman Patriot*, as one commentator summarized,

> The editors continued to publish articles in opposition to woman suffrage until the Supreme Court upheld the ratification of the Nineteenth Amendment in 1921. The newspaper continued to promote anti-feminist rhetoric until two years before it ceased publication [in 1932].[426]

As for Beatrice, she and her girls moved to England in the early 1920s. Their last time in Scituate seems to have been in 1920. In England, Beatrice hosted visits by Rose O'Neill, and Inez and Will Irwin. She occasionally returned to America and continued to give lectures.

Beatrice's public speaking included frequent appearances in the Boston area. She spoke in Boston in 1919 at the New England Congress for a League of Nations, along with ex-President Taft and other noted speakers. She was a speaker at the dinner concluding the League of Women Voters conference in New York in 1920, along with Carrie Chapman Catt, Maud Wood Park, and others. In 1921, the Feakins agency still represented her for booking lectures. At the time, Feakins also represented Meyer Bloomfield, who is covered in a separate chapter.[427]

Beatrice was the subject of a lengthy interview published in 1927 in which she highlighted women's "spiritual loneliness." Later, in 1931, Beatrice spoke in Boston on "Can a Modern Woman Afford a Husband?"[428]

Also in 1931, Sanchia, an actress living in Wellesley, was reportedly marrying Stanislaw Franchot, a Harvard junior. Further tracing Beatrice's children and descendants is beyond this book's scope.[429]

Beatrice was a loving wife and mother, despite a troubled and unfaithful husband. She traveled far and worked hard for woman suffrage, feminist ideals, and women's issues, as well as America's war effort. She was attacked by the anti-suffragists, but saw her work achieve the vote for women. Her contributions to the woman suffrage movement deserve more recognition.

6

The Glades

Suffragism was not the order of the day for summer residents of the Glades in Scituate's far north.

The Glades. Photo 2016 by Lyle Nyberg.

The Glades is a large, rocky, isolated peninsula with views of Cohasset and Boston. It is the site of a hotel building built in 1846. In the 1870s, a group of prominent Bostonians bought the property, including the old hotel building, and established the Glades Club there. It became a private enclave for summer vacations by members and their families. Family names included Adams (of the Presidential Adams family), Ames, Homans, Hunnewell, Lovering, and Saltonstall. Descendants have spent summers at the Glades ever since.[430]

Those Glades Club members whose positions can be identified were squarely anti-suffragist.

Charles Francis Adams III (1866–1954) was a Glades member, as was his wife, the former Frances Lovering. In 1914, the *Boston Globe* reported, "Mrs Charles Francis Adams opened her house in Washington last Wednesday afternoon for a meeting of the District of Columbia Association Opposed to Woman Suffrage, which was the first in a series of four addresses in favor of antiwoman suffrage."[431]

Mr. and Mrs. Richard M. Saltonstall were anti-suffragists who spent summers at the Glades, in its early years. Richard Saltonstall (1859–1922) was a prominent lawyer in Boston. His wife was the former Eleanor Brooks (1867–1961). Their son Leverett Saltonstall (1892–1979) later became Governor of Massachusetts and a US Senator.[432]

Eleanor was a member of the executive committee of the Massachusetts Association Opposed to the Further Extension of Suffrage to Women (MAOFESW) in 1907, and its successor, the Women's Anti-Suffrage Association of Massachusetts (WASAM) in 1915. She was one of those who organized resistance to the suffragist "Victory" parade in Boston on October 16, 1915. She and another woman were in charge of the hotel sale of red roses, the symbol of the anti-suffragists. Eleanor stationed herself at the Hotel Somerset, at the corner of Commonwealth Avenue and Charlesgate East.[433]

At the same time, Richard Saltonstall was a member of the executive committee of the men's auxiliary to WASAM, along with Frederick P. Fish (who had Scituate connections) and others. Evidently, Richard was one of the group's original members when it was founded in 1912. Before that, both Richard and Frederick were among about 300 men who signed a September 1910 declaration in opposition to the further extension of suffrage to women. In October 1915, the men's auxiliary spread "anti" literature, at the height of the campaigns on the suffrage referendum in Massachusetts.[434]

Eleanor and Richard's second child was Eleanor "Nora" Saltonstall (1894–1919). She did not support the woman suffrage movement, although her views were not immutable. Nora served as a volunteer with the Red Cross in France during World War I. Her brother Leverett enlisted in the US Army and he too served in France.[435]

Their father Richard, in early 1918, was one of those who sent telegrams to US Representative Frank Clark of Florida, a member of the Committee on Woman Suffrage. Richard's telegram said: "I am earnestly opposed to Federal amendment for woman suffrage. The States should settle the question individually. Certainly unpatriotic to bring up this question at this time." At this time, his children Leverett and Nora were both serving in World War I.[436]

Mrs. Thomas Nelson Perkins was another Glades summer resident who sent a telegram to the House Committee on Woman Suffrage in 1918. She wrote, "We pride ourselves on America as democracy, yet the suffragists admit that they want the Federal amendment in order to avoid submitting the question to the people." She was Chairman, Westwood Branch, Massachusetts Antisuffrage Association, and Branch Organization Chairman of that association. Previously, in early 1915, she was a patroness of a fundraiser for the association.[437]

It is doubtful that any of these views on woman suffrage disturbed summers at the Glades. As Abigail Adams Homans said in her 1966 book *Education by Uncles*, "The general tone of the Glades has always been extraordinarily simple, friendly, and democratic. ... I don't remember any political discussions or ever any mention of the stock market." Notwithstanding this, Abigail's husband, Robert Homans, was one of those men who signed the September 1910 declaration in opposition to the further extension of suffrage to women.[438]

Mrs. Charles D. Homans, undoubtedly connected with the Homans family of the Glades, was a vice president of the Massachusetts Association Opposed to the Further Extension of Suffrage to Women (MAOFESW) as late as 1911. Interestingly, her 1914 obituary in the anti-suffragist journal *The Remonstrance* said, "Mrs. Homans was generous to sincere believers in Woman Suffrage, as was shown by her continued friendship for Mrs. Julia Ward Howe."[439]

The summer residents of the Glades had more in common with the anti-suffragists in the neighboring town of Cohasset and other South Shore towns. In 1905, Cohasset had two members on the standing committee of the anti-suffrage MAOFESW. Hingham had five members, and Quincy had two, including the wife of the grandson of President John Quincy Adams. In 1910, many South Shore men opposed the extension of suffrage to women, including four men from Cohasset. One of those from Cohasset was William L. Parker.[440]

Parker's wife Elizabeth spent summers at her new estate at 180 Border Street in Scituate, which she owned from about 1901 to 1909. This was at the border with Cohasset, and not far from the Glades. She was an artist, art collector, and friend of Isabella Stewart Gardner. In 1910, she and her husband had box seats at the new Boston Opera House between the box seats of Thomas Lawson of Scituate and Richard M. Saltonstall, whose anti-suffragist stance is discussed above.[441]

Anti-suffragists in neighboring Cohasset were particularly active in opposing the 1915 Massachusetts referendum to give women the vote. Scituate, however, had no committee members on the anti-suffragist MAOFESW.[442]

7

Judith Winsor Smith & Sylvanus Smith

Judith Winsor (McLauthlin) Smith (1821–1921) was an early Massachusetts suffragist. Her interest in woman suffrage began about 1850. She and her husband Sylvanus Smith (1817–1901) were active suffrage supporters by 1877. By 1881, Judith was involved with the Massachusetts Woman Suffrage Association (MWSA). In 1885, she was a director of the Massachusetts School Suffrage Association. She

Judith W. Smith, late 1800s. Courtesy of the Duxbury Rural and Historical Society.

became a member of the executive committees of the Massachusetts, New England, and American Woman Suffrage Associations. Her lifelong dedication to the suffrage cause led her to be called the oldest suffrage orator in the world.

Judith came from Marshfield and Sylvanus came from Duxbury, neighboring towns on the South Shore of Boston. After they married, they lived on the South Shore, then moved to East Boston, where they spent most of their lives. For decades, Judith and Sylvanus and their family spent summers at Cedar Point in Scituate, first at the iconic Old Scituate Light keeper's cottage, then at their own cottage near the lighthouse. Judith was responsible for Scituate being mentioned in the suffragist *Woman's Journal.* Judith was a friend and colleague of Julia Ward Howe, Lucy Stone, Henry B. Blackwell, Alice Stone Blackwell, and other leading suffragists.[443]

The prominence of Judith's suffragist friends has long overshadowed Judith's significant contributions to the movement. The discussion below tries to remedy that and bring her contributions to light. It also explores the family's summer life in Scituate in the late 1800s and early 1900s, using Judith's diaries and other unpublished material.[444]

Background and Life in East Boston

Judith McLauthlin was born in Marshfield and became a schoolteacher in Duxbury. Sylvanus Smith was born in Duxbury and grew up there. Judith and Sylvanus likely met in Duxbury while she was teaching. Both had parents who were *Mayflower* descendants. They married in 1841 in Duxbury. By all accounts, it was a happy marriage.[445]

Sylvanus worked his way up from the South Shore of Boston to become one of America's leading shipbuilders, based in East Boston. At first, he worked in the shipyards of the North River, which meanders through Marshfield, Pembroke, and Scituate. This was a center of shipbuilding since early colonial times. In 1844, Sylvanus bought a farm close to a bend in the North River's upper reaches. Called the "Morse place," it was in Pembroke, a town just west of his hometown of Duxbury. There he raised peaches. According to a summary of early correspondence, Sylvanus "apparently bought the farm in Pembroke without her [Judith's] consent and left her isolated there with small children — overflowing cistern, scarlet fever, crops and livestock — while he went to work in East Boston." East Boston was quickly overtaking the South Shore as a shipbuilding center. Despite this description, they had a close and happy marriage, and they wrote each other often when Sylvanus was away at work. While they lived on the farm, three of their children were born: Sidney, Frances, and Zilpha. They would later add Mary, Erasmus ("Race"), and Jennie to their fold.[446]

Sylvanus Smith, age 70, photo by Notman, 1887, per Smith family chronicle. Courtesy of the Duxbury Rural and Historical Society.

Much later, Judith described life on the farm. The pump for water was across the road at the barn, far from the house, and uphill. She asked any man who visited to bring her a bucket of water. In addition, she relied (presumably for supplies) on her neighbors and any man who drove (horse-drawn wagons, etc.) from Duxbury to Boston. She said, "there was no railroad then, even from Plymouth. Three stages, each with four horses, drove up, and three down, in those days, and my husband came home once in three weeks."[447]

In 1854, after 10 years, Sylvanus sold the farm, and the family moved to East Boston. They must have been thinking about it for a while. A November 1853 letter sent from New Orleans by Sylvanus' brother Jonathan, older by seven years, said, "you had better tell Judith to get ready for I am going to turn your cows out to pasture this winter and bring your family up to live in E. Boston soon after I get home." The new town of East Boston, where speedy clipper ships were built, was perhaps the preeminent capital of shipbuilding in America.[448]

East Boston shipyards (right) in "Photographic panorama of the waterfront of Boston, from East Boston," c. 1877. Courtesy of Boston Public Library/Digital Commonwealth.

The Smiths' first house in East Boston was at what is now 56 Eutaw Street. It was one of a long row of connected houses. In 1872, the family moved a few blocks north into the house at 76 White Street, originally numbered 36. A photo of the house taken by the Smiths' son Erasmus has this note: "Built by my Father Silvanus Smith in 1871 occupied in January 1872." Given Sylvanus's experience as a ship carpenter and ship builder, it is likely that he built this house himself.[449]

This East Boston area was a bustling new town, described as follows:

> Shipbuilding and servicing industries lined East Boston's waterfront, including those of Donald McKay and Sylvanus Smith, two prominent Eagle Hill residents. McKay (1810–1880), a New Brunswick native, built over 120 sailing vessels of all classes at his Border Street yard. His most famous ship the *Flying Cloud* set speed records for encircling Cape Horn. McKay resided in the Greek Revival house at 78–80

> White Street (Boston Landmark 1977, NR 1982). Sylvanus Smith's yard also launched some of the sleekest clipper ships of the era, most notably the *North American* which set speed records for the New York to Melbourne and the San Francisco to Liverpool routes. Smith resided at 76 White Street from 1880 until his death in 1901.[450]

The Sylvanus Smith house at 76 White Street was adjacent to Donald McKay's house. They built their homes near the top of Eagle Hill, and near a reservoir that is now the site of East Boston High School. One writer said, "McKay built a mansion on top of Eagle Hill, where he could observe his Border Street shipyards. Famous people of the era visited him there, including Ralph Waldo Emerson and Henry Wadsworth Longfellow."[451]

Smith's shipbuilding yards were just a block or two west of his house, at the end of White Street. Just south of his yards were those of McKay, and farther south were those of Samuel Hall, a pioneer in East Boston shipbuilding. Even after the clipper ship era, an 1880 plan called this Halls Ship Yard.[452]

Over the course of his career, Sylvanus Smith became a highly regarded shipbuilder of more than 100 vessels. Shipbuilding was not a ticket to wealth, however, and it seems that Smith's family was not well off financially. According to the 1860 US census, his house on Eutaw Street was valued at $5,000 — a large amount — but his personal estate was valued at only $1,000. Even the famous Donald McKay had a personal estate valued at only $5,000 (and a house at $10,000). Smith and McKay's personal estates were among the four lowest amounts of any shipbuilder in the area in 1860, near the peak of shipbuilding in East Boston. (No such values were entered for Smith or McKay in the 1870 US census, and the 1880 census did not collect such values.)[453]

Sylvanus stood to lose (or gain) as both seller and part owner of the ships he built. In July 1876, for example, Sylvanus evidently had a part ownership in the *Puritan*, which wrecked at the mouth of the Hoogly River in India, bound for Calcutta. It was a $2,500 loss to Sylvanus, "who bears losses better than anyone I ever knew," according to

Judith. Later that month, Judith noted, Sylvanus sold another ship (three-fourths of it) for $15,000, less than the ship cost.[454]

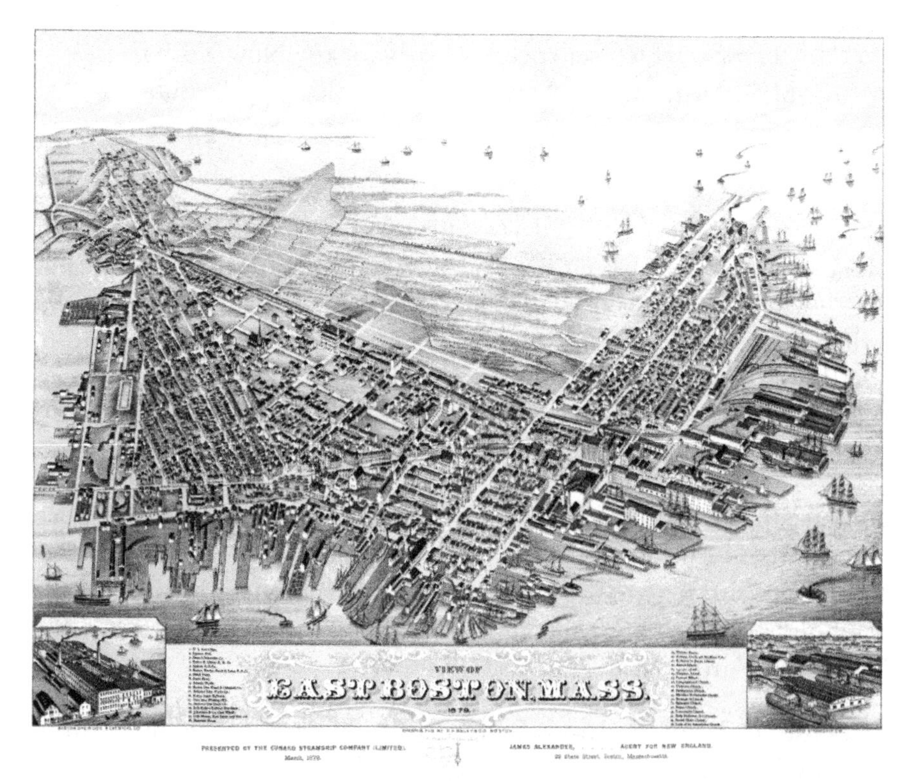

Smith house is between the Smith yards (lower left), and the rectangular reservoir several blocks above the yards. *View of East Boston, Mass.* by O.H. Bailey & Co., 1879. Map reproduction courtesy of the Norman B. Leventhal Map & Education Center at the Boston Public Library. Copies available at Digital Commonwealth and Library of Congress.

Sylvanus's last commercial vessel was the *Minnie Rowen* built in 1884. On February 1, 1894, that ship wrecked off First Cliff in Scituate, near where the Smiths by then were spending summers.[455]

Suffrage Activities

Judith was an abolitionist from an early age. She said, "My father was an abolitionist and had a station on the underground railway. I guess I follow in his footsteps in my liking for public affairs." Mr. and Mrs. Sylvanus Smith subscribed to the 28th national anti-slavery anniversary in 1862, and their names appeared in *The Liberator*, William Lloyd Garrison's abolitionist newspaper. Garrison's son, also named William Lloyd Garrison, attended a reception for the Smith's golden 50th anniversary in 1891, and was a prominent supporter of woman suffrage. Judith is a good example of how the abolition movement fostered the woman suffrage movement.[456]

Judith was socially aware and well educated, although she did not attend college. She attended many lectures and heard sermons on social issues, and she frequently discussed these with others. She belonged to a number of women's organizations. In 1875, she founded and served as the first president of the Home Club of East Boston. It was just the second women's club in Massachusetts. At meetings of the club, members listened to papers presented on various issues and then discussed those issues. In the club's first year, it heard addresses from Julia Ward Howe and Mary A. Livermore, both important figures in the woman suffrage movement. Judith had a special connection with Mary Livermore, because both had been teachers in Duxbury, and both found husbands there, in the early 1840s. Judith served as the Home Club's president for ten years.[457]

Judith was an early member of the New England Women's Club (NEWC), founded by Julia Ward Howe and others in 1868. Judith joined in 1873, and by 1891, she was a vice president. It was one of the two oldest women's clubs in America. In its interests and members, it overlapped the emerging woman suffrage movement, and it was a generally pro-suffrage organization.[458]

NEWC's headquarters at the Chauncy Hall Building, 585 Boylston Street in Boston, would reflect the women's club movement's overlap with the suffrage movement. At that location, Judith attended NEWC meetings in the former Chauncy Hall Building. When that building was replaced by another Chauncy Hall Building on the same site in 1909, NEWC was one of the first tenants. From 1909 through at least 1918, the building also housed the Massachusetts Woman Suffrage Association (MWSA), the Boston Equal Suffrage Association for Good Government (BESAGG), and the College Equal Suffrage League. The *Woman's Journal* was there from 1911 to 1916. This building was a beehive of suffrage activity.[459]

Chauncy Hall Building, October 4, 1912. Courtesy of the City of Boston Archives.

Long before the beehive, however, both Sylvanus and Judith became interested and then involved in the woman suffrage movement. Judith's diary says both of them attended a suffrage meeting in 1871, relatively early in the movement, in which they continued throughout their lives.[460]

In 1877, Sylvanus collected and sent 84 petitions for woman suffrage to the state legislature, as noted in the *Woman's Journal*, the prominent suffragist periodical. In 1878, Sylvanus outdid himself and sent in 414 more petitions, the most by far of the many persons listed in the *Woman's Journal.* In 1878, Sylvanus — not Judith — was elected an officer of the newly organized East Boston Woman Suffrage Club. In 1879, Sylvanus submitted another 112 suffrage petitions.[461]

Meanwhile, Judith was involved with the *Woman's Journal* as early as 1876, when she recommended her niece Catherine "Kate" Wilde (1844–1917) to fill a vacancy at the publication. Catherine became the clerk in charge of the journal's office and the clerk for the journal's company. She also became close friends with Julia Ward Howe and the journal's editors, Henry B. Blackwell and Alice Stone Blackwell. In 1891, the journal named Catherine as one of its two assistant editors, and her name appeared on the journal's masthead until 1906. She became a member, and later officer, of the New England Woman's Press Association. She continued as clerk of the journal's company until at least 1911. Catherine's work at the *Woman's Journal*, so important to the woman suffrage movement, came about because of Judith's recommendation.[462]

The Woman's Journal.

Vol. XXVII. BOSTON, SATURDAY, JULY 25, 1896. No. 30.

The Woman's Journal.

FOUNDED BY LUCY STONE.

A Weekly Newspaper, published every Saturday in Boston, devoted to the interests of woman—to her educational, industrial, legal and political equality, and especially to her right of suffrage.

EDITORS:

H. B. BLACKWELL.
ALICE STONE BLACKWELL.

ASSISTANT EDITORS:

FLORENCE M. ADKINSON.
CATHARINE WILDE.

OCCASIONAL CONTRIBUTORS:

Julia Ward Howe,
Mary A. Livermore,
Helen E. Villard,
Alice Wellington Rollins,
Mary Putnam Jacobi, M. D.,
Frances E. Willard,
Laura M. Johns,
Lillie Devereux Blake,
Elizabeth Stuart Phelps Ward,
Harriet Prescott Spofford,
Dr. Emily Blackwell,
Dr. Lelia G. Bedell,
Dr. Alida C. Avery,
Adelaide A. Claflin,
Candace Wheeler,
Baroness Alexandra Gripenberg,
Prof. Ellen Hayes.

Boston Office—No. 3 Park Street, where copies are for sale and subscriptions received.

SUBSCRIPTION.

Per Annum	$2.50
First year on trial	1.50
Single copies	.05
Club Rates—Five copies one year	10.00

Checks and drafts and post-office orders should be made payable to the Woman's Journal. Letters containing remittances should be addressed to Box 3638, or to the office of the Woman's Journal, 3 Park Street, Boston, Mass. Registered letters or Express Co.'s money orders may be sent at our risk. Money sent in letters not registered will be at the risk of the sender.

J. B. Morrison, Advertising Manager.

the New York Legislature—a school suffrage bill, as far back as 1877."

The writer of "Woman in Society Today," in the July *Arena*, says: "For myself I do believe with Frances Power Cobbe that any woman worth her salt sooner or later takes an interest in some question which involves legislation; and however much they may recoil from public duties, women begin to ask themselves, 'Why should I, because I am a woman, be forbidden to help achieve some public good or redress some flagrant wrong?'"

The New England Armenian Relief Committee continue to receive pressing appeals for contributions, as the situation in Turkey is described as simply heartrending. The outlook for the coming winter causes a great deal of anxiety, as little, if any, harvest can be reaped, and therefore no provision for the winter can be gathered. A letter from the interior says: "It is painful to go from house to house, and find no beds nor cooking utensils. In one place an old petroleum tin was used to cook the food in, and the houses were stripped and bare. In one village a few handfuls of flour or millet, but only enough to last a day or two at most. With no oxen for ploughing, the land soon becomes hard, and cannot be sown for fall, and in many villages passes out of the hands of the Christians. If the Christians lose their holdings, it will only be a question of time when they will have to give their houses also to the Turks and Kurds,

the sanction of the State Church and rendering it necessary to make the marriage a civil ceremony or have it performed by a Nonconformist minister.

A friend of Mrs. Stowe tells a quaint, pathetic little anecdote of later date than most of the reminiscences her going has called forth, writes "Dorothy Lundt," in the Boston *Transcript*. A welcome guest always at the homes near what was the home of her later years, it was sometimes her wont to wander, at twilight, from her own into some neighboring garden, and thence through the hospitable open door into hall or living-room. In the hall of one such house there was a fine bust of Henry Ward Beecher, in white marble, resting in a deep niche in the wainscoted wall, and near it a softly-shaded light. One summer twilight, when this light had been newly kindled, Mrs. Stowe came absently in through the open door, and stood looking at the bust. "Ah, Henry!" they heard her murmur, in her quiet, dreamful voice, "Ah, Henry, the light burns before you there, like a saint in your shrine! But—you were no saint, Henry! You were no saint!"

The American College for Girls at Constantinople has completed another year of faithful work which secured the reward of medal and diploma from the World's Columbian Exposition at Chicago, recently received. The students of the college are of various nationalities, and commencement week in June has come to be

enough, and the old adage, "Early to bed and early to rise, makes a man healthy and wealthy and wise," needs changing. There need be no reference to early rising in it. For "early to rise," "late to rise," might be substituted. The advice of that old saw was concocted in days when there were no express trains, no telegraphs, no telephones, no hurry. Where is the use of telling people to get up early whose brains are racked by anxiety and worry, and who are really being burned up by the ever-increasing rate at which things have to be done? The proper thing to say to them is to get as much sleep as they possibly can on every possible occasion.

And ah! what restful memories that brings of delicious, dreamy hours spent lying on the thick, elastic greensward of Prince Edward's enchanted isle! Nothing to do, no newspapers; no enforced talk; no thought about dress. Just

"With half-shut eyes ever to seem
Falling asleep in a half-dream."

While the breeze swept about me, softly cool from bright Bay Fortune. Mother earth is the restorer, the nurse, the blessing. Alice Brown, the wood-lover, writes:

Set the mind only upon flowing water and beautiful trees, and that in no studious mood, but the warm languor of a midday dream. Form a happy company of such as love the earth, and set up your tents by sea or lake, or even on the hilly pasture slopes at home. . . . There shall be long hours spent "in a green shade;" still, serene floating on the lake, while the sunset burns to gold, and deep dream-locked sleep under canvas or in the open air. You shall find the simplest fare ambrosial; and you shall be called to life every morning by a chiming chorus

CONCERNING WOMEN.

Mrs. L. D. Blake will take her usual summer vacation, writing only every other week.

Miss May Abraham, the new English superintendent of factory inspectors, is a beautiful woman of the Semitic type. She began her career as Lady Dilke's private secretary.

Mrs. Hiram Hunt, of Greenville, is one of Maine's renowned fisherwomen. On her first fishing expedition Mrs. Hunt caught the largest salmon ever taken from Moosehead Lake, and in addition landed five trout.

Miss Kate Sanborn, the witty author of "Abandoning an Adopted Farm," is a devotee of the wheel. In her cycling ventures Miss Sanborn tries to maintain the equilibrium fitting a niece of Daniel Webster, and really rides very well—on level ground.

Mrs. George Riggs, known to thousands of readers as Kate Douglass Wiggin, has a little cottage on the banks of the Saco River in Maine to which she repairs when she wishes to write uninterruptedly. The place is called "Quillcote," and was originally an abandoned farm.

Mrs. Charles H. Banta, who is serving her fourth year as president of the Jefferson City Union, No. 1, W. C. T. U., is one of the most faithful and efficient workers in the cause. She is county superintendent of jail work in the W. C. T. U..

Woman's Journal, detail with masthead at left, July 25, 1896. Courtesy of Schlesinger Library.

From her vantage point at the *Woman's Journal*, Catherine Wilde would undoubtedly have been interested in her Aunt Judith's activities. Perhaps this led to Scituate's early appearance in the publication. Judith spent summers at the Scituate lighthouse keeper's cottage by 1873. In 1878, the journal had a story about Scituate's Rebecca Bates and her sister Abigail. They were young daughters of the first lighthouse keeper. They were hailed as the "American Army of Two" for repelling the British in the War of 1812 by playing a fife and drum to act as an American troop.[463]

Judith was deeply involved in the suffrage movement by 1881, when she helped arrange a two-day convention of the MWSA. In 1883, she was named chair of the executive committee of the New England

Woman Suffrage Association (NEWSA). By 1885, Judith was a director of the Massachusetts School Suffrage Association.[464]

As chair of NEWSA's executive committee, Judith was involved in a one-day woman suffrage convention in the Casino at Newport, RI, on August 11, 1887. The convention featured speeches by Julia Ward Howe, Lucy Stone, and Henry B. Blackwell, among others. This was 22 years before Alva Belmont famously opened her Marble House mansion in Newport to the public, with a speech by Julia Ward Howe, and with admission fees to benefit the National American Woman Suffrage Association. At the 1887 convention, 300 people attended the afternoon session, after which local citizens organized a Newport Woman Suffrage League. The evening session featured speeches by Mary A. Livermore, Susan B. Anthony, and Julia Ward Howe. It closed with the singing of Howe's "Battle Hymn of the Republic."[465]

In 1887, MWSA, NEWSA, and the *Woman's Journal* moved from 5 Park Street to 3 Park Street, where the journal would be published for another 21 years.

Also at that location were the studios of Notman Photographic Company. William Notman established the main office in Montreal. The Boston studio was opened by William's brother, James Notman, by 1877. It photographed many famous Bostonians, including Oliver Wendell Holmes. Notman produced a photo of Lucy Stone with her baby, Alice Stone Blackwell. (The photo was taken in 1858 and probably copied by Notman later.) Notman's later portrait of Lucy Stone appeared as an engraving in 1881's *History of Woman Suffrage,* volume 2. The Boston studio made a photo collage in 1884 of eminent women, including suffragists Mary A. Livermore and Julia Ward Howe. The Boston studio also made a portrait of Sylvanus Smith in 1887. Boston suffragists would not have to go far to have their photos taken.[466]

For Judith, getting to the offices of MWSA, NEWSA, and the *Woman's Journal* in Boston would not have been difficult. A north ferry and a south ferry connected the southern end of East Boston with Boston proper. The fare to cross the harbor was only a few cents.[467]

In 1891, many noted suffragists associated with MWSA attended a reception for the Smiths' 50th wedding anniversary. The guest book had nearly 500 signatures, including Mary A. Livermore, William Lloyd Garrison (son of the famous abolitionist), Archibald H. Grimké (born a slave, nephew of the famous Grimké abolitionist sisters), Catharine "Kate" Wilde (Judith's niece, an editor of the *Woman's Journal*), Lucy Stone, Henry B. Blackwell, and Julia Ward Howe. Julia gave an opening address and wrote a poem for the occasion.[468]

In 1892, Judith reflected on her marriage in a talk at a women's club in Winchester on "How to Make a Happy Home." Her advice was:

> First, I think a man is an essential to a perfect home; although I know that good homes can be had without men. I also think that the home is more likely to be a happy one if the said man has decidedly limited means.
>
> Then every new thing brought into the house is thoroughly appreciated and enjoyed; and it is "cultivating" to plan how this and that can be had.
>
> ...
>
> I need not tell you club women that it makes home happier to join a church, or club, or both; and to help on unpopular causes. The happiest homes I have known are those of reformers, who look beyond the centre of their own homes, and try to help others to better ones.
>
> At a Golden Wedding, a newly married pair asked the aged couple how they had managed to keep so young in their looks and feelings. They said, "by joining the most unpopular causes that are good;" and you had better begin by joining the Woman Suffrage League.[469]

Alice Stone Blackwell heard the talk and published it in the *Woman's Journal*.[470]

An 1892 letter from Lucy Stone to her friend Judith reflects their closeness: it thanks Judith for the idea of using leaflets, muses about possible limits on woman suffrage (to those 21 years in the country), and complains about her rheumatism. Judith was Lucy's confidante. Lucy's daughter later called her, "Mamma's particular friend, dear Mrs. Judith W. Smith of East Boston."[471]

Judith's suffrage work continued, even as she entered old age. In 1899, she presided over MWSA's annual meeting, and the meeting elected her as the Massachusetts member of the executive committee of the national association, NAWSA. In 1901, the MWSA annual meeting again elected her as its member of the national executive committee. In 1910, Judith attended a standing-room-only meeting of BESAGG at its headquarters at 585 Boylston Street. Judith became an elder stateswoman of the suffrage movement. In 1915, at the age of 93, she was a speaker at MWSA's annual meeting. A 1919 article in NAWSA's official publication, *The Woman Citizen*, recognized her contributions to the cause, calling her "one of [MWSA's] most esteemed and beloved members."[472]

Perhaps the highest praise came from Lucy Stone's husband Henry B. Blackwell, who wrote Judith in 1905,

> I think hardly any woman in Massachusetts was so valued by my wife as Mrs. Judith W. Smith. Your family stood by the cause from its very beginning, and I have heard my wife describe her having enjoyed the hospitality of Mrs. Smith's father in Pembroke, Mass., long before I myself had the happiness to know her.[473]

Alice Stone Blackwell, the daughter of Lucy Stone and Henry B. Blackwell, worked with Judith for years, and she too was a big fan of Judith. She wrote many complimentary poems to Judith. In a 1914 postcard written presumably on the boat to her place on Martha's Vineyard, Alice wrote Judith: "As this long, Steady trip o'er the water extends — long, blessed life with the...steadfast, and straight, and Helps up us...to the heavenly Gate. With Love, Alice Stone Blackwell."[474]

Early Summers at Old Scituate Light

While Alice Stone Blackwell was spending summers in Martha's Vineyard, Judith and her family spent summers in Scituate. Judith documented in her diary the family's summer life on Lighthouse Point in Scituate in the late 1800s. While this was mostly a time for the family to enjoy each other, see friends and family from East Boston and Duxbury, and engage in outdoor activities, Judith's dedication to woman suffrage continued. A few episodes in Scituate were even written up in the *Woman's Journal.* The family would spend summers in Scituate for decades.

Scituate Harbor entrance, old lighthouse at left, with breakwater leading to its right. Postcard, early 1900s. Author's collection.

The Smiths were staying in Scituate by 1873, nearly 20 years after their move to East Boston. In July 1873, Judith wrote in her diary, "Father [Sylvanus] & Z [Zilpha] & Jennie took the cars [trains?] for Cedar Point Scituate, and Sidney & I went with horses. Very hot at home. Nice and cool at the Point. … A lovely place to spend the fourth — away from folks and firecrackers." The place was the keepers' cottage at the iconic Old Scituate Light on Cedar Point at Scituate Harbor. The federal government had discontinued and abandoned the old lighthouse.[475]

The federal government grew disenchanted with Old Scituate Light in the late 1840s and established a new light at Minot's Ledge in 1850. That light was destroyed in a storm in 1851. When a new Minot's Ledge Light became operational on November 15, 1860, Old Scituate Light went dark. The Fresnel lens installed at the top of the tower in 1855 was removed, and so was the lantern.[476]

Old Scituate Light, postcard postmarked 1911, with keeper's cottage. Author's collection.

The Smith family was probably able to stay at the discontinued lighthouse courtesy of Samuel Hall, one of their close family friends. The government hired him as the live-in caretaker of the lighthouse. The only surviving government records say this was for 1873, but he may have been involved before and after.[477]

Samuel Hall (born 1833, died before 1897) was almost certainly the son of the noted shipbuilder Samuel Hall (1800–1870) of Marshfield, Duxbury and later East Boston. He worked at his father's shipyard and lived near it in East Boston. Sylvanus Smith at one time worked for the senior Samuel Hall in East Boston, and there the families all lived near one another, and near the shipyards. Not only that, but the families were connected in other ways, including by marriage. In 1877, the Smiths' daughter Mary married Luke, a grandson of the brother of the senior Samuel Hall.[478]

The junior Samuel Hall was also president of the Cedar Point Club, named for the location of the Scituate lighthouse. The club seems to have engaged in gunning (shooting) shore birds, which were plentiful in that area. Club members included Sylvanus Smith, and they met in the lighthouse.[479]

The Smith family spent July 4th weekends at the lighthouse at first. By the 1890s, they were spending the whole month of July there, according to Judith's diary entries. Judith was a faithful diarist.[480]

On July 1, 1876, members of Judith's family sailed from East Boston to Scituate in the twilight. Three other men "sailed at the same time for the same place." They were Capt. John Bradford, Reuben Peterson, and George Manson. Manson was likely the George Manson of East Boston who, in 1860, married Mercy Ford Clapp of Scituate, where many of her family members lived.[481]

Judith did not take a sailboat to Scituate. On July 3, she packed, probably took the train, and spent a week in Scituate. The lighthouse lacked the conveniences of their city house. The boys had to go up town for water. Evidently, there was no well at the lighthouse. Judith took the train back home. The boys sailed off to Duxbury. For them, sailing must have offered the same freedom and independence as, in our time, getting a driver's license and having a car. Meanwhile, Judith sweltered. Boston had 43 straight days with temperatures above 80 degrees.[482]

The boys were not the only ones to explore the world by sea.

Stowaway

In July 1875, the Smiths' daughter Mary, then about 20 years old, hid away on a ship to Philadelphia. Here is what happened.

In 1875, Sylvanus's firm, Smith & Townsend, built a new clipper ship named *Centennial.* The name was doubtless in honor of the 100th anniversary of the signing of the Declaration of Independence in Philadelphia. On July 13, the ship was set to sail for Philadelphia and then on to San Francisco. Philadelphia was an appropriate destination, as the city was already planning centennial celebrations and constructing buildings for the Centennial International Exhibition of 1876. It was the first official World's Fair to be held in the United States.[483]

—The new ship Centennial, launched a few weeks since from the yard of Smith & Townsend, East Boston, will sail for Philadelphia, today, where she will load for San Francisco in the new line of packets to be established between San Francisco and Philadelphia. Smith & Townsend are constructing another ship of 750 tons.

Boston Globe, July 13, 1875, page 8

In what must have been a farewell gathering, Mary and her family visited the *Centennial* before the ship sailed. The captain of the 1,287-ton ship was Isaac M. Bearse. Passengers who boarded for the voyage to Philadelphia were Mary's father Sylvanus, Mary's Uncle Rufus (Judith's brother), Capt. Mayer, Capt. Sampson, and evidently Capt. Bearce's wife.[484]

During the visit, Mary hid in a closet for fun, then accidentally locked herself in as the ship sailed from Boston. Mary finally got someone's attention to let her out. Everyone was surprised to see her and laughed. During the voyage, which took less than five days, she was promoted to third mate and secretary. Upon her arrival in Philadelphia, she wrote, "The only trouble is, that I am introduced to everyone as a stowaway and have all manner of fun made of me."[485]

Her mother Judith was not amused. Her diary for July 13–14 said,

> ... then we all went to the ship Centennial, and sailed down the harbor in her — a very pleasant party — but my enjoyment of the sail up was marred very much by knowing that my dear Mary had hid herself on board, and must suffer the consequences of doing a very foolish — selfish — thoughtless act. Too bad – to mar her father's pleasure, who has gone to Philadelphia in the ship. Also Rufus, Capt. Mayo & Sampson. Luke

> [Mary's boyfriend and future husband] feels very badly about it.[486]

A week later, Judith had calmed down. She received a letter from Sylvanus. He hoped she did not worry about Mary. He and Mary had been sick but were much better. Mary was having a nice time. The *Centennial* "beat everything, and the pilot said it was the finest ship that ever came up the Delaware [River]." Sylvanus wished many times that Judith and all could have been there. He soon wrote again, July 24, giving details of their stay in Philadelphia. He tried that day to book passage home for Mary on a steamer, but all the berths were sold. He arranged for her to go home the following Saturday (July 31) on the steamer *Roman* with Capt. Crowell, a fine man related by marriage to Capt. Bearse. The *Centennial* had a hard time getting rid of its ballast. A sale fell through, and finally "Capt Bearse got the centennial folks to take it."[487]

Sylvanus and Mary went to Independence Hall and saw the council chamber. Mary sat in the President's chair, according to Sylvanus, and "decreed to have the streets in the lower part of the city repaired and cleaned, and to have sewers in the streets. It was passed unanimously." They later took a river cruise. When they got back, they saw a gang of men cleaning the street. Mary said, "you see they are carrying out our vote." They returned to the *Centennial*, which was docked about a 10 minutes' walk north of Arch Street, on the river.[488]

Instead of returning home right away, Sylvanus traveled farther south, to the Norfolk area, to inspect oak timber, evidently for use in building his ships. He was not able to return to Philadelphia in time to see Mary off. Writing Judith on Sunday, August 1, he said he expected to be home at the end of the week.[489]

Summers in Scituate

Judith did not go on the voyage to Philadelphia, so she missed Sylvanus and Mary's sightseeing tours of the city. But Judith explored the sights around Scituate during her stays at the lighthouse. For example, on July 10, 1882, on her way to visit Duxbury, she "drove to North River by the beach road, stopping to go over the large hotel and cottages being built there — and after crossing the $10,000 bridge they have built over the river, we stopped to pick flowers."[490]

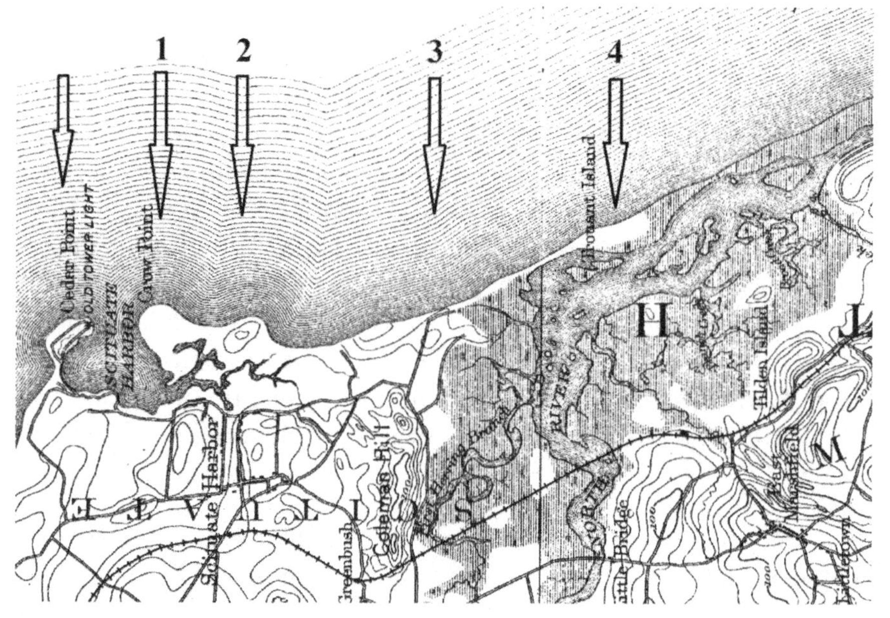

1893 USGS map, detail (sideways, ocean at top, arrows added). From left: Cedar Point, Scituate Harbor, four cliffs (numbered), with narrow beach between Third Cliff and Fourth Cliff, where Hotel Humarock was.

Judith evidently rode in a horse-drawn wagon, and the "beach road" was the road over the narrow shingle beach that then laid between Third Cliff and Fourth Cliff. The hotel being built at Fourth Cliff was the grand Hotel Humarock. Humarock was the area south of the point of Fourth Cliff. Part of Scituate, Humarock was a narrow strip of land with the ocean on one side and the North River on the other. The new bridge noted by Judith crossed the North River. It went between Humarock and Marshfield's village of White's Ferry at Sea Street. The bridge allowed mainland access to cottage lots being developed at Humarock as well as the new Hotel Humarock.[491]

Three weeks after Judith's visit, the "magnificent and palatial summer hotel known as Hotel Humarock" opened for guests. Three weeks after that, it burned to the ground. The loss was estimated at $35,000. The next year, a new Hotel Humarock was built on the same site.

Judith would have been one of the few to see the original hotel before it was destroyed by fire.[492]

In 1889, the Smiths spent practically the whole month of July at the lighthouse. Sylvanus built a canopy outside to provide cool shade. It was held up by two vertical posts that looked like tree trunks. It had cross beams, and ribs on top, supporting a striped awning that gave it the look of a tent. On July 9, Judith wrote in her diary, "Sylvanus finished the tent, which we all enjoyed very much, for it was hot." The canopy appeared in 1890 photos in a Smith family chronicle (see below), in a 1902 US government photo, and in a photo used in a postcard postmarked 1908.[493]

Canopy skeleton appears at left in this postcard (detail), "3 — Old Light Tower, Built 1811, Scituate, Mass." published by F. N. Damon Curio Co., postmarked 1908. Author's collection.

In 1890, the Smiths again spent most of July at the lighthouse. Sylvanus was busy fixing up the keeper's cottage. On July 5, Judith wrote in her diary that he "has bought boards and shingles to repair this shantie, so he will be happy." A photo in the family chronicle shows Sylvanus shingling the roof. He also cleared a path to the outhouse. This work would have been natural for him, with his years of experience as a shipbuilder, and as a house carpenter before that. For Sylvanus, this would have been a good way to spend a vacation.[494]

Sylvanus Smith (left) shingling part of keeper's cottage at Old Scituate Light, with canopy he built at right. E. F. Smith photo, 1890. Copy in Smith family chronicle.

The Smith family chronicle has two interesting photos taken at the Old Scituate Light in 1890 by Erasmus F. Smith, a son of Judith and Sylvanus. The chronicle reported:

> Mr. [Sylvanus] Smith was a member of the gunning club established by Mr. Samuel Hall, then custodian for the United States of the lighthouse property at Scituate. It gradually became the custom for each member to take his family there for a month.
>
> These photographs taken by E. F. Smith, in 1890, show (1) Mr. Smith shingling the roof at the old light, and (2) under the awning he had put up, a party of friends such as he liked to gather about him there. This party was from Duxbury.[495]

Visits from family and friends were not the only ways the Smiths spent their summers. Some sailed around Scituate's waters, even in moonlight. Some flew a kite, played in the sand hills, or fished on the breakwater next to the lighthouse. One day's catch could provide supper for the whole family. In addition, there were trips to Peggotty

Beach or into town for the shops at Scituate Harbor. The Smiths even had mail delivered or forwarded to them at the lighthouse. They also visited or had dealings with locals, like Mr. Barker, probably the man who owned the huge farm and old house not far from the lighthouse, and Mr. Prouty, Mr. Gardner, Mrs. Spencer, William Jackson, and Mrs. Hammond, who ran the Colonial Inn on Meeting House Lane.[496]

Sylvanus Smith (center, with hat?), Judith Smith, and Duxbury party, under canopy with striped awning at Scituate lighthouse, with First Cliff in background. Photo by E. F. Smith, 1890, Smith family chronicle. Courtesy of the Duxbury Rural and Historical Society.

In addition to these people, Judith's diary mentioned visiting Pembroke and calling on Dr. Collamore. This was almost certainly Dr. Francis Collamore of North Pembroke. The Smiths would have known him from their years on the farm in Pembroke, 1844 to 1854. The farm was adjacent to the property and house of Dr. Anthony Collamore. He was descended from Collamores in Scituate in the 1600s. He left his medical practice to Francis Collamore, his nephew. Francis was born in Pembroke December 7, 1825, and he attended Dartmouth Medical School. Francis and his family lived in the Collamore house or another house next door. While the Smith farmhouse is gone, the Collamore house still stands in Pembroke.[497]

In the summer of 1891, the Smiths' friend Mr. Roper came from Boston in his steam launch. With Sylvanus's background building ships, he would have been interested in this fast, powerful boat, and Scituate's harbor would have been a good showplace for it. Mr. Roper took the family for trips on his launch as far out as the Hotel Humarock, where they saluted the hotel guests, and the guests waved back. Mr. Roper was almost certainly Sylvester H. Roper, an inventor who worked with steam-powered conveyances for decades. He had two fast steam launches, the *Pickerel* and the *Toothpick*. Five years after visiting the Smiths, he would die at age 73 while testing a steam-powered bicycle on a track along the Charles River near Harvard. He became what one expert said was "the world's first motorcycle fatality."[498]

Sylvanus continued to fix up the lighthouse keeper's cottage. In 1891, Judith reported that "Sylvanus finished the window in the roof, just before the rain poured, and then went to work on the screen doors." A few days later, he was at work on the stable.[499]

The Smith family's presence at the Scituate lighthouse was even noted in the *Boston Globe*, which reported in 1892 that, "Mrs. Emma McLaughlin, late of Paris, is the guest of Mrs. Sylvanus Smith of Boston at the old lighthouse on Cedar Point."[500]

In 1893, the family celebrated July 4th at the old Scituate lighthouse. Son Sidney fired the cannon, others set off firecrackers and Roman candles, and the family had a bonfire. The family watched other fireworks all along the shore. The next day, Sylvanus and Sidney began building an annex to the stable.[501]

Back in East Boston, Sylvanus built a boat in the loft of the stable at their house. In early July 1894, the boat appeared in Scituate. It was named the *Judith*. Judith said, "Sidney took his family, I and Annie to sail in the *Judith*. It was a clear, bright morning with a good breeze that did not heel the boat over, and we sailed as far as the 4th cliff! Perfectly lovely."[502]

Judith's presence in Scituate led to articles highlighting the town in the *Woman's Journal*. An 1894 story again told readers about Scituate's "American Army of Two" (the Scituate lighthouse keeper's daughters), and it reported the following:

> A certain active member of the Mass. W. S. A. is spending her vacation at the Point, entertaining her children and grandchildren. Here she sails the seas over in a boat which her husband, seventy-five years old, built with his own hands, and named the "*Judith*," in loving honor of his faithful "first mate" of so many years. A trip was recently made to Minot's Ledge Lighthouse, where our suffrage friend was welcomed as the oldest visitor who had ever been hoisted to that dizzy height. True to her principles, she carried with her some copies of the *Woman's Journal*, the first ever seen at the Light, and left them for the benefit of the light-keepers, who, she writes, "have plenty of time to read and ponder."[503]

The "certain active member" in the 1894 article was Judith. The article's writer, "C. W." was Catherine Wilde, Judith's niece, and, as noted before, an editor of the journal. In the same issue, on the front page, Judith wrote a report on association activities as Mrs. J. W. Smith, "Chairman Ex. Com." [Executive Committee].

Meanwhile, a month after the story in the *Woman's Journal*, Judith wrote a letter telling about the boat that her husband built and their trip to Minot's Light,

> Dear Cousin, Your letter … was forwarded to us at the old light house in Scituate, where we spend July of each year. …
>
> Silvanus built a boat in his stable last spring, about sixteen feet long. She proved to be a very safe, excellent sailer, and added very much to the pleasure of each of our married children, and their families, as they came in turn to visit us.
>
> Even I, who thought I never should sail outside the harbor in an open boat again, did so and enjoyed it very much.

> The last time we sailed to Minot's Light, and I went up in the chair, tied in, with a three and a half year old granddaughter in my lap. Silvanus thinks it is ninety feet from the boat to the door we were pulled into. …
>
> [In talking with the lighthouse keeper, it appeared Judith was the oldest person who had come up there.] The lighthouse itself, the life of the five keepers; three of them there at a time, for two weeks each (if they can get ashore at the end of them) and their families on shore, are all very interesting.[504]

Judith found her own summer life in Scituate interesting as well. That same summer of 1894, family members often took the train to visit the Smiths. They included their children: Sidney and his wife Mary B and family, Frances, Mary and her husband Luke and family, Erasmus ("Race") and family, Jennie, and occasionally Zilpha. Then there were grandchildren, like Sidney's Lawrence, Jennie's Miriam, and Mary's Constance ("a little duck in the water"). One day, Judith, Mary, Lawrence, and Miriam "drove to the first and second cliff …. Saw the Lighthouse from that point of view, and the wreck of the Minnie Rowen; a schooner which father built. She went ashore last March, in a dreadful storm." Sylvanus shingled one side of the roof over the "prospect room." Often the family sailed in the *Judith*, rowed in their skiff, bathed (presumably at the beach), and fished (sometimes from the *Judith*). On July 4, in addition to fish chowder, they had watermelon, huckleberry cake, and pie.[505]

Food did not seem to be a problem. With all the fishing, they often made fish chowder. When Sylvanus made it, Judith usually described it as "a fine fish chowder." Luke's uncle, Mr. Clapp, 77 years old, brought milk to the cottage. This was probably Rufus Clapp, a milkman with a farm at Willow Street near Bay Street (today's Beaver Dam Road near Tilden Road).[506]

There was a little time for diversions after the domestic chores were done. They played whist in the evenings. At the end of July 1894, Judith finished reading *The Heavenly Twins*, a recent and controversial novel by Irish feminist writer Sarah Grand. Sylvanus took time from making new stairs to take Judith to the Glades, at low tide, where they realized what a rock-bound coast this was. At the end of their 1894 seaside vacation in Scituate, they packed and took their wagon home to East Boston.[507]

In 1896, Judith was again (somewhat anonymously) the subject of a report in the *Woman's Journal*:

> The ever-cheery spirit of the presiding member (not the President) of the M. W. S. A. will be recognized in the following bit from a private letter:
>
> Cedar Pt., Scituate, July 19.
>
> We decided to build a cottage here, knowing our children and grandchildren would enjoy coming here in their vacations, and having a nice time with little money. So we drove down two weeks ago. The lighthouse where we always stayed was occupied, so we brought our belongings into the boathouse, and here we have lived more comfortably than even we would have thought possible.
>
> . . .
>
> One morning I saw a neighbor at work on her piazza; so I took the *Woman's Journal* over and read her "Mrs. Purdy's Parquisites." She came in afterwards, and said the directors at the sewing circle took turns in reading, and asked if she could have the paper to read them that story!
>
> We have a good force at work on the house, and it rises fast day by day.[508]

By then, when the Smiths' new cottage was being built, the lighthouse keeper's cottage was probably occupied by a local lamplighter and undertaker named John E. O. Prouty. He was assigned to maintain the navigational red light, installed in 1891, on a wooden spar at the end of the breakwater next to the lighthouse. He lived in town but was allowed to stay in the keeper's cottage during summer months.[509]

The Smith family no longer had to be concerned about the lighthouse being occupied when they built their cottage in 1896. It was just a few steps away from the lighthouse. It was on the Scituate Harbor side of Cedar Point (Lighthouse Point). Later, we discuss the cottage in more detail.

The Smith cottage is the tall cottage left of center, in this view of Scituate Harbor with Lighthouse Point in background and Old Scituate Light at right, postcard, postmarked 1912. Author's collection.

With the cottage complete, it was a good place for family to visit. In September 1900, the Smiths' daughter Mary and son-in-law Luke Hall made the trip from East Boston to Scituate by horse, even though Luke had said he would never do that again. According to Mary, Luke said, "the train was good enough for him. But after many autos had whizzed by us he decided he would have one of those." They stopped in Quincy for supper with relatives, then rode from 8:20 until 11:15 to reach the cottage at Lighthouse Point.[510]

During Mary's visit, her husband Luke worked hard helping to build a boat, *The Raymond*, with Cedar Point summer neighbors Fred Bourne of Somerville and Will H. P. Harrington of Waltham. Mary went to

Scituate Harbor to run errands. In addition, she went with Mrs. Bourne and Mrs. Harrington to the Marshfield Fair and enjoyed the horse racing there.[511]

Scituate was the nation's center for harvesting Irish moss. It is a type of seaweed used in producing such items as beer and ice cream. In 1900, Judith used Irish moss from Scituate to promote woman suffrage:

> The president, Mrs. J. W. Smith of the East Boston Woman Suffrage League, has bought a quantity of Irish moss gathered in Scituate, and agrees to fill all the little silk bags the other Leagues will send her, with this cheap and nutritious article, for the National Bazar. The bags may be sent to her, care *Woman's Journal*, 3 Park Street, Boston. Each bag will contain a typewritten receipt for making delicious blanc-mange, and another for an efficient and agreeable cure for colds. The bags should be about three inches long, and made to draw together at the top.[512]

In the summer of 1901, Judith spent some time in New Hampshire for her health. Sylvanus wrote her on Friday, July 5, describing sights he saw in Scituate and the fireworks he saw on the way home to East Boston. He said:

> We drove in to the Lawson place, and saw where they were putting in the foundations for his residence. It is just to the west of the house where you and Jen [their daughter] stayed, but a little farther from the road. It is but a story and half high but quite long sort of rambling, looks like about 3 houses joined together in a crooked line.[513]

Sylvanus was describing what would be the remarkable Dreamwold home of Thomas Lawson's huge estate in Scituate. Sylvanus closed the letter by saying "So good night, Silvanus. Now Jen & I have to have our quiet before going to bed. PS I felt quite blue not getting any thing [letter] from you until Wednesday night."[514] These were some of his last words.

On July 30, 1901, Sylvanus died, at age 84. Henry B. Blackwell and Alice Stone Blackwell wrote a heartfelt letter of condolence to Judith, as did Julia Ward Howe. The *Woman's Journal* reported the death, noting that he was a native of Duxbury, and a shipbuilder in the firm of Smith & Townsend in East Boston. The journal called him "an earnest and uncompromising advocate of equal rights for women." Sylvanus "was a familiar sight at the social gatherings of the Mass. W. S. A., of which his wife has so long been a valued officer." The journal noted that he loved to gather with his family in his summer home in Scituate by the sea.[515]

A lengthy obituary of Sylvanus by Mary A. Livermore appeared in the next issue of the *Woman's Journal.*[516]

The Oldest Suffragist Orator in the World

Judith continued her suffrage work. After the death of Susan B. Anthony in 1906, a memorial fund was established in Anthony's name by the NWSA. Judith was one of nine honorary chairmen.[517]

National Woman Suffrage Association.

HONORARY CHAIRMEN:

Clara Barton,
Antoinette Brown Blackwell,
Caroline M. Severance.

Elizabeth Smith Miller.
Judith Winsor Smith.
Emily Howland.

Eliza Wright Osborne.
Charlotte L. Peirce.
Phebe A. Hanaford.

Susan B. Anthony Memorial Fund.

"If I have lived to any purpose, carry on the work I have to lay down."—Susan B. Anthony.

Judith was one of nine honorary chairmen of the Susan B. Anthony Memorial Fund. Notice, c. 1906. Courtesy of Library of Congress.

In November 1909, the New England Women's Club honored Judith on her 88th birthday. The club, located in Boston, was one of the earliest women's clubs in America. At the ceremony, Julia Ward Howe, one of the club's founders, a suffragist, and in her 91st year, gave a long address in honor of Judith. The *Woman's Journal* reported that Judith was "one of its [the club's] oldest and most highly-esteemed members, who is also a much-beloved member and officer of the Massachusetts W. S. A." The journal included a poem by Miss Blackwell (presumably Alice Stone Blackwell) with the following lines, referring to Judith's late husband Sylvanus:

> At Scituate, their summer home,
>
> Their biggest boat for sailing
>
> He named the Judith, after her,
>
> His will in this prevailing.
>
> She said, "Such partiality
>
> An evil name would gain us,
>
> And so our other boat, my dear,
>
> I'll christen the Sylvanus!"[518]

Judith's fight for suffrage was long and continued all her life. She gave many public speeches when she was in her 90s. In 1914, she was one of those "well known women who took part in the parade" of suffragists, held in May in Boston.[519]

On July 31, 1914, she spoke at a rally in Post Office Square in Boston. The *Boston Globe* reported:

> At 1 yesterday afternoon there was a big suffrage rally in Postoffice sq. Mrs. Thomas Pelham Curtis drove her automobile, with the little group of speakers, very close to the big monument which commemorates the great humanitarian, George Thorndike Angell. The square was thronged with men, wagons and automobiles. Many of the men apparently enjoyed the break in the dull routine of the day.
>
> In the rear seat of the auto was Mrs Judith W. Smith of East Boston, now in her 92d year, who has

> been identified with all the great reforms advocated by women for more than half a century.[520]

Another Boston newspaper reported on the same event:

> The burden of the 92 years of her life did not prevent Mrs. Judith Smith of 76 White street, East Boston, from making a hearty, vigorous speech in behalf of suffrage for women when she addressed a meeting in Postoffice Square yesterday afternoon under the auspices of the Boston Equal Suffrage Association.[521]

Later, in August 1914, she spoke at Liberty Square in Boston:

> Mrs Judith W. Smith of East Boston, 92 years old, spoke at a suffrage meeting this afternoon between 1 and 2 o'clock, at Liberty sq. under the auspices of the Boston Equal Suffrage Association. The other speakers were Mrs Maud Wood Park and William H. McMasters.[522]

Liberty Square is still there, just a block or two from Post Office Square and the Old State House.[523]

Judith spoke at suffrage events in 1915, a key year for woman suffrage because of the state referendum. In May, at a memorial service for Julia Ward Howe, Boston Mayor James Michael Curley spoke, and Judith paid tribute to Julia, her old friend and co-worker in the suffrage movement. In August, when a bronze tablet was unveiled to mark the birthplace of Lucy Stone, Lucy's friend Judith spoke. In October, when the suffragists held the "Victory" parade in Boston, Judith rode in Lucy Stone's carriage. Two of her grandsons walked beside the carriage as escorts. Governor Walsh reviewed the parade, presenting a bouquet of yellow roses to Alice Stone Blackwell, president of MWSA. Then Mayor Curley reviewed the parade, accepted a letter from Judith, and presented her with a bouquet of yellow roses. Yellow roses were for the suffragists, red roses were handed out by the "antis." By then, Judith was reputed to be "the oldest suffragist orator in the world."[524]

In 1916, when the home of Lucy Stone and Henry B. Blackwell was dedicated as the headquarters of the *Woman's Journal* and as a suffrage library, Lucy's friend Judith spoke.[525]

In January 1918, Judith took part in celebrating BESAGG's new headquarters in the Little Building, 74–94 Boylston Street, Boston. The opening of the new headquarters brought together hundreds of suffragists, including Alice Stone Blackwell, president of the MWSA. Judith was a special guest, and at 97 the oldest living member of MWSA.[526]

In the same month, Alice Stone Blackwell wrote a note to Judith, saying

> At the National Suffrage Convention in Washington, it was voted that a letter of greeting and affection and gratitude should be sent you, for the good work that you did for woman suffrage in the years when it had so many less friends than it has today. ... I am an enthusiastic admirer of yours, not only on suffrage grounds but on human grounds. I wish we had millions of women as level-headed and sound-hearted and high-principled as you.[527]

On August 13, 1918, Judith spoke at a luncheon at the Hotel Somerset in Boston, organized by the MWSA, celebrating the 100th anniversary of the birth of Lucy Stone. Judith had been one of Lucy's closest friends, and Judith was still considered an active worker in the cause of suffrage.[528]

By January 1919, Judith with her daughter Zilpha moved into a house in the Boston neighborhood of Jamaica Plain.[529] Later in 1919, Judith was the special guest at a gathering of the MWSA to honor her.[530]

In 1920, women got the vote with the adoption of the 19th Amendment. Now nearly 100 years old, Judith planned to vote. The *Boston Globe* quoted her as saying, "My mother and I, way back in my girlhood days, were the only people in Pembroke to sign the suffrage petition. That was 70-odd years ago, and it seems a long time for the men to make the women fight for their rights before they gained the victory."[531]

Warren Harding was elected President, with Judith's vote. August 1, 1921, was "Plymouth Day," the highlight of the town's Tercentenary celebration of the Pilgrim landing. President Harding came to the celebration, the first sitting president to visit Plymouth. Judith got to meet with him. She told the president that she waited 75 years for the opportunity to cast her ballot for the first time.[532]

As the *Boston Globe* reported, Judith was:

> one of the earliest woman suffragists, who lived to vote for him last year. Mrs Smith was dressed in white and wore a lace cap. Her hearing is impaired and she has to use an ear device, but she managed to carry on an animated conversation with the President, who said he was glad to have had the honor of meeting her, thanked her for her support in the Presidential campaign and expressed the hope that she would continue to support the Republican ticket.[533]

The Smith Cottage in Scituate

The Smith cottage is the tall one, second from left in this postcard view from Scituate Harbor of Cedar Point (Lighthouse Point), "Scene at Lighthouse Point, Sands Hill, Scituate, Mass." published by C. N. Frye, early 1900s. Author's collection.

As noted above, the Smith family built their Scituate cottage in 1896 on the Scituate Harbor side of Cedar Point (Lighthouse Point). It is now number 82 Lighthouse Road. It is close to the lighthouse where the family long spent summers. Here, Judith and Sylvanus entertained their family and visitors.[534]

The town first taxed the cottage and a stable in Sylvanus Smith's name, as recorded in the town's valuation list of May 1, 1897. At first, he did not own the land, and he probably leased the land. At the time, that arrangement was not unusual.[535]

Smith cottage in background, with Sylvanus Smith (most likely) at left, with family. Photo by Frederick N. Damon, late 1800s. Courtesy of Scituate Historical Society.

Not long after the cottage was built, the huge Portland Gale of 1898 badly damaged almost every cottage on Lighthouse Point, but the Smith family's new cottage survived intact.[536]

Smith cottage is tall one near right in this postcard, "Storm '98 Scituate Mass," c. 1899. Author's collection.

The cottage appears on a 1903 map, marked as "S. Smith Est. [Estate]" since Sylvanus had died in 1901.[537]

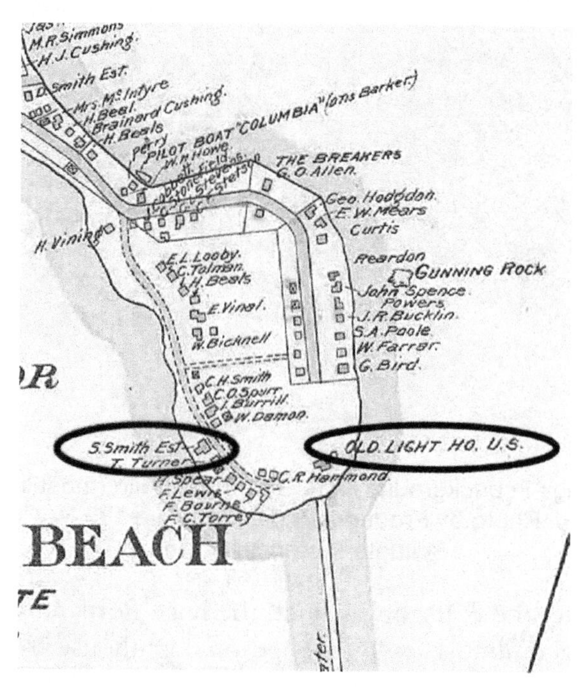

Smith cottage and old lighthouse appear on this detail of Judson, *Atlas of Plymouth County*, 1903, plate 32, Barker Farm Beach inset. Courtesy of State Library of Massachusetts.

After Sylvanus's death, Judith tried to rent their seashore cottage. She placed ads in the *Woman's Journal* in 1906 and 1915. The earlier ad said "House of nine rooms, set tubs, town water, wide piazzas and stable. Fronting on harbor."[538] In 1913, Misses Miriam Merrick and Hannah Shepard of East Boston stayed at the Smith cottage. But Judith spent time at the cottage, too, including in 1914, and evidently as late as about 1920. Many family members used the cottage.[539]

It was not until 1908, when Judith was age 87, that she acquired title to the land for the cottage. The land consisted of three lots (108, 118, and 119). The lots appeared on a 1908 plan referenced in the deed. That plan showed buildings on each of the three lots. The area was not covered by the Sanborn fire insurance maps in 1908 and 1918, but the 1926 Sanborn map showed all three buildings. The building on lot 108 (now no. 82 Lighthouse Road) was not labeled, but was the main cottage, based on tax records. A small building on lot 119 (no. 81) was called "La Casita" and the building (formerly a stable) on lot 118 (no. 83) was called "Popin." The cottages may have provided enough room for Judith's 4 children then living (of 6), 14 grandchildren, and 18 great-grandchildren at the time of her death.[540]

Smith cottage, 1911, family photo. Courtesy of the Duxbury Rural and Historical Society.

Judith Smith died December 3, 1921. She had been perhaps the oldest suffragist, and the oldest "clubwoman" in America, having been a member of the New England Woman's Club for 50 years. Judith was cheery, grateful, and determined, a woman praised by iconic people in the woman suffrage movement. She and her husband Sylvanus Smith, both *Mayflower* descendants, were buried in the Mayflower Cemetery in Duxbury.[541]

In 1922, Judith's estate separately sold the three lots at Cedar Point in Scituate, each one containing a building. The old family cottage at 82 Lighthouse Road went to Margaret O'Hare. It has remained with her descendants to this day, almost 100 years. Lot 118 at 83 Lighthouse Road went by way of a third party to Judith's son Erasmus F. Smith, who continued to sail the *Judith*. Lot 119 at 81 Lighthouse Road, with "La Casita," went to Judith's son Sidney Smith as trustee for his grandson Lothrop Smith.[542]

In 1939, Sidney wrote:

> When 72 years of age, early in 1889, he [Sylvanus] built for himself a sixteen foot sail boat – such a one as he had wanted from boyhood. He named her "The Judith", for his wife. His children, grandchildren, and now his great grandchildren have learned to sail in this staunch and trim craft. Through 45 years of continuous service she has preserved her elegance of symmetrical boat lines, such as only a master workman could combine. She is still strong, seaworthy, and the delight of his youngest son, Erasmus, who takes great pleasure, in the summer, in using her daily for the benefit and joy of all his friends.[543]

Sidney, the Smiths' oldest son, continued to enjoy living at "La Casita." Upon his death in 1941 at age 94, local papers called him the oldest resident of Scituate. His property, including "La Casita," went to Lothrop Smith in 1942.[544]

Lothrop Smith was not the only descendant of Sylvanus and Judith Smith to live on Lighthouse Road. The town's 1944 tax valuation list of property owners listed Lothrop Smith at #81 and Erasmus F. Smith at #83. Then there was Roy Hall at #65.[545]

Roy Hall fits in as follows: Sylvanus and Judith's daughter Mary (the stowaway) married Luke Hall, and among their children was Roy Hall. Roy Hall owned property at 65 Lighthouse Road from 1919 (when Judith would have been alive) until his death in 1956. Then it passed to his descendants, including his son Roy Hall, Jr., and Roy Hall, Jr.'s son Roy Hall III. In 1997, it was sold to a family trust whose trustee was Janet F. Winter, the sister of Roy Hall, Jr. In 2009, that trust sold the property to another family trust, the Winter Family Trust, probably with further descendants of the Halls. The sale in 2009 marked well over 100 years, and maybe counting, of Sylvanus and Judith Smith's family and descendants at Lighthouse Point.[546]

A card created for Sidney's 90th birthday in 1936 featured a drawing of the Scituate lighthouse and keeper's cottage, with a sailboat in the harbor. Perhaps the sailboat was the *Judith* built by Sylvanus and named for his wife. It was a fitting reminder of the summers spent in Scituate by the much-beloved suffragist Judith Smith, her suffragist husband Sylvanus, and their family.[547]

8

Women Vote

The 19th Amendment giving women the vote was ratified August 18, 1920. This was certified August 26, just in time (in most states) for women to vote for president. Below we consider how this amendment was ratified and what its impact was. We also reflect on how this historic event has been recognized, and the fight for suffrage today.

Ratification

By 1919, quite a few states allowed women to vote, with suffrage sweeping from the west toward the east. But Southern states resisted. They particularly objected to a national edict requiring them to allow women to vote. Their representatives in Congress were against the suffrage amendment.[548]

Woman suffrage map, June 4, 1919. White=full suffrage (17), dotted=Presidential suffrage (13). Source: *History of Woman Suffrage*, vol. 6, page 627.

Nevertheless, Congress passed the proposed constitutional amendment for woman suffrage on June 4, 1919. Its adoption required ratification by three-fourths — 36 — of the states. Only a handful of state legislatures were in session at the time. Massachusetts was one of them, and on June 25, 1919, Massachusetts became the eighth state to ratify. The vote in the Massachusetts House of Representatives was 185–47. Walter Haynes of Scituate, brother of Inez Haynes Irwin, was one of those who voted to ratify.[549]

A year later, ratification by a 36th state was close. In March 1920, the anti-suffrage journal *The Woman Patriot* listed ratification status state by state, and concluded, "the necessary 36 ratifications cannot be obtained in 1920."[550]

On June 22, 1920, a large delegation of the National Woman's Party, including Scituate's Mrs. Randolph Keith (Mary Moore) Forrest, met with the Republican nominee for president, Senator Warren Harding. They sought his influence to secure the 36th state. He waffled, saying, "Nothing would please me more than to have ratification made effective to give American womanhood full participation in the elections of next November. ... [but] I could not, with propriety, attempt to force any state executive to hasten action in violation of his own sense of duty."[551]

In August 1920, Tennessee was the last state to consider the constitutional amendment before the 1920 presidential election. The governor called a special session of the legislature. Suffragists, anti-suffragists, and special interests descended on the state. The outcome was in doubt. The fascinating twists and turns there are described in a book by Elaine Weiss, *The Woman's Hour*. Finally, on August 18, Tennessee became the 36th state to ratify the amendment.[552]

On August 26, US Secretary of State Bainbridge Colby certified the adoption of the amendment. He signed the proclamation at his home at breakfast without ceremony.[553]

Colby declined to have a public ceremony largely because of friction between the rival suffrage organizations over who would participate. Later on August 26, Alice Paul of the NWP and Carrie Chapman Catt, president of NAWSA, went to the State Department to meet with

Colby. Colby may have met with Carrie Catt. Alice Paul and her NWP group (which included Mary Moore Forrest of Scituate) were kept waiting, and then Colby did not meet with them. President Wilson snubbed Alice by sending a congratulatory message to Carrie Catt and not to Alice Paul. Carrie Catt and not Alice Paul met later with President and Mrs. Wilson at the White House. That evening, Colby carried the president's congratulations to a mass meeting at which Colby and Carrie Catt were the chief speakers. Many years later, Alice Paul said, "not one of us was invited or recognized in any possible [way]." That reflected NWP's militant approach, and NAWSA's careful cultivation of President Wilson and his party.[554]

Despite their rivalry, or maybe because of it, both NAWSA and NWP could take credit for gaining the right of American women to vote.

Voting

VOTE poster by League of Women Voters, 1920. Courtesy of Library of Virginia, acc. 22002, Archives and Manuscripts.

The 19th Amendment enfranchised 26 million women all at once. It was just in time (in most states) for them to vote in the 1920 presidential election on November 2. The effect was dramatic. The number of voters for president jumped from about 19 million in 1916 to almost 27 million in 1920. Warren G. Harding, Republican of Ohio,

WOMEN BY THOUSANDS POUR INTO POLLING PLACES IN BAY STATE

Vote Early, Show Great Enthusiasm and Make Few Mistakes—Outnumber Men in Some Places—All Good Natured And Quick to Learn

60,000 WOMEN CAST BALLOTS IN BOSTON

Harding Carried 17 Wards—M. A. Coolidge Leading

BAY STATE VOTE WORK OF WOMEN

Harding Carried Every City, All But Two Towns

THE BOSTON GLOBE—WEDNESDAY, NOVEMBER 3, 1920

WOMEN FEEL PROUD OF PERFORMING THEIR PATRIOTIC DUTY AS VOTERS

MRS CALVIN COOLIDGE

MRS CHANNING COX

MRS SUSAN W. FITZGERALD

MRS JAMES D. TILLINGHAST

It was the first time, yesterday, the women of the entire country took part in the choice of a President. The figures show they appreciated the opportunity. Their eagerness to exercise the newly acquired right was indicated in many other ways. They were on hand early at the polls, urged upon each other the importance of making a choice and gave thoughtful consideration to the election system. They even endured in some instances tedious waits at polling places in order to cast a vote.

There is little doubt that the share the women had in yesterday's voting was nothing if not significant. It placed upon them a new responsibility, but one which they gladly assumed. Just how they felt about it is a matter of extreme interest.

Mrs Coolidge, wife of the Vice President-Elect, had never voted before. With her husband she went to the City

MRS MABEL S. WORCESTER

MRS LUE STUART WADSWORTH

MRS A. C. WELLINGTON

Headlines in *Boston Globe*, November 3-4, 1920

won in a landslide over his Democratic opponent James M. Cox, also of Ohio. The electoral vote was 404 to 127, and the popular vote was 60% to 34%. The addition of women made for a huge increase in voters.[555]

Aside from the surge in voters, it is difficult to determine the impact of women's vote. They clearly voted heavily for Harding as did the men. Turnout for the newly enfranchised women was not as high as for the established male voters. An estimated three women voted for every five men who voted, nationally, although recent scholarship has questioned that number and provided more detailed breakdowns by state. But the estimate seems to hold for South Shore towns, based on recent analysis. Since the 1920 election, turnout by women gradually increased over the years, and it now exceeds turnout by men.[556]

Determining how women voted is hampered by limited data. Votes and/or voters were generally not recorded by gender. On the South Shore, though, most towns kept track of male and female voters separately in local elections in early 1920 and in the 1920 presidential election. Only a few (including Scituate and Marshfield) did the same for local elections in 1921. In addition, polling back then was in its infancy. Probably women voted the same way as men, and there was no "women's bloc" as some industries (like liquor) feared. That did not change until the 1950s or 1960s and the rise of the Women's Liberation movement. Women may now occupy a unique place in the electorate where they are arguably capable of exerting more political influence than ever before.[557]

We have some detail on how this played out in Scituate. Earlier in 1920, at a time when women were allowed to vote, but only in school committee contests, 525 males and 3 females voted for local offices on March 8. Most positions received 525 votes (including blanks), with only school committee receiving 528 votes. The extra three votes were presumably by women. Because women could vote only in school committee elections, it seems that most women did not show up at the polls because they were not interested in such a limited franchise.[558]

For the presidential primaries on April 27, 1920, 146 Scituate men voted for Republican delegates, all men, including local eminence

Thomas W. Lawson. Only six Scituate men voted for the Democratic slate, which had seven men as delegates and four women as alternate delegates at large: Susan W. FitzGerald (a noted suffragist), Mary A. Carson, Mary Keegan Shuman, and Helen G. Thayer. The women were from various cities in Massachusetts.[559]

Many Scituate women exercised their right to vote in the presidential election on November 2, 1920. Among the voters were 383 females, along with 615 males. The total of 998 was almost double that of the March vote for local offices. The total vote went overwhelmingly for Harding, with 756 votes versus 200 for Cox.[560]

Perhaps more significantly, the number of voters for Scituate's local offices increased dramatically from 528 in 1920 to 1,072 in 1921. In just one year, local voter turnout doubled, and other South Shore towns reported similar surges. The increase in voter participation occurred almost certainly because women were then able to vote for all offices.[561]

In addition, the total franchise expanded. In Massachusetts, in 1915, only one in five residents were qualified to vote. In 1925, about one in three residents could vote.[562]

Leaving aside statistics for a while, we now turn to what was happening with suffrage at the national level.

The National Woman's Party continued. In 1923, Alice Paul drafted an Equal Rights Amendment to the Constitution. The NWP campaigned for its passage. The amendment was introduced in every session of Congress from 1923 until it passed in 1972. As worded then, it said, "Equality of rights under the law shall not be denied or abridged by the United States or by any state on account of sex." This would have expanded women's rights beyond the right to vote. Not enough states ratified it within the stated time limit for adoption.[563]

Meanwhile, at the initiative of Carrie Chapmen Catt, NAWSA in 1919 had already decided to change its name to the League of Women Voters once the suffrage amendment was adopted. When that happened, Carrie Catt stepped down as president of NAWSA, and served as the honorary president of the League of Women Voters for the rest of her life. The organization continues today.[564]

In 1921, Judith Smith was elected an honorary vice president of the Boston League of Women Voters. As of 1919, this was the new name for the Boston Equal Suffrage Association for Good Government (BESAGG), founded in 1901.[565]

In 1922, voters elected the first women to the Massachusetts House of Representatives — Sylvia Donaldson and Susan Walker FitzGerald. Donaldson was a Republican from Brockton. FitzGerald had a long background as a suffragist. In 1908, she was executive secretary of BESAGG. She wrote a suffragist pamphlet, "Women in the Home," published 1910–1915. She was probably the Susan FitzGerald who, with a group from the Massachusetts Political Equality Union, visited Governor Foss in his office in 1913 to support woman suffrage. FitzGerald was from Jamaica Plain. She lived near the homes of two other suffragists — Pauline Agassiz Shaw, and Judith Smith (in Judith's later years when she lived with her daughter Zilpha).[566]

The advent of women voters thus started to produce women legislators.

Recognition

The fight for the vote, and the adoption of the 19th Amendment allowing women to vote, changed America forever. Many centennial events have been planned for 2020. As part of this, the participation of the summer suffragists of Scituate in the long fight for woman suffrage is worth recognizing and celebrating.

Much information documents America's major advance in democracy, including many books. But let's look at how the country has documented and recognized its important woman suffrage landmarks.

The national sites associated with the historic actions taken by women and suffragists have not been adequately documented. Look at the official list of the nation's historic places worthy of preservation, the National Register of Historic Places. It lists many properties significant for women's history.[567] But for most of the twentieth century, as one historian noted, historic preservation ignored women, and, despite later efforts:

> the number of historic sites related specifically to women remained only a small proportion of the whole, and the number of sites that dealt with suffrage was even smaller. The ten national parks that dealt directly with women, for example, made up 20 percent of the fifty-one national historical parks in the National Park Service. Only two of these — Women's Rights National Historical Park and the Belmont-Paul Women's Equality National Monument — dealt directly with woman suffrage.[568]

New York City's 166-year-old Central Park has many statues, but none of real women. In late 2019, the New York City Public Design Commission approved a memorial showing suffragists Sojourner Truth, Susan B. Anthony, and Elizabeth Cady Stanton. The memorial should be installed in 2020.[569]

The 100th anniversary is a good time to recognize suffrage sites. A starting place is The Boston Women's Heritage Trail, created in 1989. It documents sites where Boston women made history, including suffragists. It has tours of different areas of Boston, including places associated with Scituate summer resident Judith Winsor Smith.[570]

More sites could be recognized. To put women's history sites on the map, the National Collaborative for Women's History Sites has been active. Among other things, it developed a National Votes for Women Trail. The Trail now includes Scituate, with this author's input, given the town's stellar history in the woman suffrage movement. The National Collaborative also launched a historic marker program, sponsored by the Pomeroy Foundation, that commemorates the history of woman suffrage in the US.[571]

Massachusetts was a center for the woman suffrage movement. Greater Boston had the largest cluster of known women's rights properties in Massachusetts, and perhaps the Northeast, according to a National Park Service survey in 2003. The survey considered 300 sites from Washington, DC, to Portland, Maine. The survey said, "Boston's Chauncy Hall Building, the former headquarters of the New England Woman's Club, the Mary Church Terrell residence in Washington, D.C. and many other local clubhouses that survive are evidence of the far-reaching club movements."[572]

The women's clubs overlapped and supported the suffrage movement to a great degree. For example, Julia Ward Howe and Judith Smith were early club founders and suffrage activists. Boston's Chauncy Hall Building, which still exists, was home not only to the New England Women's Club, but also to the Massachusetts Woman Suffrage Association, *Woman's Journal*, Boston Equal Suffrage Association for Good Government, and College Equal Suffrage League.

Given the above, it was surprising that the Chauncy Hall Building's importance for the suffrage movement was not documented in the Massachusetts online database of cultural and historic sites, MACRIS. At least not until I added that information.[573]

When I started writing this book, I had already documented many old houses in Scituate for the state's MACRIS database. As I researched and wrote about suffragists, I could not help but document buildings that tell the story of the fight for the vote. It did not matter that they were not in Scituate. It *did* matter, to me, that a center of the national movement for woman suffrage, Boston, had not documented its historic suffrage sites. I have done what I can to remedy that.[574]

Maybe you will be inspired, as I was, to research and document other woman suffrage sites.

Reflections, and Onward

The story of suffrage is the story of challenge. It is not just about one candidate (or party) versus another; it is about who can vote. Those who are not allowed to vote, who do not have the franchise, may protest and challenge their exclusion, as the woman suffragists did. For them, it was not easy or quick, but still, they succeeded. Another challenge is by the government: voter exclusion, or suppression, based on restrictive requirements that make voting more difficult. Yet another challenge is voter apathy, or citizens simply not taking advantage of the right to vote.

The woman suffrage movement fought for women's right to vote. Once they got the vote, some questioned how many women voted, how they voted, and what other rights women should have. But unquestionably the movement elevated the importance of the vote, and the democratic ideal of who can vote for representatives in our government.

Do we measure up to that ideal? Have we taken the woman suffrage movement for granted? Do we take voting for granted? And do we have a government for the people and by the people?

We think of voting as a fundamental right. However, the US Constitution does not expressly provide a right to vote. All the 19th Amendment did was to bar the US and its states from denying the right to vote because of sex. That still left people vulnerable to state actions that exclude them for reasons other than race, color, or sex. Exclusionary examples include poll taxes, literacy tests, residency requirements, restrictive registration requirements, purging registration rolls, and gerrymandering. These actions have gone on for hundreds of years and some exist today. These actions suppress votes and may have disparate impacts on protected classes of people.[575]

These actions "that make it harder to vote," according to two political scientists, "weigh most heavily on those people who are already marginalized. Rather than asking if potential voters – women in 1920 or other groups today – are failing to fulfill their civic responsibilities, we might do better to ask if the political system is failing its citizens."[576]

Many historians suggest the suffrage fight is not over. Susan B. Ware said:

> Although the 19th Amendment dramatically increased the American electorate, the result fell far short of a universal adult franchise. Disenfranchisement remains a significant and growing problem today. Penal restrictions on voting, battles over immigration and naturalization, and the push for voter ID laws

> demonstrate that the fight for suffrage—who counts as a voter, and whose vote gets counted—is far from over.[577]

America's history of voting is overshadowed by its history of nonvoting. In America's last election for its highest office, 56% of the voting age population turned out to vote. That means that nearly 100 million Americans who were eligible to vote did not do so. And if we compare America to other developed countries, using the same measure (turnout of voting age population), America places only 26th out of 32.[578]

As if that weren't enough, there have been serious issues involving foreign interference in American elections. At the same time, questions have been raised about voting machines and other election technology being susceptible to hacking. An HBO documentary investigated "the startling vulnerabilities in America's voting systems and the alarming risks they pose to our democracy."[579]

The Covid-19 pandemic laid bare even more faults and vulnerabilities in our systems of voting. Voting safely during such a pandemic may mean voting by mail, but this required special legislation in many states. Some allowed this for primaries, but not for general elections. Some did not plan well for counting mail-in ballots. The pandemic also created challenges for legislators to vote. Legislatures are trying alternatives, some of which are unprecedented experiments. For example, the US House of Representatives' plan for voting by proxy faces serious questions about its constitutionality.[580]

Some claim that mail-in ballots invite massive fraud. However, states that have experience with them report a minuscule rate of potentially fraudulent ballots — 0.0025 percent.[581]

In 2020 — 100 years after the 19th Amendment passed — the power of voting again became a focus as the country experienced widespread protests against racial inequality and racist violence by law enforcement personnel. One such protest was in front of the White House, the same place where women suffragists protested against a President who they felt failed to provide leadership on women's rights. In both cases, the government used violence against mostly peaceful protests.[582]

How to respond to challenges that these protests raise? The late John Lewis (1940–2020), US Congressman and civil rights icon, said:

> A great many of these problems we'll be able to solve through the power of the ballot. The vote is the most powerful nonviolent tool we have in a democratic society. And it's why people didn't want people of color to come register to vote, because you have power that you can use.[583]

Another view is that "we have come to take democracy for granted, and civic education has fallen by the wayside," as US Supreme Court Chief Justice Roberts said in 2019. Have things gotten this bad? Have we already disenfranchised ourselves?[584]

Our big challenges today show that the fight for the vote did not end with the adoption of the 19th Amendment. Let us be inspired by the suffragists of a century and more ago, to act today, to perfect our government and our democracy, to provide justice, and to fight for the vote. And to vote.

NOTES ON SOURCES

Sources are meticulously provided in the notes. Important archives, manuscript collections, key primary sources, and abbreviations are listed below. Not all abbreviations here are used in the text or notes.

1903 map. J. E. Judson, *Topographical Atlas of Surveys: Plymouth County together with the town of Cohasset, Norfolk County, Massachusetts* (Springfield, MA: L. J. Richards & Co., 1903), plates 31 and 32, State Library of Massachusetts, Massachusetts Real Estate Atlas Digitization Project, http://www.mass.gov/anf/research-and-tech/oversight-agencies/lib/massachusetts-real-estate-atlases.html.

Boston Globe (or *Globe*). The *Boston Globe*, archived issues from *Boston Globe* website under "Archives," powered by newspapers.com (previously powered by ProQuest Archiver)

Brooklyn Daily Eagle. The Brooklyn Public Library has an online collection, https://bklyn.newspapers.com/.

Directories. Harold Howard published a local directory, which included Scituate, in 1915, 1918, and 1926. Copies are on file in the SHS. An 1894 directory, *Directory of Cohasset, Scituate, Marshfield, Duxbury and Norwell* (Quincy, MA: J. H. Hogan Co., 1894), is on file, SHS, and https://archive.org/details/directoryhistory00quin.

HWS. *History of Woman Suffrage* (six volumes), online, including https://catalog.hathitrust.org/Record/001142954

IHG. Inez Haynes Gillmore Papers, 1872–1945, Schlesinger Library (sometimes referred to as Papers of Inez Haynes Irwin). See "Papers of Inez Haynes Gillmore, 1872–1945," collection guide, https://hollisarchives.lib.harvard.edu/repositories/8/resources/5438 or https://id.lib.harvard.edu/ead/sch00652/catalog.

JWS. Judith Winsor Smith Papers, 1796–1945, Massachusetts Historical Society, Boston. See "Judith Winsor Smith Papers," Guide to the Collection, https://www.masshist.org/collection-guides/view/fa0063. See also *SMC*.

JWS Photos. Judith Winsor Smith family photographs, 1860–1921, Photo. Coll. 161, Massachusetts Historical Society Photo Archives, http://www.masshist.org/collection-guides/view/fap031.

LOC. Library of Congress

Local Newspapers: South Shore Mirror (1957–1979), *Scituate Herald* (1929–1967). Available from Scituate Town Library website, halfway down right side, http://www.scituatetownlibrary.org/.

MACRIS. Massachusetts Historical Commission's database, called Massachusetts Cultural Resources Information System, http://mhc-macris.net/index.htm

MHS. Massachusetts Historical Society

MWP. Maud Wood Park Papers, Library of Congress. (No abbreviation is used for the collection of her papers in the Schlesinger Library.)

PCRD. Plymouth County Registry of Deeds, online at https://www.plymouthdeeds.org/home/pages/search-records. Deed book and page references are shortened to [book #]/[page #]. Plan book references are similar: pb [book #]/[page #]/[sheet #, if applicable].

RMPC. Ralph M. Pearson Collection (1870–1930), Fray Angelico Chaves History Library, The Palace of the Governors, Santa Fe, NM. An inventory of the collection is at Rocky Mountain Online Archive, https://rmoa.unm.edu/docviewer.php?docId=nmsm1ac380.xml. It includes letters of Beatrice Forbes-Robertson Hale, letters of Swinburne Hale, and Hale family papers. Of these papers, I reviewed only Swinburne Hale letters in box 9, folder 8. Those letters are to Evelyn (last name unknown) of New York City, December 6, 1918, to

January 2, 1919, and a letter from *The New York Call* to Swinburne Hale, October 28, 1919. See also SHP.

Sanborn maps. The Sanborn Map Company made detailed maps for insurance purposes. They are on microfilm at State Library of Massachusetts, Special Collections. Those for Scituate are in film box 709, reel 37. They include *Scituate, Plymouth County, Massachusetts* [map], 1 inch = 100 feet (New York: Sanborn Map Company, December 1918); *Scituate, Plymouth County, Massachusetts* [map], 1 inch = 100 feet (New York: Sanborn Map Company, October 1926). Citations are to the year and often the sheet.

SHP. Swinburne Hale papers, Manuscripts and Archives Division, The New York Public Library, Astor, Lenox, and Tilden Foundations, New York City. See Marleen Buelinckx, finding aid, 1995/2003, http://www.nypl.org/sites/default/files/archivalcollections/pdf/hale.pdf. Includes about 140 letters by Beatrice Forbes-Robertson Hale to Swinburne Hale, 1913–1920. See also *RMPC*.

SHS. Scituate Historical Society. SHS Newsletters are online at the Society's website.

SL. Schlesinger Library, Radcliffe Institute, Harvard University, Cambridge, MA

SMC. Smith McLauthlin Collection, Drew Archival Library, Duxbury Rural and Historical Society (includes Judith Winsor Smith papers). See "Smith McLauthlin Collection," partial Finding Aid, https://drewarchives.org/finding-aids/smith-mclauthlin-collection/. See also *JWS*.

SUFF: *The Suffragist*, https://archive.org/details/thesuffragist

WRC. Woman's Rights Collection, Schlesinger Library

WJ. *The Woman's Journal*, online at "The Woman's journal and Woman's Journal and Suffrage News. Boston, 1870–1917," courtesy of Schlesinger Library, https://listview.lib.harvard.edu/lists/drs-422585198 (click on "Full Text Search" upper right to search all issues). In 1917, the journal was absorbed into *The Woman Citizen*, published in New York City. Past issues of the journal are at Hathitrust Digital Library, https://catalog.hathitrust.org/Record/008868782, and (for 1921–1922, when its title reverted to the *Woman's Journal*), at https://catalog.hathitrust.org/Record/100898354.

Valuation List. Town tax assessor records of property valuations recorded in yearly books using state formats, on file in Scituate Town Archives. Citation is to year and often to page.

Other. I tried to follow the *Chicago Manual of Style* for the most part, but the notes do not include the dates I accessed web links, or (in many cases) whether they were previews. Most were accessed in 2019–2020. If you need these details, or help on dead links, feel free to contact me. See *About the Author*. The electronic version does not include an index. It is my understanding that readers can search for particular words or phrases, and they can click on web links to see the sources listed in the notes.

Notes

[1] Chief Justice Cushing Chapter, Daughters of the American Revolution, *Old Scituate* (Boston: DAR, 1921), 262-263, https://archive.org/details/oldscituate00chapgoog.

[2] "The Seaweeds of the United States," *National Geographic Magazine*, vol. 16 (Washington, DC: National Geographic Society, May 1905), 244-245, photos from Hugh M. Smith, Bureau of Fisheries; William E. Curtis, "Home of the Old Oaken Bucket," *Boston Globe*, August 14, 1911, 11; Charles Barnard, "Rebecca, The Drummer (A True Story of the War of 1812.)", *St. Nicholas: Scribner's Illustrated Magazine for Girls and Boys* (New York: Scribner & Co., 1874), vol. 1, no. 9, July 1874, 503-505, copied in *The Woman's Journal* [*WJ*], August 29, 1874, 277, Schlesinger Library, Radcliffe Institute, Harvard University [SL].

[3] *Osgood's New England: A Handbook for Travellers* (Boston: James R. Osgood and Company, new edition, 1877), 49 (source of quote); Bushrod Washington James, Aleksandr Ivanovich Voeĭkov, *American Resorts: With Notes Upon Their Climate* (Philadelphia: F. A. Davis, 1889), 33.

[4] "Watering Place Notes," *Sunday Herald* newspaper clipping [probably *Boston Sunday Herald*], June 17, 1877, from EC Manson/Edith Manson Freeman scrapbook, copy in "Hotels, Inns" file, Scituate Historical Society [SHS]; Nicholas Kilmer, ed., "Thomas Buford Meteyard Paintings and Watercolors," Exhibition Catalog (New York: Berry-Hill Galleries, Inc., 1989); *Scenes from Vagabondia: Thomas Buford Meteyard & Dawson Dawson-Watson From Giverny to Scituate, 1890-1910*, Exhibition Catalog (Cambridge, MA: Pierre Menard Gallery, 2009); "The Bawdy House Set: A 19th Century Art Colony at Scituate, Massachusetts, 1889-1910," http://19thcenturyartcolony.com/; Inez Haynes Irwin diaries, SL; Inez Haynes Irwin, *Adventures of Yesterday*, unpublished autobiography, 1950, ch. 13 "The Adventure of Scituate," 528-532, Inez Haynes Gillmore Papers, 1872-1945 [*IHG*], SL. The "Visionists of Boston" had members associated with Scituate, including artist Thomas Meteyard, humorist Gelett Burgess, and composer Frederic Bullard. Josh Kastorf, "The Visionists of Boston: An online museum of Boston's lost bohemia," website, https://visionistsofboston.wordpress.com/. An ode to Gelett Burgess appeared in a book of poems illustrated by Tom Meteyard: "A Staccato to O Le Lupe," in Bliss Carman and Richard Hovey, *Last Songs from Vagabondia* (Boston: Small, Maynard and Company, 1900), 62, https://quod.lib.umich.edu/a/amverse/BAH8719.0001.001?rgn=main;view=fulltext. The Americus Club is shown on an 1879 map. *Town of Scituate Mass.*, in *Atlas of Plymouth County, Massachusetts* [map], 1 inch = 135 rods (Boston: Geo. H. Walker & Co., 1879), page 33 (and see 36, Village of Scituate Harbor, detail), State Library of Massachusetts, Massachusetts Real Estate Atlas Digitization Project, URI http://hdl.handle.net/2452/205573, http://www.mass.gov/anf/research-and-tech/oversight-agencies/lib/massachusetts-real-estate-atlases.html (for detailed view), and https://www.flickr.com/photos/mastatelibrary/8881938110/in/album-72157633790765207/). Beckington is mentioned in news accounts from 1913 about Inez, and in Inez's diaries as early as 1903. Meteyard attracted others to Scituate, who are mentioned in Inez's unpublished autobiography, ch. 13, 528, SL. They include poet Richard Hovey, composer Frederick Field Bullard and his wife, and Elizabeth Robins, an early radical writer, suffragist, and feminist, who visited Scituate. For more information on Robins, see "Guide to the Elizabeth Robins

Papers MSS.002," Fales Library and Special Collections, Elmer Holmes Bobst Library, NYU, http://dlib.nyu.edu/findingaids/html/fales/robins/bioghist.html. Inez's autobiography also mentions "the four painter women."

[5] Porter E. Sargent, *A Handbook of New England* (Boston: Porter E. Sargent, 1916), 529, https://books.google.com/books?id=z0AAAAAAYAAJ&source=gbs_navlinks_s.

[6] Charles W. Dow, *The Old Colony Railroad: An Historically True Narrative of One of the Pioneer Railroad Systems in America* (n. p., for Massachusetts state commission, 1949), 49.

[7] Inez Haynes Irwin to Maud Wood Park, June 25, 1938, box 4, Maud Wood Park Papers, Manuscript Division, Library of Congress, Washington, DC [*MWP*]; "With the Members Sworn to Secrecy, Forty of New York's Prominent 'Advanced' Women Band Into 'The Heterodoxy' and Meet to Eat and Decide Their Position on Problems of the Day," *New-York Tribune*, November 24, 1914, Library of Congress, https://chroniclingamerica.loc.gov/lccn/sn83030214/1914-11-24/ed-1/seq-7/.

[8] Inez Haynes Irwin to Maud Wood Park, July 1, 1938, box 4, *MWP*.

[9] Jennifer Morgan Williams and Bronwen Howells Walsh, "Osterville women 'rock the boat'" *The Barnstable Patriot* website, posted March 1, 2019, updated March 2, 2019, https://www.barnstablepatriot.com/news/20190301/osterville-women-rock-boat; Anna Howard Shaw, *The Story of A Pioneer* (New York: Harper & Brothers, 1915), 264-266, https://archive.org/details/storyapioneer00jordgoog/page/n8; Sophia Smith Collection of Women's History, Garrison family papers, Series VI, Subject Files, 1810-1966, Suffrage, Wianno, finding aid, and other items in the Garrison family papers collection, SSC-MS-00060, https://findingaids.smith.edu/repositories/2/archival_objects/71222. Other suffragists in Wianno included Elizabeth Buffum Chace and Lillie Chace Wyman. Elizabeth C. Stevens, *Elizabeth Buffum Chace and Lillie Chace Wyman: A Century of Abolitionist, Suffragist and Workers' Right Activism* (Jefferson, NC: McFarland & Company, Inc., 2003, https://books.google.com/books?id=TIF5ACdkeHQC&source=gbs_navlinks_s.

[10] Author's search of *Woman's Journal* [*WJ*]; Lillie Buffum Chace Wyman and Arthur Crawford Wyman, *Elizabeth Buffum Chace 1806-1899*, vol. 2 (Boston: W. B. Clarke Co., 1914), ch. 25.

[11] Carl MacGowan, "Suffragist movement had roots in Shoreham," *Newsday* website, updated April 27, 2017, https://www.newsday.com/long-island/suffolk/suffragist-movement-had-roots-in-shoreham-1.13520743; Antonia Petrash, *Long Island and the Woman Suffrage Movement* (Charleston, SC: The History Press, 2013), https://books.google.com/books?id=_4p_CQAAQBAJ&source=gbs_navlinks_s; Nancy Mion, "Amazing Women and How They Got the Vote," Powerpoint presentation, AAUW Islip Area (NY) Branch website, http://www.aauw-nys.org/branches/islip.htm; *WJ*, July 25, 1908, 120, col. 3-4; *WJ*, June 24, 1910, 101 (front page), col. 2; Harriot Stanton Blatch, "Suffrage Week in Suffolk," *WJ*, July 19, 1913, 227. Roslyn, on the north shore of Long Island, is mentioned about 36 times in the *Woman's Journal*, with 12 of those for Katherine Duer Mackay, who had homes in Manhattan and Roslyn, where she served on the town's Board of

Education. Johanna Neuman, *Gilded Suffragists: The New York Socialites Who Fought for Women's Right to Vote* (New York: NYU Press, 2017, 42.
[12] Papers of Edna Lamprey Stantial, 1836-1985 (inclusive), 1900-1955 (bulk), collection guide, SL, https://hollisarchives.lib.harvard.edu/repositories/8/resources/6169.
[13] Neuman, *Gilded Suffragists*, 51-54; *WJ*, August 20, 1910, 137, col. 3-4. See also *WJ*, August 10, 1912, 250.
[14] Author's analysis using full text search of all *Woman's Journal* issues. Chilmark's number excludes 30 ads for cottage rentals, and Shoreham's number excludes 9 references to the Shoreham Hotel in Washington, DC, or to Shoreham, VT.
[15] Author's analysis of Woman's Journal searches, and discussions below in this book.
[16] Author's analysis of *Woman's Journal* searches, and discussions below in this book.
[17] A photo of picketers, used at the start of this chapter and part of the cover, is by Harris & Ewing, *Pennsylvania on the Picket Line* (Washington D.C, 1917), Records of the National Woman's Party, Manuscript Division, Library of Congress, Washington, DC, https://www.loc.gov/item/mnwp000212/. Pennsylvania's day on the picket line was Thursday, January 24, 1917. *The Suffragist*, January 31, 1917, 4; "Bryn Mawr on the Picket Lines - The Radicals and Activists," Bryn Mawr College website, http://www.brynmawr.edu/library/exhibits/suffrage/pickets.html; National Woman's Party Photograph Collection, Catalog Number 1917.001.051, https://nationalwomansparty.pastperfectonline.com/photo/D88F07D5-D569-4C45-AAF8-204688222594.
[18] Sally Roesch Wagner, ed., *The Women's Suffrage Movement* (New York: Penguin Books, 2019), xxv (regain), ch. 1 "Women Voted Before the United States was Formed;" Elizabeth Cady Stanton, Susan B. Anthony, and Matilda Joslyn Gage, eds., *History of Woman Suffrage*, vol. 3: 1876-1885 (Rochester, NY: Susan B. Anthony, 1886), ch. 31, "Massachusetts," 283, https://babel.hathitrust.org/cgi/pt?id=njp.32101075729051&view=1up&seq=12; "Map: States grant women the right to vote," National Constitution Center website, https://constitutioncenter.org/timeline/html/cw08_12159.html. Wagner's book provides a panorama of primary source writings and other thought-provoking material.
[19] Wagner, *Women's Suffrage Movement*, ch. 2 "Women Organized Before Seneca Falls;" "Interview: Elaine Weiss on her book 'The Woman's Hour: The Great Fight to Win the Vote,'" 2018 (source of quote), Women's Suffrage and the Media website, http://suffrageandthemedia.org/source/interview-elaine-weiss-on-her-book-the-womans-hour-the-great-fight-to-win-the-vote/.
[20] "First Parish of Norwell History," First Parish of Norwell website, http://www.firstparishnorwell.org/history.htm; Alcott.net website, http://www.alcott.net/frame.html (click on "Reform" then "Samuel Joseph May"); Catherine L. Covert, "Saint Before His Time: Samuel J. May and American Educational Reform," Master's Thesis, Syracuse University (1964), retrieved from https://web.archive.org/web/20080111114721/http://www.mmuus.org/who-we-are/history/covert-may-thesis.html; "Samuel J. May Biography," Collection Description, Samuel J. May Anti-Slavery Collection, Cornell University,

http://dlxs.library.cornell.edu/m/mayantislavery/biography.html; Wagner, *Women's Suffrage Movement*, xxv, 13, 38 (abridged version of sermon).
[21] Elizabeth Cady Stanton, Susan B. Anthony, and Matilda Joslyn Gage, eds., *History of Woman Suffrage*, vol. 1: 1848-1861 (Rochester, NY: Susan B. Anthony, 1887), ch. 4, "New York," including 70 (text of declaration), https://archive.org/details/historyofwomansu01stanuoft/page/70.
[22] "Susan B. Anthony," in Julia Ward Howe, et al., *Representative Women of New England* (Boston: New England Historical Publishing Company, 1904), 369, https://archive.org/details/sketchesofrepres00howe/page/n495; "Suffragists' Efforts Turn to Legislatures," *Boston Globe*, June 5, 1919, 7.
[23] Barbara F. Berenson, *Massachusetts in the Woman Suffrage Movement* (Charleston, SC: The History Press, 2018), 13, 69-70; Stanton, et al, *History of Woman Suffrage*, vol. 3, 265 (woman's hour).
[24] "Lucy Stone," in Howe, *Representative Women of New England*, 191, 199 (Livermore). See Valerie A. Russo, "Getting The Vote: New book highlights Massachusetts suffragettes," *Patriot Ledger* website, posted March 31, 2018, https://scituate.wickedlocal.com/entertainmentlife/20180329/getting-votenew-book-highlights-massachusetts-suffragettes?template=ampart. An image of Lucy Stone is in Elizabeth Cady Stanton, Susan B. Anthony, and Matilda Joslyn Gage, eds., *History of Woman Suffrage,* vol. 2 (Rochester, NY: Charles Mann, 1881, 1887), 780-761, https://archive.org/details/historyofwomansu02stanuoft/page/n5/mode/2up.
[25] "Lucy Stone," in Howe, *Representative Women of New England*, 199 (Livermore); "Mary A. Livermore, LL.D.," in Howe, *Representative Women of New England*, 430; Berenson, *Massachusetts Suffrage*, 13, 69-70; Adriene Galindo, "Lucy Stone," Boston Athenaeum website, posted May 2016, https://www.bostonathenaeum.org/library/book-recommendations/athenaeum-authors/lucy-stone. The headquarters of these organizations were at 3 Tremont Place from 1868 to 1905, then 3-5 Park Street; the buildings are no longer there. Gail Lee Dubrow, ch. 4 "Women and Community," in Page Putnam Miller, ed., *Reclaiming the Past: Landmarks of Women's History* (Bloomington: Indiana University Press, 1992), 83, at 90-91. The *Woman's Journal* was published at 3 Tremont Place from 1870 to 1876, then 4 Park Street until 1879, then 5 Park Street until 1887, then 3 Park Street until 1908 (21 years at that location), then 6 Beacon Street until 1910, then 585 Boylston Street (across from Copley Square) through mid-1916, then 45 Boutwell Street in Dorchester until 1917. See author's website, www.lylenyberg.com, and forms for these sites filed in the Massachusetts Historical Commission's database, Massachusetts Cultural Resources Information System (MACRIS). A 1912 photo of 585 Boylston shows window signs on the third story for "Boston Equal Suffrage Association for Good Government," "Massachusetts Woman Suffrage Association," and "The Woman's Journal." Boston Public Works Department, "Buildings 601-585 Boylston Street," Boston Archives website, https://cityofboston.access.preservica.com/uncategorized/IO_065f8c48-aa8a-472f-b9a8-7e60a7c5f6ea/. See "Chauncy Hall Building," 585-591 Boylston Street, BOS.2651 (continuation sheet), MACRIS. Woman suffrage associations and the *Woman's Journal* had a home at 3-5 Park Street, shown in a photo from about 1903. E. Chickering & Co., copyright claimant, *One panoramic photo of Park St. Station,*

showing Park St. Church and State House in distance, Boston, Mass., ca. 1903, https://www.loc.gov/item/2007661060/.

[26] Author's sampling of *Woman's Journal* issues; "Warren Institution for Savings Building," 3 Park Street, Boston, BOS.1935 (author's continuation sheet at end), MACRIS; "Alice Stone Blackwell," in Julia Ward Howe, et al., *Representative Women of New England* (Boston: New England Historical Publishing Company, 1904), 406, https://catalog.hathitrust.org/Record/100558517.

[27] "Susan B. Anthony," in Howe, *Representative Women of New England*, 373; Berenson, *Massachusetts Suffrage*, 13, 69-70.

[28] *WJ*, July 10, 1880, 220, col. 4.

[29] Berenson, *Massachusetts Suffrage*, 73-76; "Timeline of Woman Suffrage in Massachusetts," Primary Research website, posted November 14, 2009, http://primaryresearch.org/woman-suffrage-in-massachusetts/; Valerie A. Russo, "Getting the Vote: New book highlights Massachusetts suffragettes," *Patriot Ledger* website, posted March 31, 2018, https://www.patriotledger.com/entertainmentlife/20180329/getting-votenew-book-highlights-massachusetts-suffragettes. See Votes For Women website, http://www.womansuffragema.com/events.html.

[30] *Town Records, vol. 11, 1882-1906*, 9, Article 14, March 6, 1882, Town Archives; *Town Records, vol. 11, 1882-1906*, 27, Article 23, March 5, 1882, Town Archives.

[31] *WJ*, January 16, 1886, 20, col. 1; *WJ*, March 13, 1886, 85, col. 2; *WJ*, March 7, 1891, 73.

[32] *WJ*, December 4, 1886, 388. Sarah Welch (1867-1950) was a daughter of E. Parker Welch who started the Welch Company in Scituate with his son George F. Welch.

[33] Scituate Historical Society, *Scituate*, Images of America series (Charleston, SC: Arcadia Publishing, 2000), 33.

[34] Susan B. Anthony and Ida Husted Harper, eds., *History of Woman Suffrage*, vol. 4: 1883-1900 (Rochester, NY: Susan B. Anthony, 1902), 734-738; "Timeline of Woman Suffrage in Massachusetts," Primary Research website, http://primaryresearch.org/woman-suffrage-in-massachusetts/; *Town Records, vol. 11, 1882-1906*, 356, November 5, 1895, Town Archives.

[35] Massachusetts Association Opposed to the Further Extension of Suffrage to Women records, 1894-1920, Guide to the Collection, Massachusetts Historical Society [MHS], http://www.masshist.org/collection-guides/view/fa0121; Anthony & Harper, *History of Woman Suffrage*, vol. 4, 738; *The Remonstrance*, Boston, January 1909, 1, Miller NAWSA Suffrage Scrapbooks, 1897 to 1911; Scrapbook 7 (1908 to 1909), Library of Congress, https://www.loc.gov/resource/rbcmil.scrp5011101/?sp=1; Johanna Neuman, "Who Won Women's Suffrage? A Case for "Mere Men," *The Journal of the Gilded Age and Progressive Era* (July 2017), 16. 347-367 ("coarse …"), abstract, https://www.researchgate.net/publication/317858963_WHO_WON_WOMEN'S_SUFFRAGE_A_CASE_for_mERE_MEN/citation/download, and DOI: 10.1017/S1537781417000081.

[36] Kathleen L. Endres and Therese L. Lueck, eds, *Women's Periodicals in the United States: Social and Political Issues* (Westport, CT: Greenwood Press, 1996), 331-334, preview, https://books.google.com/books?id=rHNlZkqY6w4C&source=gbs_navlinks_s;

Susan E. Marshall, *Splintered Sisterhood: Gender and Class in the Campaign against Woman Suffrage* (Madison: University of Wisconsin Press, 1997), 87, preview, https://books.google.com/books?id=h3itDekmfAIC&source=gbs_navlinks_s; Massachusetts Association Opposed to the Further Extension of Suffrage to Women, "Opinions of eminent persons against woman suffrage" (Boston, 1911), pamphlet, JK1896.S41 no. 26, MHS; 585-591 Boylston Street, BOS.2651 (continuation sheet February 2020), MACRIS. Copies of *The Remonstrance* and its place of publication are hard to find online without a subscription. The Library of Congress has a 1909 issue, https://www.loc.gov/item/rbcmiller001235/ (Cambridge address), and a 1911 issue, https://www.loc.gov/resource/rbcmil.scrp7010401/?st=gallery (Room 615, Kensington Building, Boston).

[37] *The Remonstrance*, April 1911, 1. Later photos of the Kensington Building are at Billski, "In search of the lost lion of the Kensington Building," ArchBOSTON website, posted May 18, 2013, https://archboston.com/community/index.php?threads/in-search-of-the-lost-lion-of-the-kensington-building.4565/, and in the Leslie Jones collection (1920 photo), Boston Public Library website, https://www.flickr.com/photos/boston_public_library/6285866933/in/photostream/. The Kensington Building was replaced. A 1912 photo of 585 Boylston Street is at the Boston Archives website, Boston Public Works Department, "Buildings 601-585 Boylston Street," https://cityofboston.access.preservica.com/uncategorized/IO_065f8c48-aa8a-472f-b9a8-7e60a7c5f6ea/. See also Chauncy Hall Building, 585-591 Boylston Street, BOS.2651 (continuation sheet), MACRIS.

[38] "Why Woman Suffrage Would Be Harmful," *Boston American*, February 23, 1913, Main Sheet, Part IV, and 2W, clippings in Woman's Rights Collection [*WRC*], SL. This press report was preparation for the March 3, 1913, suffrage procession in Washington, DC, and the article said the homemakers were to be dressed in gray and green. But a later report said the homemakers, let by Mrs. William Sturtevant Moore, were dressed in long purple robes over their street clothes. "Woman's Beauty, Grace, and Art Bewilder the Capital," *Washington Post*, March 4, 1913, 1, clipping in *WRC*, SL.

[39] *WJ*, March 31, 1900, 104; Berenson, *Massachusetts Suffrage*, 97-103, 118-119, 134-137, and 147-149 (Park).

[40] J. D. Zahniser and Amelia R. Fry, *Alice Paul: Claiming Power* (New York: Oxford University Press, 2014), 115-116, preview, https://books.google.com/books?id=18ukAwAAQBAJ&source=gbs_navlinks_s; "Suffrage Parade Has Police Guard; Strong Force Out to Keep Order in the March and Auto Spin Down Fifth Avenue," *New York Times*, May 22, 1910, 11; "Great Procession in New York," *WJ*, May 28, 1910, 86; Linda J. Lumsden, *Rampant Women: Suffragists and the Right of Assembly* (Knoxville: The University of Tennessee Press, 1997), 75, preview, https://books.google.com/books?id=ek30Fs1EDNgC&source=gbs_navlinks_s.

[41] Zahniser & Fry, *Alice Paul*, 126, 133; "Cavalry Called Out to Protect Suffrage Marchers from Mob," *Boston Daily Globe*, March 4, 1913, 1.

[42] Susan Ware, *Why They Marched: Untold Stories of the Women Who Fought for the Right to Vote* (Cambridge, MA: The Belknap Press of Harvard University Press, 2019),

76-79 (1914 handbill); Nancy F. Cott, *The Grounding of Modern Feminism* (New Haven: Yale University Press, 1987), 38 (Heterodoxy), preview, https://books.google.com/books?id=FeWdNQ-rLKQC&source=gbs_navlinks_s.

[43] See, generally, Brooke Kroeger, *The Suffragents: How Women Used Men to Get the Vote* (Albany: State University of New York Press, 2017); Brooke Kroeger, Susan Ware, and Johanna Neuman, "Role of Men in the Women's Suffrage Movement," panel discussion, October 17, 2019, National Archives and Records Administration, C-SPAN, https://www.c-span.org/video/?465423-1/role-men-womens-suffrage-movement.

[44] "Timeline of Woman Suffrage in Massachusetts," Primary Research website, posted November 14, 2009, http://primaryresearch.org/woman-suffrage-in-massachusetts/; Cook, "A rash and dreadful act for a woman," http://www.masshist.org/objects/2010july.php; Harper, *The History of Woman Suffrage*, vol. 6, 287-288; Ida Husted Harper, *The History of Woman Suffrage*, vol. 5, 1900-1920 [part 1] (New York: National American Woman Suffrage Association, 1922), 439, https://archive.org/details/historyofwomansu05stanuoft/; Berenson, *Massachusetts Suffrage*, 134-142; Gordon Harris, "November 2, 1915: Massachusetts women are denied the right to vote," Historic Ipswich website (with image of pamphlet), posted November 3, 2018, https://historicipswich.org/2018/11/03/november-2-1915-massachusetts-women-are-denied-the-right-to-vote/; "Anti[Suffrage Rally at Faneuil Hall," *The Remonstrance*. July 1915. 6 (source of quote), https://books.google.com/books?id=0S5JAQAAMAAJ&source=gbs_navlinks_s. See also "Voters Deny Massachusetts Women the Vote, November 2, 1915," Massachusetts Foundation for the Humanities' Mass Moments website, http://www.massmoments.org/moment.cfm?mid=316.

[45] Anna J. Cook, "'A rash and dreadful act for a woman': The 1915 Woman Suffrage Parade in Boston," MHS website, posted July 2010, http://www.masshist.org/objects/2010july.php; Harper, *The History of Woman Suffrage*, vol. 6, 288; "Antisuffragists To Have Special Train," *Boston Globe*, November 18, 1916, 3. For a description of anti-suffragist arguments and suffragist responses, see Woloch, *Women and the American Experience*, 336-343. For a broader history of anti-suffragism, see Rebecca A. Rix, "Anti-Suffragism in the United States," National Park Service website, last updated April 10, 2019, https://www.nps.gov/articles/anti-suffragism-in-the-united-states.htm.

[46] Berenson, *Massachusetts Suffrage*, 130-132, 143-144.

[47] Berenson, *Massachusetts Suffrage*, 145-146.

[48] Inez Haynes Irwin, *The Story of the Woman's Party* (New York: Harcourt, Brace and Company, 1921), 193-197, https://archive.org/details/cu31924030480556/page/n7; Mary Walton, *A Woman's Crusade: Alice Paul and the Battle for the Ballot* (New York: Palgrave Macmillan, 2010), 146-147.

[49] Doris Stevens, *Jailed for Freedom* (New York: Boni and Liveright, 1920), 58-60, https://archive.org/details/jailedforfreedo00stevgoog/page/n11.

[50] Stevens, *Jailed for Freedom*, 58-60; Zahniser & Fry, *Alice Paul*,, 76-85 (England), 255; Alice Paul, Interview by Amelia R. Fry, 1972-1973, 93, 338, Suffragists Oral History Project, Conversations with Alice Paul: Woman Suffrage and the Equal Rights Amendment, University of California Calisphere website,

http://content.cdlib.org/view?docId=kt6f59n89c&doc.view=entire_text; Nancy Woloch, *Women and the American Experience* (New York: Alfred A. Knopf, 1984), 206-212; Lumsden, *Rampant Women*, 118; Christine A. Lunardini, *From Equal Suffrage to Equal Rights: Alice Paul and the National Woman's Party, 1910-1928* (New York: New York University Press, 1986), 104-106.
[51] Irwin, *Story of the Woman's Party*, 193-197; Margaret C. Jones, *Heretics and Hellraisers: Women Contributors to The Masses, 1911-1917* (Austin: University of Texas Press, 1993), 99, quoting Inez's 1950 unpublished autobiography, *Adventures of Yesterday*, page 460, *IHG*. In the 1940s, Inez's husband Will Irwin said much the same thing as Inez's autobiography. Will Irwin, *The Making of a Reporter* (New York: G. P. Putnam's Sons, 1942), 328; Will Irwin, "Inez Haynes Irwin," biographical sketch, 1942-1943, Edna Lamprey Stantial Papers in the Mary Earhart Dillon Collection, 1870-1944, A-68, Series XI, folder 573 (quoting Inez), SL, https://nrs.lib.harvard.edu/urn-3:RAD.SCHL:37982834?n=1.
[52] Irwin, *Story of the Woman's Party*, 197, 210-211; Neuman, *Gilded Suffragists*, 129 (source of quote),
[53] Irwin, *Story of the Woman's Party*, 197, 210-211; Neuman, *Gilded Suffragists*, 134 (Eunice); James Harrison Wilson, *The Life of Charles A. Dana* (New York: Harper & Brothers, 1907), 13, 15, https://books.google.com/books?id=YlAOAAAAIAAJ&source=gbs_navlinks_s; Stevens, *Jailed for Freedom*, multiple pages (including at the end, photos of nearly 100 "silent sentinels"); Lumsden, *Rampant Women*, 126 (wartime picketing); "'Suffs,' at Faneuil Hall, Claim Victory; Freed White House Pickets Criticise President," *Boston Globe*, January 9, 1918, 3; "Alice Paul and Suffragists Were First to Picket the White House," Smithsonian Institution website, posted March 29, 2018, https://www.si.edu/newsdesk/snapshot/alice-paul-and-suffragists-were-first-picket-white-house; Matthew Costello, "Picketing the White House: The Suffragist Movement during the Great War," White House Historical Association website, originally published April 14, 2017, https://www.whitehousehistory.org/picketing-the-white-house; "Why the Suffragist Memorial," Turning Point Suffragist Memorial website, https://suffragistmemorial.org/why-the-suffragist-memorial/; Berenson, *Massachusetts Suffrage*, 149-152. A photo of sixteen suffragists who picketed on Bastille Day, July 19, 1917, and were sent to prison is at the Our Documents website, https://www.ourdocuments.gov/doc.php?flash=false&doc=63.
[54] "House for Suffrage by Bare Two-Thirds," *Boston Globe*, January 11, 1918, 1 & 7 (Tague); "Suffrage Beaten in Senate By Two Votes," *Boston Globe*, October 2, 1918, 1; Berenson, *Massachusetts Suffrage*, 155-159.
[55] Barbara F. Berenson, "Politicians beware: Crossing women comes at a hefty cost," *Washington Post* website, posted October 16, 2018, https://www.washingtonpost.com/outlook/2018/10/16/politicians-beware-crossing-women-comes-hefty-cost/.
[56] "5 Suffragists Arrested for Keeping Watchfires," *Minneapolis Star Tribune*, January 5, 1919, 2; Timeline, LOC; "Suffragists Tour of Country to Be In a 'Prison Special'" *Brooklyn Daily Eagle*, February 2, 1919, 4.
[57] *Boston Globe*, February 24, 1919, 2 (source of quote); 9-10 Park Street, BOS.1937, MACRIS (author's continuation sheet at end, April 2020); James J. Kenneally, "'I Want to Go to Jail': The Woman's Party Reception for President Wilson in Boston,

1919," *Historical Journal of Massachusetts*, vol. 45 (1), Winter 2017, 102, http://www.westfield.ma.edu/historical-journal/wp-content/uploads/2020/01/I-Want-to-Go-to-Jail.pdf.

[58] "Suffragists Claim Congress Majority; Miss Alice Stone Blackwell Says Goal Is in Sight," *Boston Globe*, May 21, 1919, 2.

[59] "House Votes For Suffrage, 304-89," *Boston Globe*, May 22, 1919, 1, 2 ("Vote in House on Suffrage") (Fitzgerald, and Republican Frederick W. Dallinger, who represented the 8th Congressional District that included Scituate); "Suffrage Wins in Senate 56-25; Forty Year Struggle by Women Crowned With Victory; Prevention of Ratification by South is Threatened," *Boston Globe*, June 5, 1919, 1; "Women's Suffrage Now Up to States," *Boston Globe*, June 6, 1919, 22; "Demand Bay State Be First to Ratify," *Boston Globe*, June 9, 1919, 1; Berenson, *Massachusetts Suffrage*, 155-159.

[60] Susan Ware, *Why They Marched: Untold Stories of the Women Who Fought for the Right to Vote* (Cambridge, MA: The Belknap Press of Harvard University Press, 2019).

[61] Barbara F. Berenson, *Massachusetts in the Woman Suffrage Movement* (Charleston, SC: The History Press, 2018).

[62] Elaine Showalter, "Irwin, Inez Leonore Haynes Gillmore," in Barbara Sicherman and Carol Hurd Green, ed., *Notable American Women: The Modern Period* (Cambridge: The Belknap Press of Harvard University Press, 1980), 368; Lumsden, *Rampant Women*, 164-165 (Inez listed as one of 23 prominent suffragists in the 1910s). Showalter's entry is probably the lengthiest and best pure biography of Inez. Inez wrote an unpublished autobiography, *Adventures of Yesterday*, *IHG*. Inez's sister Daisy wrote an unpublished account of her years with Inez. Edith ["Daisy"] Haynes Thompson, "Inez and I," c. 1964-1965, donated by William J. Williams, August 1, 1983, on file, SHS. Inez's written work was extensively treated in Jones, *Heretics and Hellraisers.*

[63] Showalter, *Notable American Women*, 368.

[64] Thompson, "Inez and I," 16, SHS (Aunt Lorenza and Aunt Maria [Haynes Johnson] on her father's side); Trigg, *Feminism as Life's Work*, 22 (her father's youngest sister Lora, who was an ordained minister). "Inez and I" includes tales of growing up in Charlestown and on Beacon Hill in Boston.

[65] "Woman Author Tells Story," *WJ*, August 9, 1913, 251. See her similar story "The Making of a Militant," in Elaine Showalter, ed., *These Modern Women: Autobiographical Essays from the Twenties* (New York: The Feminist Press at The City University of New York, 1979, rev. ed. 1989), 33-40, preview, https://books.google.com/books?id=ckHwIV8edTYC&source=gbs_navlinks_s. See Thompson, "Inez and I," which says the divinity school was in Syracuse, NY.

[66] Thompson, "Inez and I;" Frances E. Willard and Mary A. Livermore, eds., *A Woman of the Century: Fourteen hundred-seventy Biographical Sketches Accompanied by Portraits of Leading American Women in All Walks of Life* (Buffalo: Charles Wells Moulton, 1893), 366-367, https://archive.org/details/bub_gb_zXEEAAAAYAAJ/page/n1/mode/2up; Appleton's Annual Cyclopedia and Register of Important Events of the Year 1899 (New York: D. Appleton and Company, 1900), 607, https://books.google.com/books?id=9pFRAAAAYAAJ&source=gbs_navlinks_s.

[67] Thompson, "Inez and I," 5 (Blanche); Will Irwin, "Inez Haynes Irwin," biographical sketch, 1942-1943, Edna Lamprey Stantial Papers in the Mary Earhart

Dillon Collection, SL, A-68, Series XI, folder 573, https://nrs.lib.harvard.edu/urn-3:RAD.SCHL:37982834?n=1. Maud Wood Park's life in the suffrage movement is summarized in "November 2014: Suffragist of the Month," Turning Point Suffragist Memorial website, https://suffragistmemorial.org/november-2015-suffragist-of-the-month/. Her essay, "How I Came to Start My Work for Woman Suffrage," recounts her Radcliffe experiences, and is copied at "After a Historic Night, a Look Back at the Women's Suffrage Movement," ProQuest blog post July 27, 2016, https://www.proquest.com/blog/pqblog/2016/After-a-Historic-Night-a-Look-back-at-the-Womens-Suffrage-Movement.html. Maud Wood Park's papers are at the Schlesinger Library (SL), and at the Library of Congress, where they include correspondence with Inez Haynes Irwin. "Maud Wood Park papers, 1844-1979," finding aid,
http://findingaids.loc.gov/db/search/xq/searchMferDsc04.xq?_id=loc.mss.eadmss.ms012158&_start=1&_jump=con4irwin.

[68] "Woman Author Tells Story," *WJ*, August 9, 1913, 251.

[69] *Boston Directory* (Boston: Sampson & Murdock Co., 1905), http://bcd.lib.tufts.edu/view_text.jsp?urn=tufts:central:dca:UA069:UA069.005.DO.00015&chapter=d.1905.su.Gilmore. See also "Gillmore, Rufus (Hamilton)," The FictionMags Index website,
http://www.philsp.com/homeville/fmi/z/z89.htm#TOP; "Rufus Gillmore; author," Prabook website, http://prabook.com/web/person-view.html?profileId=1086660; "Rufus Gillmore; Author Began His Career on a Magazine in Boston," obituary, *New York Times*, January 23, 1935, abstract, http://query.nytimes.com/gst/abstract.html?res=9905E3D8103FE53ABC4B51DFB766838E629EDE&legacy=true.

[70] "College Women's Dramatics," *WJ*, April 28, 1900, 129 (front page); "Livermore, Mary A. (1820–1905)," Encyclopedia.com,
https://www.encyclopedia.com/women/encyclopedias-almanacs-transcripts-and-maps/livermore-mary-1820-1905. Mary Livermore Norris went on to become a Massachusetts legislator and the first woman to chair a committee. "History of Women in Massachusetts Government," Massachusetts Caucus of Women Legislators website, http://www.mawomenscaucus.com/history-of-women-in-massachusetts-government.

[71] Daisy Thompson, "I Remember Scituate," Scituate Historical Society Newsletter, vol. 8, issue 8, June/July 2004, 3-4 (long version, with last paragraph naming noted guests), at Society's website, which also has a direct link to a slightly shorter version; "Foster, Edward Road Bridge," SCI.901 (1930 bridge), MACRIS. On Second Cliff, lots were being sold and houses erected, shown by comparing the 1895 plan (Plymouth County Registry of Deeds [PCRD], plan book 1, page 153, sheet 4 of 5), with the 1903 map, plate 32, inset for Second Cliff. J. E. Judson, *Topographical Atlas of Surveys: Plymouth County together with the town of Cohasset, Norfolk County, Massachusetts* (Springfield, MA: L. J. Richards & Co., 1903), plates 31 and 32, State Library of Massachusetts, Massachusetts Real Estate Atlas Digitization Project ["1903 map"].

[72] Inez Haynes Irwin, *Adventures of Yesterday*, ch. 13, "The Adventure of Scituate," 532-533, 544, unpublished autobiography, *IHG*.

[73] J. E. Judson, *Topographical Atlas of Surveys: Plymouth County together with the town of Cohasset, Norfolk County, Massachusetts* (Springfield, MA: L. J. Richards & Co., 1903),

plates 31 and 32, State Library of Massachusetts, Massachusetts Real Estate Atlas Digitization Project. Interviewed in 1925, Inez said she dictated to secretaries. "The Irwins Agree Journalism is Good Training for Writers," *Brooklyn Daily Eagle*, April 5, 1925, 81. The locations of the Supple cottages correspond to today's 36, 38, and 40 Peggotty Beach Road, and it is possible the cottages there now were those once owned by Supple. The author's in-laws owned the cottage at 40 Peggotty Beach Road for some 70 years, with five generations spending summers there. Relatives owned 38 Peggotty Beach Road.

[74] "Stalwart Soldiers All," *Boston Globe*, January 15, 1890, 2; "To Hunt Deer in Maine," *Boston Globe*, November 7, 1903, 14; *Scituate Herald*, June 26, 1958, 6.

[75] Thompson, "I Remember Scituate;" *The South Shore Blue Book, Containing Lists of the Summer Residents of the Principal Resorts Along the South Shore including Hull, Nantasket, Jerusalem Road, Cottage City, Falmouth, Marshfield, Duxbury, Scituate, Woods Hole, Cohasset, Etc.* (Boston: Boston Suburban Book Co., 1906), 38 ("Mr. & Mrs. R. H. Gilmore"), on file in Scituate Town Library; Harold Howard, *Resident and Business Directory of Scituate and Marshfield Massachusetts* (Boston: Harold Howard, 1915), 64 (listing for Harry E. Haynes); Will Irwin and Inez Haynes Gillmore Papers, Yale Collection of American Literature, Beinecke Rare Book and Manuscript Library, and Danijela True and Jennifer Meehan, "Guide to the Will Irwin and Inez Haynes Gillmore Papers YCAL MSS 603," (New Haven: Yale University Library, 2012) (listing for series 1, box 2), http://hdl.handle.net/10079/fa/beinecke.irwin. Harold Howard directories (1915, 1918, 1926) are on file, SHS. Harry Haynes and Inez Haynes Irwin are buried in Scituate's Union Cemetery. *Deeds*: Florence M. Cushing, et al, to Harry E. Haynes, deed, September 30, 1907, PCRD, book 987, page 63 (lots 60 & 77); Florence M. Cushing, et al, to Harry E. Haynes, deed, March 27, 1909, PCRD, book 1023, page 98 (lot 76); Florence M. Cushing, et al, to Harry E. Haynes, deed, April 25, 1910, PCRD, book 1057, page 129 (lot 61); Livingston Cushing and Frank Gwen White to Inez Haynes Gillmore, deed, July 23, 1910, PCRD, book 1066, page 64 (lots 62 & 75); Livingston Cushing and Frank Gwen White to Inez Haynes Gillmore, deed, March 11, 1911, PCRD, book 1081, page 227 (lots 63 & 74). These deeds refer to Frederick T. Bailey, Surveyor, Plan of Lots on 2nd Cliff, Scituate, 1895, filed January 29, 1896, PCRD, plan book 1, page 153, sheet 4 of 5.

[76] "Won a Wife," *Boston Globe*, July 18, 1893, 1 (perhaps somewhat fictional); "Charles H. Copeland," obituary, *Cambridge (MA) Tribune*, September 20, 1913, 1, https://cambridge.dlconsulting.com/?a=d&d=Tribune19130920-01.2.7&e=-------en-20--1--txt-txIN-tribune+1913+september+20------; telephone pole authorizations, Town Records, August 3, 1904 (residence of C. H. Copeland on 2d Cliff); Evangeline Chace, "Titanic Story Reminds Many of May Futrelle," *Scituate Herald*, November 10, 1955, 7, Scituate Town Library website; "19th Century Art Colony;" Nicholas Kilmer and David Noonan, Jr., "The Scituate Connection," in *Scenes from Vagabondia*, 21 (at 24); "Exhibition by 'Satuit Crafts,'" *Boston Globe*, September 12, 1906, 8; E. Parker Welch to Elberta F. Copeland, May 1, 1907, PCRD, book 964, page 215 (2 ½ acres, north side of Meeting House Lane, former homestead of H. G. Reed); 12 Meeting House Lane, SCI.1090 (continuation sheet, filed January 2020), MACRIS.

[77] Jeffrey A. Marks, "No Escape: Jacques Futrelle and the Titanic," *Mystery Scene Magazine* (September 2002, issue #76),

https://www.mysteryscenemag.com/article/37-blurb-jaques-futrelle-and-the-titanic; Florence M. Cushing, et al, to John Heath Futrelle, deed, April 18, 1907, PCRD, book 971, page 192.
[78] *1918 Valuation List*, 129 (house on lot 62, equivalent to 10 Crescent Avenue); Town of Scituate Assessor hand-drawn plot plans, by street, around 1930-35, Town of Scituate Archives at Town Hall (house on lot 62, equivalent to 10 Crescent Avenue); *1908 Valuation List*, 30 (Futrelle, new house $2,500, as of May 1), 38 (Harry Haynes, new house, $2,200); *1912 Valuation List*, 100 (Inez Gilmore [sic], house $3,000); Inez Irwin, autobiography, ch. 13, SL; Robert V. Hudson, *The Writing Game: A Biography of Will Irwin* (Ames: The Iowa State University Press, 1982), 75; "Futrelle, Jacques," and "Futrelle, (L.) May (Peel)," in A. N. Marquis, ed., *Who's Who in America: A Biographical Dictionary of Notable Living Men and Women of the United States*, vol. 7 (1912-1913) (Chicago: A. N. Marquis & Company, 1912), 764, https://books.google.com/books?id=9OkDAAAAYAAJ&source=gbs_navlinks_s .l; Inez's autobiography, ch. 13, 536-537, 545A, 547-548, SL.
[79] Thompson, "I Remember Scituate" (both houses designed); Inez's autobiography, ch. 13, 537 (Gelett designed, Supple built), and ch. 14 "The Adventure of Will Irwin," 550, SL.
[80] Hudson, *The Writing Game*, 33-34, 44-47; Gelett Burgess and Will Irwin, *The Picaroons* (New York: McClure, Phillips & Company, 1904), http://www.gutenberg.org/files/55164/55164-h/55164-h.htm.
[81] "Two Nearly Drown," *Boston Globe*, September 18, 1908, 8.
[82] Marilyn J. Ziffrin, *Carl Ruggles: Composer, Painter, and Storyteller* (Urbana: University of Illinois Press, 1994), 14-15, 27, 36, 38, preview, https://books.google.com/books?id=oH2AesrNyGkC&source=gbs_navlinks_s; Winona (MN) *Republican-Herald*, August 29, 1912, as quoted in Marilyn J. Ziffrin, "Interesting Lies and Curious Truths About Carl Ruggles," published October 1, 1979, last modified September 11, 2018, College Music Symposium website, n.5, https://symposium.music.org/index.php/19/item/1828-interesting-lies-and-curious-truths-about-carl-ruggles#x5; Inez's autobiography, ch. 13, 541, SL.
[83] Brooks Robards, "Barn Housing: A communal summer home with a lively past and present gains historical recognition," *Martha's Vineyard Magazine*, August 1, 2013, http://www.mvmagazine.com/news/2013/08/01/barn-housing; Jones, *Heretics and Hellraisers*, 100 (cartoon of picketing suffragists by Boardman Robinson); Inez's autobiography, ch. 13, 541, SL; "The Masses," Encyclopedia Britannica, https://www.britannica.com/topic/The-Masses, "The Masses," Spartacus Educational, https://spartacus-educational.com/ARTmasses.htm; "A Short History of THE MASSES," LaborArts/Bobst Library NYU, http://www.laborarts.org/exhibits/themasses/history.cfm; Madeleine Baran, "A Brief History of The Masses," *The Brooklyn Rail*, April-May 2003, https://brooklynrail.org/2003/04/express/a-brief-history-of-the-masses.
[84] Marks, "No Escape: Jacques Futrelle and the Titanic;" "Charles H. Copeland," *Cambridge (MA) Tribune*, September 20, 1913, 1; "Funeral of C. H. Copeland," *Boston Globe*, September 17, 1913, 3.
[85] Ziffrin, *Carl Ruggles*, 38, quoting from *Boston Sunday Post*, August 24, 1913. See also Samuel V. Kennedy III, *Samuel Hopkins Adams and the Business of Writing* (Syracuse, NY: Syracuse University Press, 1999), 60-62, 92-93 (Adams roomed with

Irwin in two places in New York), preview, https://books.google.com/books?id=1TkZl3vObC8C&source=gbs_navlinks_s.

[86] *Boston Globe*, October 21, 1977, 46, obituary; Thompson, "Inez and I," 6 (1875); Thompson, "I Remember Scituate" (source of quote).

[87] Thompson, "I Remember Scituate" (extended version); "Harvey," review, *Variety*, December 31, 1949, https://variety.com/1949/film/reviews/harvey-2-1200416661/; "Stage Star Josephine Hull Dies," *The Pittsburgh Press*, March 12, 1957, 35, https://news.google.com/newspapers?nid=djft3U1LymYC&dat=19570312&printsec=frontpage&hl=en.

[88] "Scituate: The Cup, All Right, is Out of Sight in Tennis Play on Labor Day," *Boston Globe*, August 24, 1913, 7.

[89] *The Bookseller, Newsdealer and Stationer* (New York: Edwin O. Chapman), May 15, 1913, 395, https://books.google.com/books?id=hahUAAAAYAAJ&source=gbs_navlinks_s. Many of these names were repeated in a 1916 guidebook. Sargent, *A Handbook of New England*, 529.

[90] "Irwin, Inez Haynes (Gillmore)," in Jones, *Heretics and Hellraisers*, 178; *The Writer* (Boston: The Writer Publishing Company), December 1914, 187, https://books.google.com/books?id=n2pJAQAAMAAJ&source=gbs_navlinks_s; "Will Irwin Has Followed His Brother's Lead, And Claimed a Bride, Is News," *Oakland Tribune*, February 13, 1916, 45, clipping, https://www.newspapers.com/clip/4796901/oakland_tribune/.

[91] Zahniser & Fry, *Alice Paul*, 115-116; "Suffrage Parade in New York City, ca. 1912," DocsTeach website from the National Archives, https://www.docsteach.org/documents/document/suffragette-parade-nyc. See also "Inez Milholland," photo, May 3, 1913, Bain News Service, Library of Congress, https://www.loc.gov/pictures/item/2014692616/.

[92] Showalter, *Notable American Women*, 368; "With the Members Sworn to Secrecy, Forty of New York's Prominent 'Advanced' Women Band Into 'The Heterodoxy' and Meet to Eat and Decide Their Position on Problems of the Day," *New-York Tribune*, November 24, 1914, 7, Library of Congress, https://chroniclingamerica.loc.gov/lccn/sn83030214/1914-11-24/ed-1/seq-7/; Dee Garrison, *Mary Heaton Vorse: The Life of an American Insurgent* (Philadelphia: Temple University Press, 1989), 67-69, JSTOR, https://www.jstor.org/stable/j.ctv6mtdr2 and doi:10.2307/j.ctv6mtdr2; Cott, *The Grounding of Modern Feminism*, 38; *Heterodoxy to Marie* [1920], collection guide, SL, https://hollisarchives.lib.harvard.edu/repositories/8/archival_objects/1532478; Lynne Masel-Walters and Helen Loeb, "Irwin, Inez Haynes," in Taryn Benbow-Pfalzgraf, ed., *American Women Writers: A Critical Reference Guide from Colonial Times to the Present* (Detroit: St. James Press), Encyclopedia.com, http://www.encyclopedia.com/arts/news-wires-white-papers-and-books/irwin-inez-haynes; Laura Quilter, ed., "An Inez Haynes Gillmore Irwin Bibliography," Feminist Science Fiction, Fantasy and Utopia website, http://www.feministsf.org/authors/ihgi.html; Ware, *Why They Marched*, 255-256; Holmes, "Will Irwin – Ace Among Writers."

[93] "Nation Rolls Up Huge Petition," *WJ*, July 12, 1913, 217 (front page); "Storm Congress With Petitions," *WJ*, August 9, 1913, 249 (front page). See W. R. Ross,

"Reception to U.S. Senate Petitioners, Hyattsville, MD, July 31, 1913," photo, Records of the National Woman's Party, Manuscript Division, Library of Congress, https://www.loc.gov/item/mnwp000441/.

[94] Berenson, *Massachusetts Suffrage*, 134-135; "Women Give Great Parade," *Boston Daily Globe*, May 3, 1914, 1; SantaFeKate, "Boston Suffrage Parade - May 2, 1914," Dateline: Boston 1905 website, posted July 27, 2009, http://boston1905.blogspot.com/2009/07/boston-suffrage-parade-may-2-1914.html.

[95] John Galluzzo, "Galluzzo: Woman's Suffrage takes hold in Scituate," *Quincy (MA) Patriot Ledger* website (containing news reports from 100 years before), posted June 20, 2015, http://www.patriotledger.com/article/20150620/NEWS/150629802.

[96] "Miss Etta Seaver Died at Cohasset," *Scituate Herald*, August 32, 1934, 5; 1915 directory, 49-50.

[97] John Galluzzo, "In July 1912, 1,200 crustaceans stolen from Mr. Prouty's lobster car," Scituate Wicked Local website, posted July 26, 2015, https://scituate.wickedlocal.com/article/20150726/NEWS/150728318.

[98] John Galluzzo, "1915 primary drew 376 voters in Scituate," *Quincy (MA) Patriot Ledger* website, posted October 23, 2015, http://www.patriotledger.com/article/20151023/news/151028531.

[99] "Friday 'Suffrage Day' at Red Sox-Indians Game," *Boston Globe*, August 4, 1915, 2.

[100] "Scituate Leader Confident," *Boston Globe*, October 16, 1915, 3.

[101] "Timeline of Woman Suffrage in Massachusetts," Primary Research website, posted November 14, 2009, http://primaryresearch.org/woman-suffrage-in-massachusetts/; Cook, "A rash and dreadful act for a woman," http://www.masshist.org/objects/2010july.php; Harper, *The History of Woman Suffrage*, vol. 6, 286; "Massachusetts Woman Suffrage Victory Parade, Instructions to Marchers," broadside, "Can She Do It?" exhibition, MHS, 2019, see http://www.masshist.org/features/suffrage; "Scituate Leader Confident," *Boston Globe*, October 16, 1915, 2 (source of quote); *Town Records, vol. 12, 1906-1925*, 325, November 2, 1915, Town Archives; *Annual Report of the Officers of the Town of Scituate for the Year Ending December 31, 1915* (North Scituate: The Boundbrook Press, 1916), 91; Berenson, *Massachusetts Suffrage*, 137-142. See also "Voters Deny Massachusetts Women the Vote, November 2, 1915," Massachusetts Foundation for the Humanities' Mass Moments website, http://www.massmoments.org/moment.cfm?mid=316.

[102] *Annual Report of the Officers of the Town of Scituate for the Year Ending December 31, 1915* (North Scituate: The Boundbrook Press, 1916), 89.

[103] For example, *The Suffragist*, vol. 3, no. 1, January 2, 1915 (Washington, DC: Congressional Union for Woman Suffrage), 4, https://archive.org/details/suffragist03cong/page/4; *The Suffragist*, vol. 8-9, January-February 1921 (Washington, DC: National Woman's Party, 1921), 334, https://books.google.com/books?id=nJszAQAAMAAJ&source=gbs_navlinks_s.

[104] "Blossomed Once More for France," *Boston Globe*, September 22, 1918, 43; "Mrs. Irwin to Tell of Scenes at Front," *Boston Post*, September 22, 1918; "Mrs. Irwin to Speak on War Experiences," *Boston American*, September 22, 1918; "Suffrage Meeting Ordered Postponed," *Boston American*, September 26, 1918;

Dugan Arnett, "In the Grip of an Epidemic," *Boston Globe*, March 15, 2020, and https://www.bostonglobe.com/2020/03/14/metro/100-years-ago-another-epidemic-terrorized-city/. All 1918 clippings are in Maud Wood Park Papers, *WRC*, SL (2690_038_1 to 39). See also Alisha Haridasani Gupta, "When Women's Suffrage Battled a Pandemic," *New York Times*, May 4, 2020, A20.
[105] Showalter, *Notable American Women*; Lynne Masel-Walters and Helen Loeb, "Irwin, Inez Haynes," in Taryn Benbow-Pfalzgraf, ed., *American Women Writers*; Quilter, "An Inez Haynes Gillmore Irwin Bibliography," "Maud Wood Park" in Femilogue blog, January 25, 2013, http://femilogue.blogspot.com/2013/01/maud-wood-park.html; Ware, *Why They Marched*, 255-256; Fred L. Holmes, "Will Irwin – Ace Among Writers of Fact and Fiction," *The Dearborn Independent* (The Ford International Weekly), vol. 22 (Dearborn, MI: Dearborn Publishing Co.), September 2, 1922, 6 [258 at website], https://books.google.com/books?id=y2Y6AQAAMAAJ&source=gbs_navlinks_s; Claire Delahaye, "Deconstructing and Reconstructing Woman Suffrage History: The Story of the Woman's Party" *American Studies Journal* (Göttingen: Göttingen University Press, 2019), 68, DOI 10.18422/68-03.
[106] Elizabeth Thomsen, "Maida's Little Website" website, http://www.ethomsen.com/maida/.
[107] Inez Haynes Irwin, *Angels and Amazons: A Hundred Years of American Women* (New York: Arno Press, 1974, originally published by Doubleday, 1933).
[108] Andrea Kempf, "Shared Lives: Women Who Wrote for Women" (Sabbatical Projects, Paper 1, Johnson County Community College, 1994), 82, 101 (source of quote), http://scholarspace.jccc.edu/sabbatical_projects/1.
[109] "Will Irwin Dead; Noted Journalist; Former War Correspondent, Biographer of Hoover, Gained Fame as Reporter, Author." *New York Times*, February 25, 1948, 23; *Scituate Herald*, Feb. 27, 1948, 5; Will Irwin, *The Making of a Reporter* (New York: G. P. Putnam's Sons, 1942); Inez's autobiography, ch. 14 "The Adventure of Will Irwin," 569, SL.
[110] Inez's autobiography, ch. 14 "The Adventure of Will Irwin," 553-554, SL.
[111] "Will Irwin Dead," obituary, *New York Times*, Irwin, *The Making of a Reporter*; Gelett Burgess and Will Irwin, *The Picaroons* (New York: McClure, Phillips & Company, 1904), http://www.gutenberg.org/files/55164/55164-h/55164-h.htm.
[112] Hudson, *The Writing Game*, 44-47; Inez Haynes Irwin's diary, January 21, 1905, p. 217 (met with Will), September 12 and following, 1905, pp. 122-124 (visit to New York City), papers of Inez Haynes Gillmore, 1872-1945, SL.
[113] Gretchen and Penny, September 26, 2016, comment on Elizabeth Thomsen, *Maida's Little Website*, http://www.ethomsen.com/maida/; *1918 Harold Howard Directory*, 79 (Will & Inez Irwin); Harold Howard, compiler, *Towns of Scituate and Marshfield Massachusetts Directory 1926: Containing Alphabetical List of Inhabitants and a Street Directory Classified Business Directory; a list of Town Officials; Churches, Schools, Teachers, Societies, Associations, Clubs, Institutions and Summer Resident Directory* (Boston: Harold Howard, 1926), 99 (Will & Inez Irwin); Mary K. Trigg, *Feminism as Life's Work: Four Modern American Women through Two World Wars* (New Brunswick, NJ: Rutgers University Press, 2014), 108, preview, https://books.google.com/books?id=8n2LAwAAQBAJ&source=gbs_navlinks_s; Thompson, "I Remember Scituate;" Will Irwin and Inez Haynes Gillmore Papers, Yale Collection of American Literature, Beinecke Rare Book and Manuscript

Library, and Danijela True and Jennifer Meehan, "Guide to the Will Irwin and Inez Haynes Gillmore Papers YCAL MSS 603," (New Haven: Yale University Library, 2012) (listing for series 1, box 2), http://hdl.handle.net/10079/fa/beinecke.irwin; Will Irwin to Hamlin Garland, letter, August 5, 1909, University of Southern California Library, Hamlin Garland Papers, http://digitallibrary.usc.edu/cdm/ref/collection/p15799coll81/id/18274; Livingston Cushing and Frank Gwen White to Will H. Irwin, deed, December 30, 1912, PCRD, book 1138, page 301 (lots 46 & 47, with 47 being approximately 14 Prospect), referring to Frederick T. Bailey, Surveyor, Plan of Lots on 2nd Cliff, Scituate, 1895, filed January 29, 1896, PCRD, plan book 1, page 153, sheet 4 of 5; "Will Irwin Has Followed His Brother's Lead, And Claimed a Bride, Is News," *Oakland Tribune*, February 13, 1916, 45, clipping, https://www.newspapers.com/clip/4796901/oakland_tribune/. Will sold his lots in 1923. Will H. Irwin and Inez Haynes Irwin to Sarah Baldwin, deed, October 13, 1923, PCRD, book 1451, page 176. Valuation lists show he built no house on the lots.

114 Irwin, *The Making of a Reporter*, 138, 196-199 (suffrage, with 198 source of quote); *WJ*, September 9, 1911, 1, col. 5.

115 Irwin, *The Making of a Reporter*, 196-199 (suffrage, with 198 source of quotes). This was probably the May 4, 1912, parade. Will also marched in the torchlight parade in New York City in November 1912, in which Beatrice Forbes-Robertson Hale was Grand Marshal. Kroeger, *The Suffragents*, 113.

116 "15,000 Women March in America's Greatest Suffrage Parade," *Boston American*, May 5, 1912 ("splendid" reception, 2,000 men); "Women Parade; Crowds Applaud," *Brooklyn Daily Eagle*, May 5, 1912, 1 ("greatest procession," 1,000 men); *Harper's Weekly*, May 11, 1912 (photo caption says 619 men marched, compared with 94 men in 1911); "10,000 Women and Men March for Equal Suffrage," *New York Times*, May 5, 1912, part 9; all clippings (except *Brooklyn Daily Eagle*) in *WRC*, SL (002690_029_0218_0005_From_201_to_250). See also Neuman, *Gilded Suffragists*, 91-95.

117 Irwin, *The Making of a Reporter*, 328; Kroeger, *The Suffragents*, 84 (photo), 113, 143, 172-173, 324 (page 192 note, citing 1915 letterhead of Men's League); Ware, *Why They Marched*, 76 (copy of handbill), 7; discussion elsewhere in text.

118 Irwin, *The Making of a Reporter*, 192.

119 Irwin, *The Making of a Reporter*, 194. The farmhouse would have been at 3 Elm Park, but is no longer there.

120 Irwin, *The Making of a Reporter*, 194-195.

121 Irwin, *The Making of a Reporter*, 195; "Estate of H. Haynes Esq., Scituate, Mass." map/drawing, copy courtesy of Priscilla Haynes; "Around the Town," *Boston Globe*, February 14, 1914, 6; "Schauffler, Robert Haven House," 322 Cushing Hwy, SCI.1248, MACRIS.

122 Will Irwin, "Togo, Mayor of Scituate: A True Dog Story, Illustrations by Henry J. Soulen," *The American Magazine*, vol. 78, no. 2, August 1914 (New York: Phillips Pub. Co., 1914), 11-16 & 83-86, https://books.google.com/books?id=9Vg_AQAAMAAJ&source=gbs_navlinks_s.

123 Irwin, *Togo Mayor*; Henry James Soulen [1888-1965], "Moss Houses Peggoty Beach," 10 x 18 inch oil on board color illustration for *American Magazine* story, offered for sale March 1-2, 2012, by MutualArt.com,

http://www.mutualart.com/Artwork/-Moss-Houses-Peggoty-Beach---American-Ma/A48D07B21FC511E5.

[124] Irwin, *Togo Mayor*, 13.

[125] Irwin, *The Making of a Reporter*, 204-205, 217-222, 236-237, 293-294.

[126] Hudson, *The Writing Game*, 97. Inez's autobiography, ch. 13, 537, SL, says he gave her the two lots next to hers. But it must have been the two lots that he owned, on the next street over.

[127] Inez's autobiography, ch. 14 "The Adventure of Will Irwin," 558, and page toward end of chapter, SL; Irwin, *The Making of a Reporter*, 299-300; Lynne Masel-Walters and Helen Loeb, "Irwin, Inez Haynes," in Taryn Benbow-Pfalzgraf, ed., *American Women Writers*; Quilter, "An Inez Haynes Gillmore Irwin Bibliography."

[128] Dee Garrison, *Mary Heaton Vorse: The Life of an American Insurgent* (Philadelphia: Temple University Press, 1989), ch. 7, incl. n. 15, https://temple.manifoldapp.org/read/mary-heaton-vorse-the-life-of-an-american-insurgent/section/bab4f71b-b5aa-4d19-9266-51b42a5a354f; Gregg Wolper, "Woodrow Wilson's New Diplomacy: Vira Whitehouse in Switzerland, 1918," *Prologue* (Washington, DC: National Archives, Fall 1992), 226, incl. 231, https://books.google.com/books?id=l4uTqTCEizwC&source=gbs_navlinks_s; Neuman, *Gilded Suffragists*, 76, 152-153 (Whitehouse).

[129] Inez Haynes Irwin letter to Jane and Sam, June 25, 1918 (third summer away from Scituate), offered for sale on eBay, https://www.ebay.com/itm/1918-Autograph-Signed-Letter-Suffragette-Feminist-Inez-Haynes-Gillmore-Irwin-/264104353865; "Scituate," *Boston Globe*, August 6, 1918, 5; "Blossomed Once More for France," *Boston Globe*, September 22, 1918, 43.

[130] "Scituate," *Boston Globe*, August 6, 1918, 5.

[131] "Lawson Reiterates Senate Aspiration," *Boston Globe*, August 24, 1918, 5.

[132] Showalter, *Notable American Women*, 368 (source of quote).

[133] Inez's autobiography, ch. 13, 542-543, SL; author's research.

[134] Charlotte Rich, "From Near-Dystopia to Utopia: A Source for *Herland* in Inez Haynes Gillmore's *Angel Island*," in Cynthia J. Davis, Denise D. Knight, eds., *Charlotte Perkins Gilman and Her Contemporaries: Literary and Intellectual Contexts* (Tuscaloosa: The University of Alabama Press, 2004), 157, preview, https://books.google.com/books?id=zKxUNUcnopUC&source=gbs_navlinks_s; 1921 correspondence cited by Charlotte Rich: Series III ("General Correspondence"), section C (Chronological), folder 143, of the Charlotte Perkins Gilman Papers, 1846-1961, Mf-1, 143, SL, starting at https://iiif.lib.harvard.edu/manifests/view/drs:13350845$1i.

[135] Trigg, *Feminism as Life's Work*, 19; Showalter, *Notable American Women*, 368. Mary K. Trigg's 2014 book appears to be an outgrowth of her 1989 doctoral dissertation at Brown University, discussed in Kempf, "Shared Lives: Women Who Wrote for Women."

[136] 1930 US census, "Edith Thompson," Manhattan, New York, New York, T626, roll 1558, page 8A, enumeration district 0249, image 364.0, FHL microfilm 2341293, HeritageQuest (W. 11th St.); *1926 Harold Howard Directory*, 99 (2d Cliff and 240 W. 11th St., New York City); *The South Shore Social Register and Who's Who on Cape Cod* (Boston: Davis Pub. Co., 1938), 124; Trigg, *Feminism as Life's Work*, 108; Thompson, "I Remember Scituate." Daisy Thompson's daughter Inez "Ebie" Sturges (1919-1997) is buried in Scituate's Union Cemetery. She attended Stephens

College in Columbia, Missouri, and first married Lawrence Cookman in 1941. *Scituate Herald*, January 24, 1941, 1.
[137] Inez's autobiography, ch. 13, 538, SL.
[138] "Maude Emma Haynes [Duganne]," *Provincetown Advocate*, August 24, 1967, 2, obituary, RootsWeb.com website, http://wc.rootsweb.ancestry.com/cgi-bin/igm.cgi?op=GET&db=oldmankew&id=I8814; Thompson, "Inez and I."
[139] "Walter Haynes of Scituate is Laid to Rest," *Scituate Herald*, May 22, 1936, 1, 4; Deaths Registered in the Town of Scituate, vol. 34, 1931-1963, 17 (Walter Haynes death May 20, 1936, occupation editor), Scituate Town Archives; "Haynes, Walter," legislative biographical card file, State Library of Massachusetts, Special Collections; Ray Zucker email, June 23, 2017 (Margaret was an O'Neil); Harry E. Haynes [and his wife Elizabeth Iverson Haynes], Gideon Haynes [and his wife Christina Iverson Haynes], Maude Haynes Duganne, widow, Inez Haynes Irwin [and her husband Will Irwin], and Edith Haynes Thompson, unmarried, to Margaret J. Haynes, deed, February 23, 1938, PCRD, book 1745, page 123 (property on Hazel Avenue); *1918 Harold Howard Directory*, 39; *1926 Harold Howard Directory*, 55. Walter Haynes and Margaret Haynes are buried in Scituate's Union Cemetery.
[140] *1918 Harold Howard Directory*, 39; Jarvis Freymann, *Scituate's Educational Heritage 1630-1990* (Scituate Historical Society, 1990), 176; *Scituate, Plymouth County, Massachusetts* [map], 1 inch = 100 feet (New York: Sanborn Map Company, December 1918), sheet 3; *1926 Harold Howard Directory*, 55; *Scituate, Plymouth County, Massachusetts* [map], 1 inch = 100 feet (New York: Sanborn Map Company, October 1926), sheet 3; Margaret Cole Bonney, *My Scituate* (n.p., 1988), 21-22. Sanborn maps for Scituate are on microfilm at State Library of Massachusetts, Special Collections, film box 709, reel 37.
[141] "Haynes, Gideon," legislative biographical card file, State Library of Massachusetts, Special Collections; *Souvenir of the 50th Anniversary of the Dedication of Bunker Hill Monument, 1843-1893* (Charlestown, MA: The Bunker Hill Times, 1893), 38 (with photo and biography stating he died in 1892 at Nantasket Beach in Hull), http://hdl.loc.gov/loc.gdc/scd0001.00140695269, and https://archive.org/details/souvenirof50than00char; "Maude Emma Haynes [Duganne]," *Provincetown Advocate*, August 24, 1967, 2, obituary, RootsWeb.com website, http://wc.rootsweb.ancestry.com/cgi-bin/igm.cgi?op=GET&db=oldmankew&id=I8814.
[142] "News Happenings in Drugdom – Boston Briefs," *N.A.R.D. Journal* (Chicago: National Association of Retail Druggists, 1916), vol. 23, no. 7, November 16, 1916, 293,
https://books.google.com/books?id=FBgzAQAAMAAJ&source=gbs_navlinks_s. H. M. Macdonald is listed in the 1918 New England Telephone directory with residence on Allen Place, and Harry M. Macdonald is listed in the *1918 Harold Howard Directory*, 46 (wife Mabel P.) as druggist, Front Street, home, Allen Place.
[143] "Haynes, Walter," legislative biographical card file, State Library of Massachusetts, Special Collections. The card mentions Harvard College under "Additional Information" but he is not listed as a graduate of Harvard. Harvard University, *Quinquennial Catalogue of the Officers and Graduates of Harvard University 1636-1905* (Cambridge: Harvard University, 1905), https://archive.org/details/quinquennialcata00harviala.

[144] "Dedication, Soldiers' and Sailors' Monument, Scituate, Massachusetts, June 17, 1918," program, on file, SHS.
[145] "On this day … June 25, 1919 – Massachusetts Ratifies the 19th Amendment," Massachusetts Secretary of State website, http://www.sec.state.ma.us/mus/pdfs/Suffrage-June-25-panels.pdf.
[146] "Walter Haynes of Scituate is Laid to Rest," *Scituate Herald*, May 22, 1936, 1, 4; *Boston Globe*, May 23, 1936, 15.
[147] Inez Haynes Irwin, *Adventures of Yesterday*, ch. 13 "The Adventure of Scituate," 524-527, unpublished autobiography, SL; *Scituate Herald*, October 7, 1949, 5 (Inez speaking on Old Scituate at Scituate Woman's Club); Will Irwin, "The Story of Scituate," in *Scituate, 1636-1936* (Scituate: Scituate Tercentenary Committee, 1936, reprinted 1973), with booklet's credits on last page, and listing of historic houses on page 45; "Address by Miss Perkins Arouses Enthusiasm; One of Principal Closing Events of Anniversary Week," *Scituate Herald*, September 11, 1936, 1, 8; Irwin, *The Making of a Reporter*, 197; Ware, *Why They Marched*, 76.
[148] "Zoning Variance Hearing, Scituate," *Scituate Herald*, August 13, 1937, 1 and 5; Mary Ann Ford to Judith W. Smith, November 24, 1919, box 1, Judith Winsor Smith Papers, 1796-1945 [*JWS*]. MHS; Judith Smith diary, July 11, 1893 (Sylvanus & Mary visit to Mary Ann Ford), *JWS*; *Annual Report of the Town Officers and Committees of the Town of Scituate for the Year Ending December 31, 1922* (Scituate: Town of Scituate, 1923), 11-12 (report of Scituate Historical Society), Scituate Town Library website.
[149] "Zoning Variance Hearing, Scituate," *Scituate Herald*, August 13, 1937, 1 and 5.
[150] "Debate Greenbush Zoning Rules," *Scituate Herald*, October 1, 1937, 1, 8; Greenbush area form, SCI.C, MACRIS.
[151] Inez Haynes Irwin to Maud Wood Park, July 1, 1938, box 4, *MWP*.
[152] Inez Haynes Irwin to Maud Wood Park, June 25, 1938, box 4, *MWP*.
[153] Inez Haynes Irwin to Maud Wood Park, June 25, 1938, box 4, *MWP*.
[154] *Scituate Herald*, August 20, 1937, 5; *Scituate Herald*, May 5, 1955, 5; *Scituate Herald*, December 5, 1957, 3; "Mrs. Irwin Opens Home to League," May 10, 1956, 5; "Charming Homes Selected for League Tour," *South Shore Mirror*, July 2, 1959, 17; "Tea and Tour," *South Shore Mirror*, July 9, 1959, 16.
[155] *Scituate Herald*, June 26, 1958, 6.
[156] See also Trigg, *Feminism as Life's Work*, 108.
[157] "Biographical Note," Sophia Smith Collection, Smith College, Phyllis Duganne Papers website, https://asteria.fivecolleges.edu/findaids/sophiasmith/mnsss87_bioghist.html, and https://asteria.fivecolleges.edu/findaids/sophiasmith/mnsss87_main.html. A few candid photos of Phyllis with her new son Eben in 1929-1940 are on file in the Grace Parthenia Atwell Papers, SL. Copies of the photos can be found by using the search engine at http://via.lib.harvard.edu/via/deliver/advancedsearch?_collection=via, and entering "Edith" and "Haynes" and "Thompson."
[158] *The Publishers' Weekly*, September 11, 1920, 566, https://books.google.com/books?id=n2wyAQAAMAAJ&source=gbs_navlinks_s.
[159] "Maude Emma Haynes [Duganne]," *Provincetown Advocate*.
[160] Jones, *Heretics and Hellraisers*, 136-137, 140.

[161] Assessor's database, 6 Bridge Avenue (Harry Haynes house), and 64 Edward Foster Road (Futrelle house); Haynes, Harry E. House, 6 Bridge Avenue, SCI.1228, MACRIS; 64 Edward Foster Road, SCI.__ (filed November 2019), MACRIS.
[162] *Boston Globe*, October 1, 1970, 48.
[163] Author's visit October 2, 2017. The words were selected by Inez from an essay on medieval Italy by John Addington Symonds, according to Hudson, *The Writing Game*, 180, citing Inez's autobiography, "Adventures of Yesterday," 589.
[164] Author's visit October 2, 2017.
[165] Quilter, "An Inez Haynes Gillmore Irwin Bibliography."
[166] Zahniser & Fry, *Alice Paul*, 126, 133.
[167] Harriet Connor Brown, ed., "Official Program, Woman Suffrage Procession, Washington, D. C., March 3, 1913" (Washington, 1913), 16 of 20, Library of Congress, https://www.loc.gov/item/rbpe.20801600/; "Caro Garland *Burwell* Moore," Find A Grave website, http://findagrave.com/cgi-bin/fg.cgi/http=://www.findagrave.com/cgi-bin/fg.cgi?page=gr&GRid=160483257.
[168] Justin Winsor, *History of the Town of Duxbury, Massachusetts, with Genealogical Registers* (Boston: Crosby & Nichols, 1849), 210 (Josiah 1834), in chapter "History of the Church of Duxbury," https://catalog.hathitrust.org/Record/009577937; *Vital Records of Duxbury, Massachusetts, to the Year 1850* (Boston: New England Historic Genealogical Society, 1911), 111 (William birth), 158, 309 (Smith 1841 marriage), 318 (Moore 1831 marriage), 396 (Rebecca Moore death), https://archive.org/details/vitalrecordsofdu00duxb/page/n7; *The Mayflower Descendant: Volume 30, 1932* (Boston: Massachusetts Society of Mayflower Descendants, 1932), 86, https://books.google.com/books?id=l_71cOEKvlwC&source=gbs_navlinks_s.
[169] SLGMSD, "Como William Sturtevant Moore, Sr," Find A Grave website, https://findagrave.com/cgi-bin/fg.cgi?page=gr&GRid=42930827; *Quinquennial Catalogue of the Officers and Graduates of Harvard University 1636-1920* (Cambridge: Harvard University, 1920), 93 (A.B. 1873), https://hdl.handle.net/2027/iau.31858027489990; Ada T Hayden and John E. V. Hayden, husband, to Caro G. Moore of Boston, deed ("formerly the homestead estate of Rev. Josiah Moore deceased, near Partridge Academy"), March 6, 1906, PCRD, book 930, page 262; "Bradford, Capt. Gamaliel House," DUX.3, MACRIS (also listed on the National Register of Historic Places); Carolyn Ravenscroft email, June 15, 2020 (Bradford House).
[170] *The National Cyclopaedia of American Biography*, vol. 16 (New York: James T. White & Company, 1918), 162-163 (photograph), https://archive.org/details/nationalcyclopae16newy; *A Souvenir of Massachusetts Legislators 1909* (Stoughton, MA: A. M. Bridgman, 1909), 45 (photograph), 63 (photograph), 159 (biography), Massachusetts State Archives, archives.lib.state.ma.us/bitstream/handle/2452/43359/ocm08580879-1909.pdf; *A Souvenir of Massachusetts Legislators 1910* (Stoughton, MA: A. M. Bridgman, 1910), 45 (photograph), 63 (photograph), 153 (biography), Massachusetts State Archives, archives.lib.state.ma.us/bitstream/handle/2452/43360/ocm08580879-1910.pdf; *Who's Who in State Politics 1909* (Boston: Practical Politics, 1909), 45 & 63, 125 (photo), https://archives.lib.state.ma.us/handle/2452/43359, and *Who's Who in State Politics 1910* (Boston: Practical Politics, 1910) ("Bird book"), 234 (photo), State

Library of Massachusetts, https://archives.lib.state.ma.us/handle/2452/423323; *Journal of the House of Representatives of the Commonwealth of Massachusetts 1910* (Boston: Wright & Potter Printing Co., State Printers, 1910), 128, 858, 1175 (seawall); 203, 692, 715 (pollution);
https://books.google.com/books?id=odJBAQAAMAAJ&source=gbs_navlinks_s.
[171] *Massachusetts Men's League for Woman Suffrage* (Boston: Massachusetts Men's League for Woman Suffrage [T. Todd Co., Printers], January 1, 1911), statement of objectives, constitution, and membership list, SL, in Nineteenth Century Collections Online; Kroeger, *The Suffragents*, 118 (photo of W. S. Moore), 135 (W. S. Moore met with others to form a local men's league in Washington, mention of his testimony on mistreatment of 1913 marchers).
[172] Brown, "Official Program, Woman Suffrage Procession," 16 of 20.
[173] "Mrs. Owens and Mrs. C.G. Moore," digital file from original negative, 1913, Library of Congress, http://www.loc.gov/pictures/item/ggb2005012548/ and http://hdl.loc.gov/loc.pnp/ggbain.12512; *Pittsburgh Post-Gazette*, February 2, 1913, 1, https://www.newspapers.com/newspage/85732393/; *Lima News* [OH], February 14, 1913, 7, https://www.newspapers.com/newspage/38780706/; *The Roanoke Beacon* [Plymouth, NC], February 21, 1913,
http://newspapers.digitalnc.org/lccn/sn92074055/1913-02-21/ed-1/seq-1/ocr/; *San Bernardino County Sun* [CA], February 28, 1913, 6,
https://www.newspapers.com/newspage/49186283/.
[174] Brown, "Official Program, Woman Suffrage Procession," 8 (image) and 15 (bio). Mary Forrest (also known as Marie) was the daughter of naval officer William S. Moore and Virginia Eastman, who died in 1892. William S. Moore in 1901 married Caro Moore, who was not much older than his daughter Marie. Marie married Keith Forrest in 1910. SLGMSD, "Marie Henderson *Moore* Forrest," Find A Grave website, https://findagrave.com/cgi-bin/fg.cgi?page=gr&GRid=160372098.
[175] Brown, "Official Program, Woman Suffrage Procession," 17; Nicholas Kilmer, "Thomas Buford Meteyard: A Biography," in Nicholas Kilmer, ed., *Thomas Buford Meteyard Paintings and Watercolors*, exhibition catalog (New York: Berry-Hill Galleries, Inc., 1989), 28-34; Nicholas Kilmer and David Noonan, Jr., "The Scituate Connection," in *Scenes from Vagabondia*, 21 (at 22).
[176] "To See Suffrage Parade," *Boston Daily Globe*, February 2, 1913, 10; Edward F. Burns, "Cavalry Called Out to Protect Suffrage Marchers from Mob," *Boston Daily Globe*, March 4, 1913, 1; "Women in Tears at Struggle," *Boston Daily Globe*, March 4, 1913, 1; "Police Heads Appear Today," *Boston Daily Globe*, March 8, 1913, 8; "Woman Suffrage," *Index to Dates of Current Events Occurring or Reported During the Year 1912[-1913]* (New York: R. R. Bowker Co., July 1913) ("mauled by crowd"), 237,
https://books.google.com/books?id=HWI9AAAAYAAJ&source=gbs_navlinks_s
; Irwin, *Story of the Woman's Party*, 29, republished as *The Story of Alice Paul and the National Woman's Party* (Fairfax, VA: Denlinger's Publishers, 1977); Sheridan Harvey, "Marching for the Vote: Remembering the Woman Suffrage Parade of 1913," Library of Congress, American Memory website,
https://memory.loc.gov/ammem/awhhtml/aw01e/aw01e.html; "Alice Paul (1885-1977)," National Women's History Museum website, https://www.nwhm.org/; Donald L. Haggerty, ed., *National Woman's Party Papers: The Suffrage Years, 1913-1920: A Guide to the Microfilm Edition* (Microfilming Corp. of America, 1981),

http://cisupa.proquest.com/ksc_assets/catalog/2609.pdf; Ware, *Why They Marched*, 194-201; Zahniser & Fry, *Alice Paul*, ch. 7 "A Procession of Our Own;" Johanna Neuman, "Women On the March," Nursing Clio website, posted August 24, 2017, https://nursingclio.org/2017/08/24/women-on-the-march/. Inez Haynes Irwin described the parade as succeeding beyond the suffragists' wildest hopes, and called it "the monster procession" in Irwin, *Story of the Woman's Party*, 28-31, 35. A description of the march and a wonderful set of photos of the march from the Library of Congress (including Caro Moore's "Homemakers" at images 18 and 20) are at Alan Taylor, "The 1913 Women's Suffrage Parade," *The Atlantic* website, posted March 1, 2013 (a century after the march) https://www.theatlantic.com/photo/2013/03/100-years-ago-the-1913-womens-suffrage-parade/100465/.

[177] "Superb Gowns at Antis' Rally: Their Meeting Here is a Notable One; Frederick D. Fish Speaks Against Votes for Women," *Boston Daily Globe*, March 6, 1913, 9.

[178] 1880 US census; 1903 map, plate 31, main map ("J. Livermore" and "Mrs. Livermore"), inset for Mann Hill ("Mrs. Livermore" and "J. I. Livermore"); *1907 Cambridge Directory* (Boston: W. A. Greenough & Co., 1907), 715, et al (Henry in law practice with Joseph), https://archive.org/details/cambridgedirecto1907unse; "Frederick P. Fish, Noted Lawyer, Dies. Was President of American Telephone and Telegraph Co. for Many Years. An Overseer of Harvard. Also a Leading Member of Massachusetts 'Tech's' Board and a Bank Director," *New York Times*, November 7, 1930, 25, *1915 Harold Howard Directory*, 67 (Joseph, Henry); *1918 Harold Howard Directory*, 81 (Joseph); *Turner's Public Spirit* (Ayer, MA), November 21, 1914, 4, obituary, https://religiondocbox.com/Latter_Day_Saints/86635052-Turner-s-public-spirit.html; "Mrs. Clara P. Fish Dead," *Boston Globe*, Nov. 14, 1914, 12.

[179] "Como William Sturtevant Moore, Sr," FindAGrave memorial; "An Act Granting pensions and increase of pensions to certain soldiers and sailors of the Regular Army and Navy …," US Statutes at Large, 63d Cong., 3d sess., Ch. 196, March 4, 1915 [S. 7509] (Private, No. 240), 1574, https://books.google.com/books?id=_T83AAAAIAAJ&source=gbs_navlinks_s; "Caro Garland Burwell Moore," Find A Grave website, http://findagrave.com/cgi-bin/fg.cgi/http=://www.findagrave.com/cgi-bin/fg.cgi?page=gr&GRid=160483257.

[180] "Scituate," *Boston Daily Globe*, June 20, 1915 (erroneously listing both Mr. and Mrs. Moore); *1915 Harold Howard Directory*, 68; *1918 Harold Howard Directory*, 83; *1911 Valuation List*, 87 (Bijou on lot 222); Caro G. Moore to Edith G. Bittinger, deed (Duxbury estate), December 10, 1914, PCRD, book 1207, page 327; George F. Welch to Caro G. Moore and Mary H. M. Forrest, deed (Scituate), December 12, 1914, PCRD, book 1207, page 340 (lot 222 "with the buildings thereon"); Howard R. Guild to Caro G. Moore and Mary H. M. Forrest, deed, November 4, 1919 (lot 221), PCRD, book 1338, page 298; Caro G. Moore and Mary H. M. Forrest, to Harriet N. Thomas, deed, August 6, 1921, PCRD, book 1395, page 147. The house is shown on lot 222 on the 1926 Sanborn Map, sheet 8. Lot 222 corresponds to today's 11 Collier Road, according to Scituate Town Assessor's Maps.

[181] *The Suffragist*, including July 1920, 129 ("Senator Harding 'Listens' and Evades"), at 143 (called "Mrs. Randolph Keith Forrest, of Scituate, Mass."), October 1920, 248 (author of "A Pageant: The Victory Goal"), December 1920, 303 (pageantry

for memorial), and January-February 1921, 334 (masthead), 338, https://books.google.com/books?id=nJszAQAAMAAJ&source=gbs_navlinks_s. Both Inez Haynes Irwin and Mary (Marie) Forrest were listed on letterhead stationery of the National Advisory Council of the National Woman's Party by 1919. Dora Kelly Lewis to Louise Lewis, letter, January 10, 1919, "Selected Dora Kelly Lewis Correspondence, July 4, 1917-April 14, 1920," item 3 of 10, at Preserving American Freedom, a Historical Society of Pennsylvania digital history project, website, http://digitalhistory.hsp.org/pafrm/doc/selected-dora-kelly-lewis-correspondence-july-4-1917-april-14-1920.SLGMSD, "Marie Henderson Moore Forrest," Find A Grave website, https://findagrave.com/cgi-bin/fg.cgi?page=gr&GRid=160372098, and obituaries quoted; Ware, *Why They Marched*, 238 (arrests and jail). Mary Moore Forrest is not mentioned in the 1920 book by Doris Stevens, *Jailed for Freedom*, or the 1921 *Story of the Woman's Party*.

182 Emily J. Harris, ed., "William Mankins House," Historic American Buildings Survey, National Park Service, HABS No. DC-190, reiterated in "Georgetown Architecture--Northwest, Northwest Washington, District of Columbia: Historic American Buildings Survey Selections, Number 6" (Washington: US Commission of Fine Arts, 1970), 182-201, including 188 ("spectaculars," "dynamic"), https://archive.org/details/georgetownarchit06comm.

183 Inez Haynes Gillmore Papers, Harvard; Will Irwin and Inez Haynes Gillmore Papers, Yale, and True and Meehan, "Guide to the Irwin-Gillmore Papers."

184 George F. Welch to Margaret C. Colgate, deed, August 3, 1908, PCRD, book 996, page 482; *1909 Valuation List*, 106; Margaret C. Colgate to Albert E. Lynch, deed, July 20, 1928, PCRD, book 1556, page 386; Robert E. Moody, ed., *Bostonia: The Boston University Alumni Magazine*, vol. 7, no. 2 (Boston: Boston University, November 1933), 22, https://hdl.handle.net/2144/19438; *1926 Sanborn Map*, sheet 8; *Journal of the House of Representatives of the United States, 63d Congress, 2d Session*, vol. 63, issue 2 (Washington, DC: Government Printing Office, 1913), 725 (July 1, 1914: "By Mr. Mitchell: Petition of A. Gertrude Dudley, Margaret C. Colgate and others, of Rockland, Mass., urging woman-suffrage legislation; to the Committee on the Judiciary."), https://books.google.com/books?id=g01RAQAAMAAJ&source=gbs_navlinks_s.

185 *Winchester Star,* August 16, 1918, 8, col. 2 (spending August on Third Cliff), https://archive.org/details/WinStar_070518_092718/page/n55/mode/2up; Lyle Nyberg, "100 years ago: Locals spent the summer in Scituate," *Daily Times Chronicle*, posted April 18, 2017, http://homenewshere.com/daily_times_chronicle/news/winchester/article_60944e74-244a-11e7-be59-c7455a2d5540.html; "Equal Suffragists Meet; Women of Third District Hold Annual Session, with Interesting Addresses," *Cambridge Tribune*, vol. 40, no. 13, May 26, 1917, 6, http://cambridge.dlconsulting.com/cgi-bin/cambridge?a=d&d=Tribune19170526-01.2.44.

186 Beatrice to Swinburne, August 13, 1918, *SHP.*

187 "In Memoriam: Meyer Bloomfield, February 11, 1878 – March 12, 1938," *Occupations: The Vocational Guidance Journal* (now *Journal of Counseling & Development*), vol. 16, no. 7 (Blackwell Publishing Ltd, April 1938), 666, 694-695, online by John Wiley & Sons, Ltd, https://onlinelibrary.wiley.com/doi/abs/10.1002/j.2164-5892.1938.tb00354.x, doi:10.1002/j.2164-5892.1938.tb00354.x.

[188] Sanford M. Jacoby, "Origins of Vocational Guidance," in Sanford M. Jacoby, *Employing Bureaucracy: Managers, Unions, and the Transformation of Work in the 20th Century* (Mahwah, NJ: Lawrence Erlbaum Associates Publishers, 2004, revised ed.), 55-56, https://books.google.com/books?id=xCt6AgAAQBAJ&source=gbs_navlinks_s.
[189] "In Memoriam;" Henry Eilbirt, "The Development of Personnel Management in the United States," *The Business History Review*, vol. 33, no. 3 (Cambridge, MA: Harvard College, Autumn, 1959), 345-364, at 357, stable URL: http://www.jstor.org/stable/3111950; "Bloomfield, Meyer," in John N. Ingham, *Biographical Dictionary of American Business Leaders, A-G*, vol. 1, (Westport, CT: Greenwood Press, 1983), 78-79 ("the founder of the science of industrial relations), https://books.google.com/books?id=KRjPBj19i-4C&source=gbs_navlinks_s; "Meyer Bloomfield," Palmer Coates website, http://palmercoates.com/meyer-bloomfield/.
[190] "In Memoriam;" Judith Arlene Bookbinder, *Boston Modern: Figurative Expressionism as Alternative Modernism* (Hanover, NH: University Press of New England, 2005), 18-19, https://books.google.com/books?id=r47Hc8Ai7lEC&source=gbs_navlinks_s; Finding aid for the Alice Paul Archive, https://www.alicepaul.org/documents-from-the-alice-paul-archives/; "Papers of Alice Paul, 1785-1985 (inclusive), 1805-1985 (bulk)," Biography in Collection Overview, SL, https://hollisarchives.lib.harvard.edu/repositories/8/resources/5012. The history of settlement houses, with a group photo including Meyer Bloomfield, is described in John E. Hansan, "National Federation of Settlements," website of The Social Welfare History Project, Virginia Commonwealth University, http://socialwelfare.library.vcu.edu/settlement-houses/national-federation-of-settlements-and-neighborhood-centers/; "New Settlement Work," *Boston Globe*, October 27, 1901, 6. See also 112 Salem Street, Boston, BOS.16863 (January 2020), MACRIS.
[191] *Pauline Agassiz Shaw: Tributes Paid Her Memory at the Memorial Service Held on Easter Sunday, April 8, 1917, at Faneuil Hall, Boston* (Boston: privately printed, 1917), 78, https://babel.hathitrust.org/cgi/pt?id=hvd.hxt9jg&view=1up&seq=21.
[192] "Sylvia Palmer Bloomfield, 1881-1949," Palmer Coates website (naming her as a co-founder of the Civic Service House of Boston, and a founder and president of the Boston League of Women Voters), http://palmercoates.com/palmer-coates/; "Mrs. Meyer Bloomfield," obituary, *New York Times*, March 4, 1949 (helped found Civic Service House, former president and founder of the Boston League of Women Voters); Ingham, *Dictionary of American Business Leaders*, vol. 1, 78-79; *Boston Directory* (Sampson & Murdock, 1905), 112 Salem Street, https://bcd.lib.tufts.edu/view_text.jsp?urn=tufts:central:dca:UA069:UA069.005.DO.00015&chapter=d.1905.su.Bloomfield; "Experimenting Upon Apes," *Boston Globe*, December 28, 1909, 9.
[193] "Closing Exercises Held," *Boston Globe*, April 1, 1909, 3; "Civic Service House," *Boston Globe*, December 18, 1909, 7. A 1910 news account of a dispute at the Civic Service House does not mention Meyer, who, evidently, had moved on to other things. "Say Demands Were Refused," *Boston Globe*, December 12, 1910, 2.

[194] Robert A. Woods and Albert J. Kennedy, eds., *Handbook of Settlements* (New York: Charities Publication Committee, for Russell Sage Foundation, 1911), 108-109, https://archive.org/details/handbooksettlem00woodgoog.
[195] Geoffrey Blodgett, "Shaw, Pauline Agassiz," in Edward T. James, Janet Wilson James, and Paul S. Boyer, eds., *Notable American Women 1607-1950: A Biographical Dictionary*, vol. 3, P-Z (Cambridge: the Belknap Press of Harvard University Press, 1971), 278.
[196] Beacon Building, 6 Beacon Street, Boston, BOS.1545 (continuation sheet February 2020), MACRIS.
[197] Beacon Building, 6 Beacon Street, Boston, BOS.1545 (continuation sheet February 2020), MACRIS); *WJ*, January 1, 1910, 1 (editor).
[198] Maud Wood Park, "Boston Equal Suffrage Association For Good Government (1901-1907) Introductory Note," *WRC*, Subseries C. Suffrage and Women's Rights, #Pa-94, 1943, SL (Meyer on the original board, chair of the Committee on Clean Streets and Civic Sanitation).
[199] Blodgett, "Shaw, Pauline Agassiz;" Jamaica Plain Women's History Trail, number 12 and detail on Pauline Agassiz Shaw, part of Boston Women's Heritage Trail, https://bwht.org/jamaica-plain/ and https://bwht.org/pauline-agassiz-shaw/; *Old Colony Trust Co. v. Shaw*, 261 Mass. 158 (Mass. Supreme Judicial Court, 1927), https://casetext.com/case/old-colony-trust-co-v-shaw. See also Berenson, *Massachusetts Suffrage*, 102-103, 111, 121; Mark B., "Quincy A. Shaw - Very Rich Guy," Remember Jamaica Plain? website, http://rememberjamaicaplain.blogspot.com/2008/02/quincy-shaw-very-rich-guy.html.
[200] Blodgett, "Shaw, Pauline Agassiz."
[201] Blodgett, "Shaw, Pauline Agassiz;" Ida Husted Harper, ed., *The History of Woman Suffrage*, vol. 6, 1900-1920 (New York: National American Woman Suffrage Association, 1922), 268, https://babel.hathitrust.org/cgi/pt?id=njp.32101075729036&view=1up&seq=9; Sharon Hartman Strom, *Political Woman: Florence Luscomb and the Legacy of Radical Reform* (Philadelphia: Temple University Press, 2001), 69, preview, https://books.google.com/books?id=VzoQLrsyEbcC&source=gbs_navlinks_s; BESAGG meeting notice, November 14, 1907, Charlotte Perkins Gilman speaking on "Equal Suffrage," Library of Congress, https://www.loc.gov/item/rbcmiller001128/; "6 Marlborough," Back Bay Houses: Genealogies of Back Bay Houses website, https://backbayhouses.org/6-marlborough/; "Index to Deeds: 6 Marlborough," Back Bay Houses website, https://backbayhouses.org/index-to-deeds-6-marlborough/; "Suffrage Convention," *Boston Globe*, October 23, 1907, 2; *Minutes of the Suffrage Conventions of the National American Woman Suffrage Association* (Washington, DC: NAWSA, various years), 82 (1904), 98 (1906) (search for "Marlboro"), https://books.google.com/books?id=gqMLAAAAIAAJ&source=gbs_navlinks_s. For a fascinating look at Maud Wood Park's inner turmoil during this time, see "Who I Am and What I Believe," [1903], included in Maud Wood Park Archive: The Power of Organization, Part One: Maud Wood Park and the Woman Suffrage Movement, Documents for Part One selected and interpreted by Melanie Gustafson (Alexandria, VA: Alexander Street Press, 2013). She refers to her

husband Charles E. Park's speculative purchase of a farm in Scituate, but, alas, there are no recorded deeds in his name, at least for Scituate, Massachusetts.
[202] "Ahead of All Others," *Boston Globe*, December 2, 1903, 11; "Susan Walker FitzGerald papers," Bryn Mawr College, finding aid on Philadelphia Area Archives Research Portal (PAARP), http://dla.library.upenn.edu/dla/pacscl/ead.html?q=susan%20walker%20fitzgerald&id=PACSCL_BMC_USPBmBMCM19&; Strom, *Political Woman*, 69, 71; BESAGG meeting notice, November 14, 1907; "In Flourishing Condition," *Boston Globe*, March 27, 1908, 8; Lumsden, *Rampant Women*, 46-49. The *Woman's Journal* had a big profile of Susan FitzGerald with photos in 1912, when she ran for Boston School Board. "Why Not Elect a Woman," *WJ*, January 6, 1912, 1. There was internal dissension in BESAGG leadership about FitzGerald's performance, discussed in Joan C. Tonn, *Mary P. Follett: Creating Democracy, Transforming Management* (New Haven: Yale University Press, 2003), 171-179, preview, https://books.google.com/books?id=51MZS7ixyf0C&vq=hutcheson&source=gbs_navlinks_s. And there was criticism in 1910 (when he was on the board) of Meyer Bloomfield's ability to follow through, a criticism that followed him to his later work at the Vocation Bureau. Tonn, *Mary P. Follett*, 216-217, 537. A collection of colorized photos includes a photo of Susan Fitzgerald riding in an automobile with Harriot Stanton Blatch and others, in a New York City parade on July 30, 1913. Lily Rothman, Liz Ronk, Sanna Dullaway, "Colorized Photos From Early Suffrage Marches Bring Women's History to Life," March 8, 2017, TIME magazine, https://time.com/4643297/colorized-suffrage-photos/.
[203] "Suffrage Convention," *Boston Globe*, October 23, 1907, 2; Chauncy Hall Building, 585-591 Boylston Street, Boston, BOS.2651, MACRIS; Harper, *History of Woman Suffrage*, vol. 6, 275 (Blackwell meeting).
[204] "Massachusetts Men's League for Woman Suffrage," *WJ*, February 26, 1910, 36; "Report on Equal Suffrage," *Boston Globe*, April 30, 1910, 12.
[205] *Massachusetts Men's League for Woman Suffrage* (1911), SL.
[206] "Women Will Ride Horses in Parade: Mounted Suffragists in March of 7000 Today," *Boston Daily Globe*, May 2, 1914, 1 ("Among the men who will be in the men's division are … Myer Bloomfield …."); Harper, *History of Woman Suffrage*, vol. 6, 286 (1914 parade description). See "Women Give Great Parade," *Boston Daily Globe*, May 3, 1914, 1, which lists paraders including the men's league but does not include Meyer Bloomfield. Meyer's name appears along with other prominent Massachusetts men in a 1910-1911 list of men's suffragists. *Men's League for Woman Suffrage, Miller Scrapbook* (New York, 1910 [and 1911], photograph, clipping at top center of second page, Library of Congress, https://www.loc.gov/item/2002719620/.
[207] *Boston Globe*, November 8, 1912, 5; *Boston Globe*, November 12, 1912, 5.
[208] "Funeral of Mrs Shaw," and "Memorial Services for Mrs Quincy A. Shaw," *Boston Globe*, February 13, 1917, 2 (different editions). See also "Tribute to Memory of Pauline A. Shaw," *Boston Globe*, April 9, 1917, 9, and *Pauline Agassiz Shaw: Tributes.*
[209] "Sylvia Palmer Bloomfield, 1881-1949," Palmer Coates website (naming her as a co-founder of the Civic Service House of Boston, and a founder and president of the Boston League of Women Voters), http://palmercoates.com/palmer-coates/; "Mrs. Meyer Bloomfield," obituary, *New York Times*, March 4, 1949 (helped found

Civic Service House, former president and founder of the Boston League of Women Voters); "Table Gossip," *Boston Globe*, March 16, 1913, 54 & 60 (BESAGG play); printed announcement of play (undated, but 1913), Maud Wood Park Papers, *WRC*, SL; "Women Organize for City Election," *Boston Globe*, September 27, 1921, 15.

[210] 112 Salem Street, Boston, BOS.16863, MACRIS.

[211] Savickas, "Meyer Bloomfield: Organizer," 260-261.

[212] Richard Greenwald, *The Triangle Fire, The Protocols of Peace, and Industrial Democracy in Progressive Era New York*, (Philadelphia: Temple University Press, 2005), 58, preview, https://books.google.com/books?id=3FCF_iad60kC&source=gbs_navlinks_s. Chapter 2 of Greenwald's book has an extensive discussion of the strike and the efforts to settle it.

[213] Greenwald, *The Triangle Fire*, chapter 2, "The Making of Industrial Democracy in the Ladies' Garment Industry," 57-75 (hero); Maud Wood Park, "Busy Hive Full of Workers for Women," *Boston American*, February 23, 1913, 2W, clipping in *WRC*, SL; Maud Wood Park, "Boston Equal Suffrage Association For Good Government (1901-1907) Introductory Note," *WRC*, Subseries C. Suffrage and Women's Rights, #Pa-94, 1943, SL.

[214] Woloch, *Women and the American Experience*, 210-211; Brown, "Official Program, Woman Suffrage Procession," 14 of 20, 18 of 20; Jones, *Heretics and Hellraisers*, 74-77.

[215] *Industrial Relations: Bloomfield's Labor Digest* , August 1, 1919 (Boston: Meyer Bloomfield & Daniel Bloomfield), 1 (source of quote), and other examples, https://books.google.com/books?id=rT02AQAAMAAJ&source=gbs_navlinks_s. The August 1, 1919, issue was a specimen, and the vol. 1, no. 1 issue was dated October 18, 1919.

[216] Mark L. Savickas, "Meyer Bloomfield: Organizer of the Vocational Guidance Movement (1907-1917)," *The Career Development Quarterly*, March 2009, vol. 57, no. 3, 259-273 (excellent survey of Meyer Bloomfield's work), http://www.freepatentsonline.com/article/Career-Development-Quarterly/196723355.html; Anne Mackin, "Boston on the Eve of the Great Depression: A Social Portrait," in Krieger and Cobb, *Mapping Boston*, 220 (immigration).

[217] "Davis, James John (1873-1947)," Biographical Directory of the United States Congress, website, http://bioguide.congress.gov/scripts/biodisplay.pl?index=D000111.

[218] Roger W. Babson, letter in *The Jewish Tribune*, as quoted in "Boom Meyer Bloomfield As Next Secretary of Labor," Jewish Telegraphic Agency, July 27, 1930, http://www.jta.org/1930/07/27/archive/boom-meyer-bloomfield-as-next-secretary-of-labor.

[219] "Boom for Bloomfield As Secretary of Labor Growing," Jewish Telegraphic Agency, August 8, 1930 (Bloomfield interviewed by Pres. Hoover), http://archive.jta.org/1930/08/08/archive/boom-for-bloomfield-as-secretary-of-labor-growing; "William N. Doak" in "Hall of Secretaries," US Department of Labor website, https://www.dol.gov/oasam/programs/history/doak.htm; "Doak Favored for Secretary of Labor; Virginian Editor, Hoover First Choice in 1928," *Daily Boston Globe*, November 23, 1930, A19.

[220] "William N. Doak" in "Hall of Secretaries."
[221] Steven Mintz and Sara McNeil, "Repatriation During the Great Depression," Digital History website, http://www.digitalhistory.uh.edu/disp_textbook.cfm?smtID=3&psid=3699; Steve Boisson, "Immigrants: The Last Time America Sent Her Own Packing," HistoryNet website, posted July 27, 2006, http://www.historynet.com/immigrants-the-last-time-america-sent-her-own-packing.htm. Hoover's National Commission on Law Observance and Enforcement (the Wickersham Commission) had a broad scope (law enforcement), but most public interest focused on its evaluation of widespread violations of national alcohol prohibition. "Wickersham Commission: Pro- or Anti-Repeal? You Decide," Alcohol Problems and Solutions website, https://www.alcoholproblemsandsolutions.org/wickersham-commission-pro-or-anti-repeal/. The commission's deportations report, "The Enforcement of the Deportation Laws" (vol. 5 of 14), Harvard University Library Open Collections Program, http://ocp.hul.harvard.edu/dl/immigration/009735419. The report is summarized and discussed in Francis Fisher Kane, "Challenge of the Wickersham Deportations Report," 23 *Am. Inst. Crim. L. & Criminology* 575, vol. 23, no. 4 (1932-1933), http://scholarlycommons.law.northwestern.edu/cgi/viewcontent.cgi?article=2323&context=jclc.
[222] Ingham, *Dictionary of American Business Leaders*, vol. 1, 78-79.
[223] Hingham Cooperative Bank to Meyer Bloomfield, deed, August 16, 1919, PCRD, book 1331, page 552 (Collier Road, lots 1 & 2, the site of the house at today's 3 Driftway); Edward J. Ball to Meyer Bloomfield, deed, October 18, 1919, PCRD, book 1342, page 17 (Collier Road, lot 3), in which the deed said: "It is hereby understood and agreed that the building on the said premises shall be removed by the grantor within 30 days from the date hereof" (this could be a structure shown on the 1918 Sanborn map, sheet 8); Bridget A. Mahon to Meyer Bloomfield, deed, August 10, 1934, PCRD, book 1669, page 112 (parcel to the east of Bloomfield's property and bordering Water Street/Driftway), referring to Lewis W. Perkins, *Plan of Land at Third Cliff, Scituate, Mass., August 6, 1934, 20 ft.=1 in.*, PCRD, plan book 5, page 425; Sylvia Palmer Bloomfield to James F. O'Hara and Mary F. O'Hara, May 1, 1944, PCRD, book 1862, page 399 (lots 1-3 and additional Mahon property). The garage or structure on lot 3 was absent from the 1926 Sanborn map, but a garage appeared there by the time of the 1930 *Valuation List*, A-L, 17.
[224] *1926 Harold Howard Directory*, 84; 1930 US census; "Miss Bloomfield to Wed Nicholas T. Rogers," *Daily Boston Globe*, February 4, 1934, A14 (315 Central Park West); Landmarks Preservation Commission's Upper West Side/Central Park West Historic District Designation Report, vol. 2, 50, www.nyc.gov/html/lpc/downloads/pdf/reports/uwscpwvol2.pdf. The latter building ("The Brookford") is still there, according to Google Street View, and StreetEasy website, http://streeteasy.com/building/the-brookford; *1938 South Shore Social Register*, 131.
[225] "Noted Author To Speak In Scituate," *Scituate Herald*, September 8, 1939, 1; Sylvia Palmer Bloomfield to James F. O'Hara and Mary F. O'Hara, May 1, 1944, PCRD, book 1862, page 399 (lots 1-3 and additional Mahon property).
[226] Palmer Coates website, http://palmercoates.com/; author's observations.

[227] *Owego Gazette*, October 18, 1917 ("sought after"), as quoted in Ed Nizalowski, "Vote For Women: How Tioga County Women Actively Participated in This Worldwide Struggle," *Owego Pennysaver Press* website, posted August 17, 2017, http://www.owegopennysaver.com/PS/2017/08/17/vote-for-women-how-tioga-county-women-actively-participated-in-this-worldwide-struggle/; Clare A. Pickard, "The United States Food Administration in Chautauqua County," in John Phillips Downs, Fenwick Y. Hedley, eds., History of Chautauqua County, New York, and Its People, vol. 1 (Boston: American Historical Society, Inc., 1921), 309 ("world"), https://books.google.com/books?id=7vUpAQAAMAAJ&source=gbs_navlinks_s.
[228] Marleen Buelinckx, biographical note, 1995/2003, in finding aid, Swinburne Hale papers, Manuscripts and Archives Division, The New York Public Library, Astor, Lenox, and Tilden Foundations, http://www.nypl.org/sites/default/files/archivalcollections/pdf/hale.pdf; Inez's autobiography, ch. 13, 539, SL. The NYPL has an extensive collection of about 140 of Beatrice's letters, 1913-1919, in the Swinburne Hale papers collection [*SHP*]. Other letters are in the Ralph M. Pearson Collection, 1870-1930 [*RMPC*], New Mexico History Museum, Fray Angelico Chaves History Library, inventory at Rocky Mountain Online Archive, https://rmoa.unm.edu/docviewer.php?docId=nmsm1ac380.xml. Beatrice's going to Scituate because of Inez is implicit in Beatrice's letters and their circumstances, including their membership in Heterodoxy.
[229] "Miss Forbes-Robertson to Lecture," *New York Times*, June 7, 1911. Beatrice's family was English, although she was born in New York City. "Husband to Be Equal Partner – Miss Forbes-Robertson's Idea," news clipping, unknown paper, about April 20, 1910, *SHP*.
[230] Inez Haynes Gillmore to Maud Wood Park, March 29, 1910, NAWSA Papers, reel 11, Manuscripts Division, Library of Congress, as quoted in Neuman, *Gilded Suffragists*, 4.
[231] Item 71, "Gilman, Charlotte Perkins. The Yellow Wall Paper," New York ABAA Book Fair 2017, listing, https://www.luxmentis.com/images/upload/nyabaa2017showlist.pdf.
[232] "Fiancé Meets Her at Pier. Beatrice Forbes Robertson and Swinburne Hale Married." *Boston Globe*, July 1, 1910, 8 (with photos); "Miss Forbes-Robertson to Lecture," *New York Times*, June 7, 1911, http://query.nytimes.com/gst/abstract.html?res=9C06E4DD1E3EE233A25754C0A9609C946096D6CF&legacy=true.
[233] Buelinckx, Finding aid, *SHP*; "Guide to the William Gardner Hale Papers circa 1880-1928," University of Chicago Library, https://www.lib.uchicago.edu/e/scrc/findingaids/view.php?eadid=ICU.SPCL.HALEWG; "Fiancé Meets Her at Pier," *Boston Globe*, July 1, 1910, 8.
[234] Christine Woodworth, "'Equal Rights by All Means!': Beatrice Forbes-Robertson's 1910 Suffrage Matinee and the Onstage Junction of the US and UK Franchise Movements," in Sara Freeman, ed., *Theatre History Studies 2018, Volume 37* (Tuscaloosa: University of Alabama Press and Mid-America Theatre Conference, 2018), 209-224, preview, https://books.google.com/books?id=At98DwAAQBAJ&source=gbs_navlinks_s.
[235] Harper, *The History of Woman Suffrage*, vol. 5, 289.

[236] Elizabeth Robins, "Come and See (The Coronation Suffrage Pageant)," *Westminster Gazette*, June 15, 1911, in *Way Stations* (London: Hodder and Stoughton,, 1913), ch. 14, 250 (Beatrice), https://archive.org/details/waystations00robigoog/page/n8/mode/2up; W. T. Stead, "Woman's Suffrage in the Ascendant," *The Review of Reviews*, vol. 44, July, 1911, 18-19, in W.T. Stead Resource Site, https://www.attackingthedevil.co.uk/.
[237] "With the Members Sworn to Secrecy, Forty of New York's Prominent 'Advanced' Women Band Into 'The Heterodoxy' and Meet to Eat and Decide Their Position on Problems of the Day," *New-York Tribune*, November 24, 1914, Library of Congress, https://chroniclingamerica.loc.gov/lccn/sn83030214/1914-11-24/ed-1/seq-7/; Inez Haynes Gillmore Papers, Harvard; Judith Schwarz, *Radical Feminists of Heterodoxy: Greenwich Village, 1912-1940* (Lebanon, NH: New Victoria Publishers, 1982), ii, 24-25, 30, 32, 43, 73, 88, 90, 115-128; Thompson, "Inez and I," 27-32, 36-37 (love of theater). A photograph of Beatrice Hale, furnished for a 1920 booklet from Heterodoxy members to its founder, is at the Inez Haynes Gillmore Papers, Harvard, seq. 43, https://iiif.lib.harvard.edu/manifests/view/drs:50684112$43i.
[238] *WJ*, March 9, 1912, 77 (March 11 event with 25 speakers);"Twenty-Five Answers to Antis: Five-Minute Speeches on Votes for Women by Eminent Suffragists," booklet (New York City: NAWSA, 1912), *WRC*, SL (002690_043_0001_0002_From_51_to_100).
[239] "Men's League for Woman Suffrage, First District Dinner, 1912," March 21 program (with list of speakers and menu) and announcement, Harriet Wright Burton Laidlaw Papers, 1851-1958, A-63, 135, SL, https://id.lib.harvard.edu/ead/c/sch00682c00166/catalog; discussion in text above about *The Masses*.
[240] Kroeger, *The Suffragents*, 84 (photo), 101, 148, 161; *WJ*, May 11, 1912, 150, col. 1; Lucie Levine, "How the Men's League for Women's Suffrage helped win voting rights in New York," 6sqft website, posted November 5, 2018, https://www.6sqft.com/how-the-mens-league-for-womens-suffrage-revolutionized-voting-rights-in-new-york/. Max Eastman was the organizer of the Men's League for Women Suffrage of the State of New York, according to Garrison, *Mary Heaton Vorse*, 72. Swinburne was not mentioned in documents about the formation of the league. *Men's League for Women's Suffrage: Constitution and Charter Members* (1910), pamphlet, Library of Congress, https://www.loc.gov/item/rbcmiller002561/. By 1912, the league's pamphlet listed Swinburne as one of 12 members of the Executive Committee. The pamphlet is included in a Powerpoint presentation by Nancy Mion, "Amazing Women and How They Got the Vote," AAUW Islip Area (NY) Branch website, http://www.aauw-nys.org/branches/islip.htm.
[241] *The Harvard Graduates' Magazine*, vol. 20, 1911-1912 (Boston: The Harvard Graduates' Magazine Association, December 1911), 364 (class of 1905 notes), https://books.google.com/books?id=JC9YAAAAYAAJ&source=gbs_navlinks_s; Kroeger, *The Suffragents*, 100-101; "Suffrage Army Out on Parade: Perhaps 10,000 Women and Men Sympathizers March for the Cause," *New York Times*, May 5, 1912, 2; "15,000 Women March in America's Greatest Suffrage Parade," *Boston American*, May 5, 1912, clipping in *WRC*, SL (mentions Max Eastman, Swinburne

Hale, and others); "10,000 Women and Men March for Equal Suffrage," *New York Times*, May 5, 1912, part 9 (with many photos) (Beatrice).
[242] "Women Parade; Crowds Applaud," *Brooklyn Daily Eagle*, May 5, 1912, 1 (72 riders); Mary Alden Hopkins, "Women March," *Collier's*, May 18, 1912, 13, https://babel.hathitrust.org/cgi/pt?id=njp.32101079822522&view=1up&seq=357; "Marching for Suffrage," *Harper's Weekly*, May 11, 1912 Part II (with photos); Anna C. Simonson, "Féminisme Oblige: Katharine Susan Anthony and the Birth of Modern Feminist Biography, 1877-1929" (PhD dissertation, City University of New York, 2017), 155, notes 35-37, CUNY Academic Works, https://pdfs.semanticscholar.org/1f71/3c44ab411831b314c47836b3a7caa1efaece.pdf.
[243] "15,000 Women March in America's Greatest Suffrage Parade," *Boston American*, May 5, 1912; *WJ*, May 11, 1912, 145-147 (with photos); "10,000 Women Marching for Votes," *The Literary Digest*, May 18, 1912, 1024 ("largest demonstration," with photo of cavalcade), clipping, Ann Lewis Women's Suffrage Collection, https://lewissuffragecollection.omeka.net/items/show/1253.
[244] *WJ*, May 11, 1912, 146; *WJ*, May 25, 1912, 164.
[245] Margaret W. De Peyster, "Women Walk for Suffrage," *Los Angeles Times*, November 10, 1912, 7 (20,000 women and several thousand men), https://www.newspapers.com/clip/25829461/new_york_suffrage_parade_nov_1912/; "Brooklyn Suffragists Enthusiastic About Parade," *Brooklyn Daily Eagle*, November 8, 1912, 28; "15,000 Women March Down Fifth Avenue in Suffrage Cause," *Brooklyn Daily Eagle*, November 10, 1912, 64 (Chinese lanterns and flaring torches); "Half Million Cheer Parade," *WJ*, November 16, 1912, 362 (front page) (20,000 marchers); Kroeger, *The Suffragents*, 113; Lauren Santangelo, "5,000 Lanterns: The Radicalism of Suffrage Parades," Behind the Scenes website of the New-York Historical Society Museum & Library, posted July 28, 2015, http://behindthescenes.nyhistory.org/radicalism-suffrage-parades/; Men's League letterhead on announcement, WSMS collection, Series 1, Woman's Suffrage, Part B, New York, folder 002685-002-0338-0417, SL.
[246] Search of *Woman's Journal* in 1911-1913), including issues of March 18, 1911, 88, col. 5 (comedy); April 15, 1911, 114 (Pankhurst spoke in 40 US cities, Beatrice & others to tour next season); July 1, 1911, 202 (to debate in December in Newark); August 19, 1911, 264 (Montclair, NJ); October 21, 1911, 336 (return from England); November 11, 1911, 359 (Kalamazoo, Nov. 16); November 18, 1911, 367 (Detroit, Nov. 8); December 16, 1911, 398 ("Mrs. Beatrice Forbes-Robertson Hale will fill engagements in the Pacific Coast States for three weeks beginning Feb. 13. Mrs. Hale is an ardent and accomplished suffragist."); January 6, 1912, 3 (Baltimore, raising $2100); January 20, 1912, 22 (to speak in Connecticut); January 27, 1912, 27 (Pittsburgh, while her uncle spoke on west coast); February 10, 1912, 45 (Chicago, Feb. 9); February 17, 1912, 1 (Milwaukee); February 24, 1912, 63 (Chicago); March 9, 1912, 77 (NYC, March 11, with 25 speakers including Inez Haynes Gilmore); March 30, 1912, 99 (NYC); April 20, 1912, 123 (Cincinnati); April 27, 131 (Grand Rapids, Mich., May 7); May 11, 1912, 146 (May 4 march, she was one of the conspicuous figures in the leading cavalry brigade); May 25, 1912, 164 (Kalamazoo); September 14, 112, 289 (one of speakers when "New York Has Big Suffrage Week" with photo of her on front page with others); October 5, 1912, 317 (Williamsport, PA, Oct.); October 19, 1912, 333 (Detroit, Sept.); April 5, 1913,

111 (Michigan); also *Boston Globe*, March 30, 1912, 9 (Malden); *Boston Globe*, April 12, 1912, 10 (Chestnut Hill).
[247] *WJ*, September 13, 1913, 295; *Boston Globe*, September 6, 1913, 2.
[248] Ware, *Why They Marched*, 76.
[249] Beatrice to Swinburne, August 31, 1916 ("Rose O'N."), *SHP*; Beatrice to Swinburne, February 8, 1918 (glad "Rose" helped him with "Pan," which became one of the poems in his 1923 book illustrated by Rose), *SHP*; Miriam Formanek-Brunell, ed., Rose Cecil O'Neill, *The Story of Rose O'Neill: An Autobiography* (Columbia: University of Missouri Press, 1997), 11 (posters), 116-117 (friends with feminist Charlotte Perkins Gilman), 117 (mention of Swinburne), 121 (source of quotes), 122 (photo with placard), 123 (second oration), 124-125 (stayed with Beatrice in England), https://books.google.com/books?id=NFW8nIW3Q_IC&source=gbs_navlinks_s; Betsy Gomez, "She Changed Comics: Rose O'Neill, Champion of Suffrage," CBLDF website, posted March 10, 2017, http://cbldf.org/2017/03/she-changed-comics-rose-oneill-champion-of-suffrage/; "Inductee's Name: Rose Cecil O'Neill … Biographical Information," National Women's Hall of Fame, https://www.womenofthehall.org/wp-content/uploads/2019/03/O_Neill-bio-long-version.pdf.
[250] Beatrice to Swinburne, November 17, 1916, *SHP*.
[251] Lucie Levine, "How the Men's League for Women's Suffrage helped win voting rights in New York," 6sqft website, posted November 5, 2018, https://www.6sqft.com/how-the-mens-league-for-womens-suffrage-revolutionized-voting-rights-in-new-york/; Neuman, *Gilded Suffragists*, 104 (torchlight), 114-115, 154.
[252] Sandra Gail Teichmann, "Rachel Crothers (1878-1958)," in Laurie Champion and Emmanuel S. Nelson, eds, *American Women Writers, 1900-1945: A Bio-bibliographical Critical Sourcebook* (Westport, CT: Greenwood Press, 2000), 82-86, https://books.google.com/books?id=Qltu-Bw0hcUC&source=gbs_navlinks_s.
[253] Daisy Thompson had a shop in Greenwich Village. Photos there show her standing in the doorway of "Her Shop," with a sign above the door that reads "Containing Many Quaint & Beautiful Things," and then showing off items for sale inside the store. Jessie Tarbox Beals, "Edith Hayes [sic] Thompson standing in the doorway of Her Shop …," photo, c. 1912-1926, and Jessie Tarbox Beals, "Daisy Thompson standing inside of her shop …," photo, c. 1912-1926, SL, Hollis number olvgroup1002268, items PC60-60f-10 and PC60-60f-11, http://id.lib.harvard.edu/via/olvgroup1002268/catalog. The first photo is also on the Schlesinger Library's Flickr Commons page, https://www.flickr.com/photos/schlesinger_library/9628001921/in/photolist-mdCmMT-fEN2x8-mdDRyg.
[254] Beatrice Forbes-Robertson Hale, *What Women Want: An Interpretation of the Feminist Movement* (New York: Frederick A. Stokes Company, 1914), with description on 182-184, https://archive.org/details/whatwomenwantint00haleuoft.
[255] Hale, *What Women Want*, chapter 18 ("The New Man"), 231 (antis).
[256] Blodgett, "Shaw, Pauline Agassiz," 278; Neuman, *Gilded Suffragists.*, 51-53.
[257] Sargent, *A Handbook of New England*, 529 (source of quote).
[258] *SHP*, generally; *1918 Harold Howard Directory*, 38 (listing home address simply as Washington, DC). The Hales were not listed in the *1915 Harold Howard Directory*. As

noted later in the text, Swinburne Hale bought the Barber property in Scituate in 1919 and sold it by March 1925. See Marcus N. Barber to Swinburne Hale, deed, June 12, 1919, PCRD, book 1333, page 232. This was the equivalent of about 26 or 30 Peggotty Beach Road on Second Cliff. According to the *1921 Valuation List*, 120, Swinburne Hale owned "House (Barbour)" valued at $1,000 and "House #2 (ditto)" valued at $700. This was after he and Beatrice divorced in 1920.
[259] *SHP*, generally.
[260] Beatrice to Swinburne, July 12, 1913, *SHP*. The July 12 letter is Beatrice's earliest letter in the *SHP* collection, and it appears this was her first time in Scituate ("I have not yet seen the village"). The mention of Mr. Gillmore is interesting since, at the start of the summer, as mentioned in the text, he departed for a separate trip instead of joining Inez, and they were divorced in 1913 or 1914. Beatrice was planning to stay until about September 15, although the Hales had rented the cottage for longer. Beatrice to Swinburne, July 25, 1913, *SHP*.
[261] Beatrice to Swinburne, July 12, 1913, *SHP*. Based on her descriptions, the Merwins may have been staying nearby, but further away from Peggotty Beach, at 97 Edward Foster Road. See "Doherty, Cornelius House (Kliffhurst)," SCI.1153, MACRIS. Also, the well was probably on the property of Annie M. Supple or Mary F. Supple, at the equivalent of 34 Peggotty Beach Road. See Mary F. Supple to Christopher O'Neil, Jr., deed (equivalent of 36 Peggotty Beach Road), September 25, 1919, PCRD, book 1338, page 503.
[262] Beatrice to Swinburne, July 12, 1913, *SHP*. People named may be described in more detail in the chapter on Inez and Will Irwin.
[263] Beatrice to Swinburne, July 12, 1913, *SHP*.
[264] Thompson, "I Remember Scituate" (extended version).
[265] Al Jennings and Will Irwin, *Beating Back* (New York, D. Appleton and Company, 1914), https://archive.org/details/beatingback011714mbp/page/n3/mode/2up. The book was made into a movie in 1951. "*Al Jennings of Oklahoma*," Wikipedia entry, https://en.wikipedia.org/wiki/Al_Jennings_of_Oklahoma.
[266] Beatrice to Swinburne, July 14, 1913, *SHP*.
[267] Beatrice to Swinburne, July 14, 1913, *SHP*.
[268] Beatrice to Swinburne, July 14, 1913, *SHP*; Ziffrin, *Carl Ruggles*, 2.
[269] Beatrice to Swinburne, July 15, 1913, *SHP*.
[270] Beatrice to Swinburne, July 23, 1913, *SHP*. Rufus Gillmore was a journalist who became a writer of detective stories. Of all the men in the group, Beatrice liked him the best. Beatrice to Swinburne, July 25, 1913, *SHP*.
[271] Beatrice to Swinburne, July 28, 1913, *SHP*.
[272] Beatrice to Swinburne, July 26, 1913, *SHP*. William B. Feakins had a prominent booking agency for speakers. "Three New York Managers of Celebrities," *The Lyceum Magazine* (Chicago: The Lyceumite Company), July 1912, 22 (with photo), https://books.google.com/books?id=Pg0cAQAAMAAJ&source=gbs_navlinks_s; R. Scott Williams, The Forgotten Adventures of Richard Halliburton: A High-Flying Life from Tennessee to Timbuktu (Charleston, SC: The History Press, 2014), various, preview, https://books.google.com/books?id=V8SACQAAQBAJ&source=gbs_navlinks_s.
[273] Isabelle Keating, "Noted 'Suffrage Twin' Arrives With Mother: Miss Clemency Hale Who, When 18 Months Old Bathed in the Nude and Caused National

Hubbub, Comes Quietly for a Season of Acting," *Brooklyn Daily Eagle*, January 17, 1933, 2, https://bklyn.newspapers.com/image/59870880/?terms=scituate.
[274] Beatrice to Swinburne, October 20 and May 22, 1914, *SHP*.
[275] Beatrice to Swinburne, May 12, 1914, *SHP*; "Many Will Hear Mrs. Hale Speak," *Oswego Palladium*, May 8, 1914, 2, copied at https://www.rbhousemuseum.org/wp-content/uploads/2017/06/SuffMtgMrsHaleVisitsWR.pdf.
[276] Beatrice to Swinburne, June 2, 1914, *SHP*. The Waldo Hotel building is still there, corner of W. Pike St. and N. 4th St. For its history and attempts to preserve it, see Sherman Cahal, "Waldo," on Abandoned website, posted after 2010, https://abandonedonline.net/location/waldo-hotel/; Waldo Hotel Preservation Society Facebook page, https://www.facebook.com/WHPS1904/, and its 2014 YouTube video, https://www.youtube.com/watch?v=DMFaTdOzH8w.
[277] Beatrice to Swinburne, July 12 & 16, September 21, October 20, 21, 28, and November 5 (source of quotes), 1914, *SHP*.
[278] "The Woman Suffrage Party Dinner; Initial Banquet of New Organization an Unparalleled Success – 200 People Listen to Brilliant Address of noted Lecturer and Authoress." *Maryland Suffrage News* (Baltimore), February 27, 1915, 378, https://chroniclingamerica.loc.gov/lccn/sn89060379/1915-02-27/ed-1/seq-2/ocr/; Rosie Meile, "Biography of Dr. Fannie Hoopes, 1860- ," citing *Baltimore Sun*, Alexander Street website, https://documents.alexanderstreet.com/d/1009656364; Caitlin Munzer, "Biographical Sketch of Anna Herkner," Alexander Street website, https://documents.alexanderstreet.com/d/1008297965. Munzer said that Herkner was deeply involved in immigration issues as well as woman suffrage, and she was one of those arrested for picketing the White House.
[279] A. S. B. [Alice Stone Blackwell], "Mrs. Hale on Feminism," *WJ*, June 5, 1915, 178.
[280] April C. Armstrong, "This Week in Princeton History for September 25-October 1," blog post with link to *Daily Princetonian* of September 29, 1915, https://blogs.princeton.edu/mudd/tag/beatrice-forbes-robertson-hale/.
[281] *Boston Globe*, June 4, 1915, 4; *Boston Globe*, August 29, 1915, 50 (Manchester-by-the-Sea); *Boston Globe*, September 30, 1915, 2; *Boston Globe*, August 8, 1915, 50 (Scituate); *Boston Globe*, November 1, 1915, 5.
[282] "Women Raise $100,000," *Boston Globe*, November 5, 1915, 2.
[283] *WJ*, January 29, 1916, 37, col. 5; *Journal of the House of the General Assembly of the Commonwealth of Kentucky, Sess. 124, v. 1* (Frankfort: State of Kentucky, 1916), hdl:2027/nyp.33433004439422; Beatrice to Swinburne, February 22, 1916, *SHP*; Beatrice to Swinburne, March 15, 1916 (source of quote), *SHP*.
[284] Beatrice to Swinburne, October 3 & 9, 1916, *SHP*.
[285] A. S. B., "Mrs. Hale Attacked." *WJ*, October 21, 1916, 340.
[286] A. S. B., "The Bogey of Feminism," *WJ*, October 28, 1916, 348.
[287] Marguerite Mooers Marshall, "Nest for One is Cage for the Other; That's Why Marriage Fails, Sometimes, But Nest Makers and Rovers will Mate," *Boston Globe*, December 14, 1916, 10. The article refers to what was evidently Beatrice's new novel, *The Nest Builder* (1916).
[288] *WJ*, December 30, 1916, 421.
[289] "Suffragists Will Continue to Lobby," *Boston Globe*, January 24, 1917.
[290] Beatrice to Swinburne, January 13, 1917, *SHP*.

[291] Beatrice to Swinburne, January 15 & 18, February 1, March 17, 1917, *SHP*.
[292] Beatrice to Swinburne, May 24, 1917, *SHP*.
[293] "Our History," Chautauqua Institution website, https://chq.org/about-us/history; *The Chautauquan*, August 10 & 11, 1917, both on page 1, Chautauqua Institution Digitized Collections, http://digitizedcollections.archives.chq.org/virtualimage/cust/cust.aspx. At the time, Henry Turner Bailey of North Scituate was Director of Arts and Crafts at Chautauqua (1906-1917), per photo record, catalog number 2015.08.13.n, Chautauqua Institution Photographic Collection, online collections database.
[294] *The Chautauquan*, August 11, 1917, 1.
[295] "Historical Timeline of the National Womans Party, 1917," Library of Congress, https://www.loc.gov/collections/women-of-protest/articles-and-essays/historial-timeline-of-the-national-womans-party/1917/; Sarah Pruitt, "The Night of Terror: When Suffragists Were Imprisoned and Tortured in 1917," History Channel website, updated April 17, 2019, https://www.history.com/news/night-terror-brutality-suffragists-19th-amendment.
[296] Beatrice to Swinburne, August 12, 1917, *SHP*.
[297] Beatrice to Swinburne, August 12, 1917, *SHP*; "Artists" file, SHS. The Mary Gawthorpe papers are archived at the Tamiment Library & Robert F. Wagner Labor Archives, New York University. "Guide to the Mary E. Gawthorpe Papers TAM.275," http://dlib.nyu.edu/findingaids/html/tamwag/tam_275/.
[298] Beatrice to Swinburne, August 14, 1917, *SHP*; "Trumbull White," *Boston Globe*, December 15, 1941, 9 (obituary); White, Trumbull 1868-1941," WorldCat, http://www.worldcat.org/identities/lccn-no99037100/.
[299] Beatrice to Swinburne, September 20, 1917, *SHP*.
[300] Beatrice to Swinburne, October 13 & 15 (source of quotes), 1917, *SHP*. The map detail accompanying text here and on her 1918 tour is based on National Railway Publication Company, *General railway map engraved expressly for the Official guide of the railways and steam navigation lines of the United States, Porto* [sic] *Rico, Canada, Mexico and Cuba: comprising maps of the United States, Cuba, Porto* [sic] *Rico* (New York: National Railway Publications Co., 1918), retrieved from the Library of Congress, https://www.loc.gov/item/2006627696/.
[301] *Owego Gazette*, October 18, 1917, as quoted in Ed Nizalowski, "Vote For Women: How Tioga County Women Actively Participated in This Worldwide Struggle," *Owego Pennysaver Press* website, posted August 17, 2017, http://www.owegopennysaver.com/PS/2017/08/17/vote-for-women-how-tioga-county-women-actively-participated-in-this-worldwide-struggle/ (an extremely long and detailed study of woman suffrage going back to 1654).
[302] Beatrice to Swinburne, October 18, 1917, *SHP*; Stan Hywet Hall & Gardens, website, https://www.stanhywet.org/, and https://www.stanhywet.org/history; "Gertrude Penfield Seiberling (1866-1946)," https://www.stanhywet.org/sites/default/files/assets/docs/Bio-Gertrude%20Seiberling.pdf. Stan Hywet Hall is Akron's first and largest National Historic Landmark, also the nation's 6th largest historic home open to the public.
[303] Beatrice to Swinburne, October 18, 1917, *SHP*.
[304] Beatrice to Swinburne, October 27, 1917, *SHP*.
[305] Beatrice to Swinburne, October 30, 1917, *SHP*.
[306] Beatrice to Swinburne, December 11, 13, 14, & 16, 1917, *SHP*.

[307] Beatrice to Swinburne, February 5, 1918, *SHP*.
[308] Beatrice to Swinburne, February 8, 1918, *SHP*; "Women's Political Union of New Jersey," New Jersey Women's History website, http://www.njwomenshistory.org/Period_4/politicalunion.htm; Photograph 4-PS-122D; Mrs. Mina C. van Winkle of Newark, New Jersey, in uniform of Food Administration, Records of the U.S. Food Administration, Record Group 4; National Archives, https://www.docsteach.org/documents/document/mina-c-van-winkle, and Library of Congress website, https://lccn.loc.gov/2016650259; "Mrs. Mina C. Van Winkle," photo, Food Administration, National Archives Identifier: 31481065, https://catalog.archives.gov/id/31481065;
[309] Maxcy R. Dickson, "The Food Administration: Educator," *Agricultural History* 16, no. 2 (1942), 91-96, at 91, 94 (slogan), www.jstor.org/stable/3739290. Food posters are included in a history of the agency, "Meatless, Wheatless . . . and Patriotic: Posters of the United States Food Administration," New-York Historical Society, posted March 7, 2018, http://blog.nyhistory.org/meatless-wheatless-patriotic/.
[310] Beatrice to Swinburne, February 8, 1918 (source of quote), *SHP*; Neil O. Buschman, "The United States Food Administration During World War I: The Rise of Activist Government Through Food Control During Mobilization for Total War" (M. A. diss., Auburn University, 2013), https://etd.auburn.edu/bitstream/handle/10415/3861/FoodAdminthesis.pdf;sequence=2. The Food Administration was led by Herbert Hoover, a friend of Will Irwin, who later profiled him in a biography. A photo of Mrs. Mina Van Winkle is at the Library of Congress, https://www.loc.gov/item/2016650259/.
[311] Edward F. Trefz to Mrs. Mina C. Van Winkle, chief of the Speakers Bureau, Feb. 11, 1918, as cited in Dickson, "The Food Administration: Educator," 93, note 9. Within a month or so after this letter, Trefz and Beatrice had become "very good friends," according to Beatrice to Swinburne, March 14, 1918, *SHP*.
[312] Beatrice to Swinburne, February 8, 1918.
[313] Inventory of the United States Food Administration records, Hoover Institution Archives, Stanford University, Herbert Hoover, U.S. Food Administrator Files 1914-1927, Online Archive of California, reel 20, https://oac.cdlib.org/findaid/ark:/13030/kt1n39r4r8/dsc/; "Food Administration - Administrators and Staff - U.S. Food Administration, Washington, D.C. States Administration Division - NARA - 31480983.jpg," photo of men including Milne, https://commons.wikimedia.org/wiki/File:Food_Administration_-_Administrators_and_Staff_-_U.S._Food_Administration,_Washington,_D.C._States_Administration_Division_-_NARA_-_31480983.jpg; Beatrice to Swinburne, various, February-March, 1918, *SHP*.
[314] Beatrice to Swinburne, March 14, 1918, *SHP*. Trefz later that year went to Europe for the Food Administration, stayed with the troops for weeks, and came back to give talks. "Will Tell About Work at Front," *San Diego Union and Daily Bee*, October 8, 1918, 3, California Digital Newspaper Collection, https://cdnc.ucr.edu/?a=d&d=SDDU19181008.2.34&e=-------en--20--1--txt-txIN--------1; "Back from the Trenches," image, https://commons.wikimedia.org/wiki/File:Back_from_the_Trenches._Everett_Co

lby, Dan Reed, Edward F. Trefz, Roscoe Mitchell, John B. Lord, Julius Lincoln. State L - NARA - 512524.jpg.

[315] Beatrice to Swinburne, May 4, 1918, *SHP.*

[316] Beatrice to Swinburne, May 8 & 22, 1918, *SHP.*

[317] Beatrice to Swinburne, May 22, 1918, *SHP.*

[318] Beatrice to Swinburne, July 2, 8, 9, 12 (source of quote), & 17, 1918, *SHP.*

[319] Beatrice to Swinburne, August 8, 1918, *SHP*; *The Chautauquan*, August 9, 1918, 1 & 4; Pickard, "The United States Food Administration in Chautauqua County," 309 (source of quote).

[320] Beatrice to Swinburne, August 13, 1918, *SHP.*

[321] University of Michigan Center for the History of Medicine, "The American Influenza Epidemic of 1918-1919: Boston, Massachusetts," *Influenza Encyclopedia* 2.0, 2016, https://www.influenzaarchive.org/cities/city-boston.html#.

[322] Beatrice to Swinburne, October 17, 1918, *SHP.*

[323] Beatrice to Swinburne, October 17, 1918, *SHP*; "Mass Meeting on the Common," *Boston Globe*, October 17, 1918, 8; "Change of Space" notice, *Boston Globe*, October 18, 1918, 1 (meeting moved to Tremont Temple);"Subscribe $25,000 at Women's Mass Meeting," and "Women's Committee Gets $3,524,000 Subscriptions," *Boston Globe*, October 19, 1918, 3. See "Liberty bond," Wikipedia entry, https://en.wikipedia.org/wiki/Liberty_bond.

[324] Beatrice to Swinburne, October 22, 1918, *SHP.*

[325] "Food Conservation Needed Because of Pledge of Twenty Million Tons to Europe," *Chicago Commerce* (Chicago: The Chicago Association of Commerce, Fri., November 29, 1918), 24, https://books.google.com/books?id=8QubVmRZYkwC&source=gbs_navlinks_s.

[326] Beatrice to Swinburne, December 8, 1918, *SHP.*

[327] Beatrice to Swinburne, January 31, 1919, *SHP*; *Clark's Boston Blue Book, 1918* (Boston: Sampson & Murdock Company, 1917), 292, 424, https://babel.hathitrust.org/cgi/pt?id=hvd.hn4hnt&view=1up&seq=426.

[328] *Boston Globe*, August 29, 1915, 50.

[329] Beatrice to Swinburne, October 4 & 20 (boring), 1919, *SHP.*

[330] Beatrice to Swinburne (Sanchia birthday), May 22, 1914, *SHP*; Isabelle Keating, "Noted 'Suffrage Twin' Arrives With Mother: Miss Clemency Hale Who, When 18 Months Old Bathed in the Nude and Caused National Hubbub, Comes Quietly for a Season of Acting," *Brooklyn Daily Eagle*, January 17, 1933, 2, https://bklyn.newspapers.com/image/59870880/?terms=scituate.

[331] "Much-Talked-Of 'Suffrage Twins.' Clemency and Rosemary Hale, Whose Bathing Suits, or Their Lack of Suits, Have Been a Subject of Discussion at Scituate." *Boston Globe*, Sunday, August 15, 1915, 51 (with photo of twins on beach, clothed).

[332] "Seldom September Morns; Mrs. Hale's Babies Were Undressed on Beach Only for Few Minutes," *New York Times*, August 12, 1915, 18, http://query.nytimes.com/gst/abstract.html?res=9400E5DC1138E633A25751C1A96E9C946496D6CF&legacy=true; "Suffrage Twins in Nude Give Shock," *Sacramento Union*, October 3, 1915, https://cdnc.ucr.edu/cgi-bin/cdnc?a=d&d=SU19151003.2.192&e=-------en--20--1--txt-txIN--------1; Keating, "Noted 'Suffrage Twin'," *Brooklyn Daily Eagle*. January 17, 1933; Thompson, "Inez and I," 38, noting that Will Irwin showed guests the lawn of

then-postmaster Peter F. Tague and told them to remove their hats, since on those hallowed grounds, John L. Sullivan trained for a boxing match. Based on a review of deeds, mortgages, and plans relating to Peter Tague (who acquired property from the Tobin family), this would have been at the ocean end of Peggotty Beach Road, overlooking Peggotty Beach. See Josephine T. Tague to Joseph A. Butler, mortgage, May 19, 1926, PCRD, book 1504, page 512, naming plans at plan book 1, page 153 [sheet 4 of 5] (showing lot 21 and adjacent large lot owned by Tobin), and plan book 3, page 309 [sheet 2 of 2]. Beatrice's letters from this period are noticeably not included in the Swinburne Hale Papers. They may be in other collections, but were not reviewed for this book.

[333] Beatrice to Swinburne, July 10, 1915, and June 21, 1916 (source of quote), *SHP*. The June 21 letter deeply disturbed Swinburne, who wanted a real separation, as stated in his unsent letter of June 26, discussed and quoted separately in this chapter.

[334] Beatrice to Swinburne, June 21, 1916, *SHP*.

[335] Beatrice to Swinburne, June 21, 1916, *SHP*.

[336] 1910 US census; *1915 Harold Howard Directory*, 32; chapter on Inez Haynes Irwin and Will Irwin.

[337] Beatrice to Swinburne, June 21, 1916, *SHP*.

[338] Beatrice to Swinburne, June 28, 1916, *SHP*.

[339] Beatrice to Swinburne, November 17, 1916, *SHP*.

[340] Beatrice to Swinburne, telegram, August 20, 1916, and letters, August 30 & 31, 1916, *SHP*.

[341] Beatrice to Swinburne, August 31 and September 22, 1916, *SHP*. See "House Acts to Avert Strike," "Temporary Strike Injunction Granted," and "Strike Fears Start Crush on Railroads," *Boston Globe*, September 2, 1916, 1 & 2.

[342] Beatrice to Swinburne, September 22, 1916; "Shark at Scituate," *Boston Globe*, Friday, September 22, 1916, 8.

[343] Beatrice to Swinburne, May 21 & 24, June 28, 1917, *SHP*. Futrelle is discussed in the chapter on Inez and Will Irwin.

[344] Beatrice to Swinburne, September 6 (source of quote), 7, & 8, 1917, *SHP*.

[345] Beatrice to Swinburne, September 10, 1917, *SHP*.

[346] Beatrice to Swinburne, October (various dates), 1917, *SHP*. The decision to stay in Scituate is implicit in these (and later) letters, since Swinburne was staying in the cottage after the summer season.

[347] Beatrice to Swinburne, October 13, 15, 16 ("movies"), & 17 (other quotes), 1917, *SHP*.

[348] Beatrice to Swinburne, various, including October 31, November 2, 4, & 27, 1917, *SHP*.

[349] Beatrice to Swinburne, November 27, 1917, *SHP*.

[350] Beatrice to Swinburne, November 28, 1917, *SHP*.

[351] Beatrice to Swinburne, November 28, 1917, *SHP*; *1915 Harold Howard Directory*, 25.

[352] Beatrice to Swinburne, November 28, 1917, *SHP*.

[353] Beatrice to Swinburne, November 30, 1917, *SHP*.

[354] Beatrice to Swinburne, December 3, 1917, *SHP*; "Forbes-Robertson is Honored by his Company," *Boston Globe*, April 26, 1916, 10.

[355] Beatrice to Swinburne, December 11, 13, 14, & 16, 1917, *SHP*.

[356] Beatrice to Swinburne, August 11, 1919, *SHP*; "Friends" in *The Demon's Notebook — Verse and Perverse* (New York: Nicholas L. Brown, 1923), 20, https://books.google.com/books?id=BWk6AQAAIAAJ&source=gbs_navlinks_s.
[357] Beatrice to Swinburne, August 13, 1918, *SHP*; *1918 Harold Howard Directory*, 59 (Charles M. Wagner, "milk"); 1903 map (C. M. Wagner at Main Street (now Country Way) and unmarked road (now Cudworth Road) leading to cemetery near Scituate Centre.
[358] Scituate Historical Society, *Scituate*, 55; "Scituate Man Drops Dead in His Home," *Boston Globe*, December 17, 1921, 5.
[359] *Handbook of Ordnance Data* (Washington: US War Dept., 1919), 425, https://archive.org/details/handbookordnanc00unkngoog/page/n4/mode/2up; John Galluzzo, "January 22, 2009 - Proving Grounds, Scituate, Massachusetts," Half an Hour a Day with the Dead, blog, posted January 22, 2009, http://halfanhouraday.blogspot.com/2009/01/january-22-2009-proving-grounds.html; Beatrice to Swinburne, October 17 (source of quote), 1918, *SHP*.
[360] Beatrice to Swinburne, October 21, 1918, *SHP*.
[361] Beatrice to Swinburne, October 22, 1918, *SHP*. Rent was $60 a month, presumably for two cottages.
[362] Beatrice to Swinburne, October 22 & 23, and December 8, 1918, *SHP*; Swinburne to Evelyn, December 6, 1918, *RMPC*;
[363] Beatrice to Swinburne, March 29, 1919, *SHP*; Marcus N. Barber to Swinburne Hale, deed, June 12, 1919, PCRD, book 1333, page 232.
[364] Beatrice to Swinburne, July 4 (source of quote), August 11 & 14, October 4 (dull), 6, 8 (children), 20 (dormouse), 24, & 25, 1919, *SHP*.
[365] Beatrice to Swinburne, October 20 & 24 (visit), 1919, *SHP*.
[366] Swinburne Hale to John Fenton, deed, March 27, 1925, PCRD, book 1483, page 165 (last of three deeds out).
[367] Beatrice to Swinburne, May 22, 1914 (Sanchia birthday), *SHP*; Isabelle Keating, "Noted 'Suffrage Twin' Arrives With Mother: Miss Clemency Hale Who, When 18 Months Old Bathed in the Nude and Caused National Hubbub, Comes Quietly for a Season of Acting," *Brooklyn Daily Eagle*, January 17, 1933, 2, https://bklyn.newspapers.com/image/59870880/?terms=scituate; Rose O'Neill, "Together for Home and Family," poster, New-York Historical Society, Center for Women's History, Women & the American Story, https://wams.nyhistory.org/modernizing-america/woman-suffrage/together-for-home-and-family/.
[368] Beatrice to Swinburne, May 20, 1914, *SHP*.
[369] Beatrice to Swinburne, May 24, 1914, *SHP*.
[370] Beatrice to Swinburne, February 19, 1916, *SHP*.
[371] Swinburne (unsent), June 26, 1916, *SHP*.
[372] Beatrice to Swinburne, June 28, 1916, *SHP*. Swinburne was on his way to Europe on business. He returned August 20. Beatrice to Swinburne, telegram, August 20, 1916, *SHP*.
[373] Beatrice to Swinburne, November 16, 1916, *SHP*. It is unclear if his scheme was for them to live apart, or together (with him being more caring).
[374] Beatrice to Swinburne, November 16, 1916, *SHP*.
[375] Beatrice to Swinburne, November 16, 1916, *SHP*.
[376] Beatrice to Swinburne, November 16, 1916, *SHP*.

[377] Beatrice to Swinburne, March 17, 1917, *SHP*.
[378] Beatrice to Swinburne, May 24 and September 6 (source of quotes), 1917, *SHP*.
[379] Beatrice to Swinburne, May 22, 1918, *SHP*.
[380] Beatrice to Swinburne, undated, not posted, probably June 1918, *SHP*.
[381] Beatrice to Swinburne, June 18, 1918, *SHP*.
[382] Beatrice to Swinburne, July 2, 1918, *SHP*.
[383] Beatrice to Swinburne, August 19, 1918, *SHP*.
[384] Beatrice to Swinburne, December 8, 1918, *SHP*.
[385] Beatrice to Swinburne, December 8, 1918, *SHP*.
[386] Beatrice to Swinburne, December 9, 1918, *SHP*.
[387] Beatrice to Swinburne, December 17, 1918, *SHP*.
[388] Swinburne to Evelyn, various, Ralph M. Pearson Collection, Fray Angelico Chaves History Library, The Palace of the Governors, Santa Fe, NM [*RMPC*], inventory at Rocky Mountain Online Archive, https://rmoa.unm.edu/docviewer.php?docId=nmsm1ac380.xml. His December 11, 1918. letter to Evelyn contains an early version of his poem "You Are The Day," which appeared in his 1923 book *The Demon's Notebook — Verse and Perverse*, 40.
[389] Swinburne to Evelyn, December 11, 1918 (source of quotes), *RMPC*.
[390] Beatrice to Swinburne, January 15, 1919, March 29, 1919 (their friend Rose, probably Rose O'Neill, considering joining him at B. B.), and August 14, 1919 (source of quotes), *SHP*.
[391] *Social Register Summer 1919* (New York City: Social Register Association, June 1919), 486 (Bay End Farm), https://hdl.handle.net/2027/wu.89058297144.
[392] Evelyn Scott to Otto Theis, May 3, 1921, in hort4short, "A Life in Letters," ch. 7 "Back to the USA," posted October 13, 2017, https://alifeinletters2017.wordpress.com/2017/10/13/back-home/. Evelyn was married to the superintendent of the Garland's estate in Buzzards Bay and later Bermuda. She was an early suffragist, and was considered one of America's pioneer feminist writers, who went on to achieve much more fame for her work than Swinburne did. Her son in 1940 married the daughter of Swinburne's sister Margaret.
[393] Bob Seay, "Preserving The Place Where Kahlil Gibran's 'The Prophet' Was Written," WGBH News, posted October 3, 2017, https://www.wgbh.org/news/2017/10/03/arts/preserving-place-where-kahlil-gibrans-prophet-was-written; Divya John, "The cybernetics of love: A study of Kahlil Gibran" (Thesis, Department of English, Vimala College, University of Calicut, 2007), 157-158, http://14.139.116.20:8080/jspui/bitstream/10603/21602/10/10_chapter%203.pdf; Dick Cowan, *The Garland Book* (unpublished, after 1995), Yale Law School, 29-30, http://documents.law.yale.edu/sites/default/files/garland%20unpublished%20bio.pdf.
[394] "Marie Louise Tudor Garland," FindAGrave memorial, https://www.findagrave.com/memorial/205984359/marie-louise-garland; "Mrs. Frederic Tudor, 89, is Dead," *Boston Globe*, October 10, 1934, 5; Jack Coleman. "Rebuilding on a historic site," *Cape Cod Times*, December 7, 2003, updated January 6, 2011, https://www.capecodtimes.com/article/20031207/NEWS01/312079960. Genealogical information is provided by Janice Brown, "Webster New Hampshire

Author and Illustrator: Tasha Tudor aka Starling (Burgess) McCready (1915-2008)," on Cow Hampshire blog, posted April 24, 2006, updated August 2012, http://www.cowhampshireblog.com/2006/04/24/webster-new-hampshire-author-and-illustrator-tashua-tudor-aka-starling-burgess-mccready-1915-2008/. Tasha Tudor's mother Rosamond was Marie's sister.

[395] Arthur H. Phippen and Robert D. Weston, executors under will of Charles P. Horton, to Marie T. Garland, deed, May 6, 1908, Barnstable County Registry of Deeds, book 288, page 396; Arthur H. Phippen and Robert D. Weston, executors under will of Charles P. Horton, to Marie T. Garland, deed (wharf), July 31, 1908, Barnstable County Registry of Deeds, book 285, page 482; "Grazing Fields Farm - Bourne, Bethuel Tavern," Head of the Bay Road, BOU.28, MACRIS; MACRIS Maps; *Social Register Summer 1919* (New York City: Social Register Association, June 1919), 486 (Bay End Farm), https://hdl.handle.net/2027/wu.89058297144; Bob Seay, "How Grazing Fields Farm Changed How We Build Highways," WGBH News, posted October 2, 2017 (900 acres), https://www.wgbh.org/news/2017/10/02/local-news/how-grazing-fields-farm-changed-how-we-build-highways. See "Head of the Bay," BOU.C, MACRIS, and "Gibbs, Capt. Henry House (Meadowbrook)," Old Head of Bay Road, BOU.30, MACRIS. The latter may be at 30 Old Head of the Bay Road, per Google Maps (Satellite View and Street View), or 21 Old Head of the Bay Road, per MACRIS Maps. This may be part of the Overbrook House and lodge at 5 Old Head of the Bay Road, and along with the "Grazing Fields Farm," this may be part of the current Bay End Farm, although there are multiple parcels. See "Overbrook House," http://www.overbrookhouse.com/about#abouts; "Bay End Farm, home of Marie Tudor Garland, Bourne, MA," photographic print, ca. 1916, Historical Society of Old Yarmouth, Digital Commonwealth, https://www.digitalcommonwealth.org/search/commonwealth:xg94jm278; "Old Gibbs Place at Head of Bay, Bourne," in E. G. Perry, *A Trip Around Buzzard's Bay Shores* (Monument Beach, MA: E. G. Perry, 1903), 196, https://hdl.handle.net/2027/wu.89064065824. The Garland estate in 1910 is shown in *Atlas of Barnstable County, Massachusetts: towns of Bourne, Mashpee, Falmouth, Sandwich, Barnstable, Yarmouth, Dennis, Harwich, Brewster, Chatham, Orleans, Eastham, Wellfleet, Truro & Provincetown* (Boston: Walker Lithograph & Publishing Co., 1910), Index Map of the Town of Bourne (before plate 1), scale: 1 inch = 3000 feet, Massachusetts Real Estate Atlas Digitization Project by the State Library of Massachusetts, https://archives.lib.state.ma.us/handle/2452/205555. In late 1921, Marie acquired the Old Field Pond Cranberry Bog and other land in this Head of the Bay area from her brother Frederic Tudor, perhaps as a present on her wedding to Swinburne. Frederic Tudor to Marie T. Garland, deed, December 7, 1921, Barnstable County Registry of Deeds, book 385, page 288.

[396] Evelyn Scott to Lola Ridge, July 30, 1921, in hort4short, "A Life in Letters," ch. 7 "Back to the USA."

[397] "Old Colony Union Women's Club of Bourne," monograph, Bourne Historical Society. "Afternoon tea," photographic print, Historical Society of Old Yarmouth, Digital Commonwealth, https://www.digitalcommonwealth.org/search/commonwealth:xg94jm29t.

[398] Dick Cowan, *The Garland Book*, 27 (quoting her speech), 28 (source of quote).

[399] Dick Cowan, *The Garland Book*, 25; "Marie Louise Tudor Garland," FindAGrave memorial; "Staked $10,000,000 For Love – And Lost Both," *The Times-Dispatch* (Richmond, VA), October 25, 1914, https://chroniclingamerica.loc.gov/data/batches/vi_yellow_ver01/data/sn85038615/00296020102/1914102501/0434.pdf.
[400] *New York Evening World*, March 8, 1920, 15, https://www.newspapers.com/newspage/50680359/; Margaret C. Robinson, ed., "Anti-Suffrage Notes," *The Woman Patriot*, vol. 4, no. 12 (Washington, DC: The Woman Patriot Publishing Co., March 20, 1920), 7, https://books.google.com/books?id=J9NBAQAAMAAJ&source=gbs_navlinks_s.
[401] "Married to Swinburne Hale of New York," *Boston Globe*, March 3, 1921, 4; "Swinburne Hale is Married Again," *Brooklyn Daily Eagle*, April 4, 1921, 9; *Social Register Boston 1922* (New York City: Social Register Association, November 1921), 85 (at 8 East 8th St, NYC), 209, https://hdl.handle.net/2027/wu.89066401647.
[402] Evelyn Scott to Lola Ridge, January 7, 1922, in hort4short, "A Life in Letters," ch. 8 "Bermuda," posted October 20, 2017, https://alifeinletters2017.wordpress.com/2017/10/20/bermuda/.
[403] Evelyn Scott, excerpt from lengthy document of April 1956 (narrative of the years in Buzzard's Bay and later Bermuda), in hort4short, "A Life in Letters," ch. 8 "Bermuda." It is unclear whether the estate was owned by Marie, as suggested by Evelyn Scott, or Swinburne, as stated in Walter Nelles to Bob (Swinburne), October 24, 1923 ("your burdensome and expensive real estate – Bermuda"), *SHP*.
[404] Solon DeLeon with Irma C. Hayssen and Grace Poole,(eds., *The American Labor Who's Who* (New York: Hanford Press, 1925), 170, https://hdl.handle.net/2027/mdp.39015012841634; Harvard University, *Quinquennial Catalogue of the Officers and Graduates of Harvard University 1636-1920* (Cambridge: Harvard University, 1920), 434 (Hale LL.B.), 874 (Hale A B.); 632 & 884 (Nelles A.B.); 431 (Baldwin A.B. 1904, A.M. 1905), https://hdl.handle.net/2027/iau.31858027489990.
[405] Beatrice to Swinburne, July 14, 1913 ("I look forward to hearing the news of your anarchist weekend!"), *SHP*.
[406] "Application for Further Hearing by Isaac Shorr, July 7, 1924," Supreme Court, Appellate Division, Third Department (n.p., n.d), 228, https://books.google.com/books?id=RQW1Ssf-tLgC&source=gbs_navlinks_s.
[407] John Sayer, "Art and Politics, Dissent and Repression: The Masses Magazines versus the Government, 1917-1918," *American Journal of Legal History* 32.1 (Oxford University Press, 1988):42-78, at 67, https://academic.oup.com/ajlh/article/32/1/42/1805033; "The Masses," Spartacus Educational website, https://spartacus-educational.com/ARTmasses.htm; Madeleine Baran, "A Brief History of The Masses," The Brooklyn Rail website, April-May 2003, https://brooklynrail.org/2003/04/express/a-brief-history-of-the-masses; "Old Fashioned Radical Feminist," Vassar College, https://web.archive.org/web/20110508215249/http://innovators.vassar.edu/innovator.html?id=23; Frank Luther Mott, *American Journalism, A History 1690-1960* (New York: The Macmillan Company, Third Ed., 1962) 623-625.

[408] Beatrice to Swinburne, October 4 and October 20 ("two poor creatures"), 1919, *SHP*; *The New York Call* to Capt. S. Hale, Esq., Buzzards Bay, October 28, 1919 (thanking him for his work), *RMPC.*
[409] "Sec Wilson to Decide Communist Cases Soon," *Boston Globe*, January 22, 1920, 4; Richard Gid Powers, *Secrecy and Power* (New York: Simon and Schuster, 2020), https://books.google.com/books?id=Q77JDwAAQBAJ&source=gbs_navlinks_s.
[410] Alfred Bettman, Swinburne Hale, American Civil Liberties Union, *Do we need more sedition laws?: testimony of Alfred Bettman and Swinburne Hale before the Committee on Rules of the House of Representatives* (New York: American Civil Liberties Union, 1920), https://catalog.hathitrust.org/Record/005599352; Powers, *Secrecy and Power*; Curt Gentry, *J. Edgar Hoover: The Man and the Secrets* (New York: W. W. Norton & Company, 1991, 2001), 98-99, https://books.google.com/books?id=Tu86exHKPvMC&source=gbs_navlinks_s; Donald L. Smith, *Zechariah Chafee, Jr., Defender of Liberty and Law* (Cambridge: Harvard University Press, 1986), 48-50, https://books.google.com/books?id=s35PyOnr0XYC&source=gbs_navlinks_s; Samuel Walker, *In Defense of American Liberties: A History of the ACLU* (Carbondale: Southern Illinois University Press, 2d ed., 1999), 44, preview, https://books.google.com/books?id=hdkrBVJ37I4C&source=gbs_navlinks_s.
[411] Swinburne to Tom Mooney, September 23, 1920, Mooney MSS, Box 5, as quoted and cited in Richard Polenberg, Fighting Faiths: The Abrams Case, the Supreme Court, and Free Speech (Ithaca, NY: Cornell University Press, 1999, first pub. 1987), 75-76, https://books.google.com/books?id=UCvOpLFFVSgC&vq=nelles&source=gbs_navlinks_s.
[412] "American Civil Liberties Union facts for kids," Kids Encyclopedia Facts, https://kids.kiddle.co/American_Civil_Liberties_Union; Robert McNamara, "ACLU: Purpose, History, and Current Controversies," ThoughtCo. website, updated December 12, 2019, https://www.thoughtco.com/aclu-4777664. As noted above, Baldwin was in the class ahead of Hale and Nelles at Harvard, but stayed on for a year to get another degree.
[413] Walter Nelles to Bob (Swinburne), October 24, 1923, *SHP.*
[414] Walter Nelles to Bob (Swinburne), October 24, 1923, *SHP.*
[415] "Guide to the William Gardner Hale Papers circa 1880-1928," University of Chicago Library (divorce in 1924). See also Swinburne to Renehan & Gilbert, handwritten letter (probably draft), January 4, 1924 (asking to represent him in divorce, giving basis for complaint, including Marie's deserting him from Taos at end of 1922), *SHP*; Renehan & Gilbert to Swinburne, January 7, 1924 (glad to handle his case), *SHP.*
[416] Swinburne Hale to John Fenton, deed, March 27, 1925, PCRD, book 1483, page 165 (last of three deeds out).
[417] Buelinckx, finding aid, *SHP*; Jim Rosenthal, "Ralph M. Pearson – Etcher, Businessman, Adventurer, Modernist, Farmer, Author – (1883-1958)," posted February 17, 2017, "In Praise of Prints" blog, https://www.inpraiseofprints.com/ralph-m-pearson-etcher-businessman-adventurer-modernist-farmer-author-1883-1958/; Frieda Lawrence to Mabel [Luhan], July 14, 1924, and D. H. Lawrence to Harriet Monroe, September 3, 1924, in James T. Boulton and Lindeth Vasey, *The Letters of D. H. Lawrence, Volume V,*

March 1924-March 1927 (New York: Cambridge University Press, 1989, 2002), 74 (letter), 90 (footnote 1), 115 (letter), https://books.google.com/books?id=2C-SmgtKjrEC&source=gbs_navlinks_s.
[418] Beatrice to Swinburne, December 11, 1917, and December 12, 1917, *SHP*; Douglas A. Anderson, "Swinburne Hale," on Lesser-Known Writers blog, posted January 23, 2012, http://desturmobed.blogspot.com/2012/01/swinburne-hale.html; Dan Woog, "What Do Evelene Parsell, Swinburne Hale, The Westport Sanatorium And Kewpie Dolls Have In Common?" 06880 blog, posted December 27, 2013, https://06880danwoog.com/tag/swinburne-hale/. Swinburne appears to have been friends with Rose in New York, meeting with her as early as 1916. Beatrice to Swinburne, August 31, 1916 ("Rose O'N."), *SHP*.
[419] Beatrice to Swinburne, November 16, 1916, November 17, 1916, and September 10, 1917, *SHP*.
[420] Beatrice to Swinburne, undated, not posted, probably June 1918, *SHP*.
[421] Beatrice to Swinburne, December 8, 1918, and January 15, 1919, *SHP*; Swinburne to Evelyn, December 13, 1918, *RMPC*.
[422] "When Did Manic Depression Become Bipolar," Alvarado Parkway Institute website, https://apibhs.com/2019/05/30/when-did-manic-depression-become-bipolar; Philip B. Mitchell and Dusan Hadzi-Pavlovic. "Lithium treatment for bipolar disorder," *Bull. World Health Organ.* (2000), 78 (4) (lithium was not approved by the US Food and Drug Administration until 1970), https://www.who.int/docstore/bulletin/pdf/2000/issue4/classics.pdf.
[423] Buelinckx, finding aid, *SHP*; Woog, "What Do Evelene Parsell, Swinburne Hale, The Westport Sanatorium And Kewpie Dolls Have In Common?" 06880 blog; Douglas A. Anderson, "Swinburne Hale," on Lesser-Known Writers blog. Swinburne's friend and illustrator of his book, Rose O'Neill, lived in Westport starting in 1922. O'Neill, *The Story of Rose O'Neill*, 14, 128-130.
[424] Dick Cowan, *The Garland Book*, 25 (source of quote) (murder in a tub), and generally 25-35; Mike Maddigan, "Free Love at East Middleborough, 1922," Recollecting Nemasket blog, posted November 12, 2009, http://nemasket.blogspot.com/2009/04/free-love-at-east-middleborough-1922.html; Kathaleen Roberts, " O'Keeffe painting now a U.S. stamp in new art series," *Albuquerque Journal*, posted April 19, 2013, https://www.abqjournal.com/190758/okeeffe-painting-now-a-us-stamp-in-new-art-series.html; Sally Eauclaire, "Louisa McElwain slathers paint with the passion of pastry chef," *The Santa Fe New Mexican* (Santa Fe, NM), September 4, 1992, 55, https://www.newspapers.com/clip/32867701/marie-tudor-garland-murder/; "Mrs. Marie Garland Dies of Injuries After Fall," *Boston Globe*, December 22, 1949, 29; "Garland," *Boston Globe*, January 9, 1950, 49.
[425] Robinson, ed., "Anti-Suffrage Notes," *The Woman Patriot*, 7.
[426] "The Woman Patriot: A National Newspaper for Home and National Defense Against Woman Suffrage, Feminism and Socialism. (Washington, D.C.) 1921-1927," Ann Lewis Women's Suffrage Collection website, last updated: May 2015, https://lewissuffragecollection.omeka.net/items/show/1138. See "113 Commonwealth," Back Bay Houses website (Harriet Frothingham president of "extremely conservative group"), https://backbayhouses.org/113-commonwealth/.

[427] *Boston Globe*, February 3, 1919, 3; *Boston Globe*, February 9, 1919, 11 (with photo of Beatrice); *The Woman Citizen*, November 20, 1920, 694, https://babel.hathitrust.org/cgi/pt?id=inu.30000098651080&view=1up&seq=660; *Official Register and Directory of Women's Clubs in America* (Shirley, MA: Helen M. Winslow, 1921), various, including supplement, IX and XXIII (Mrs. Forbes-Robertson Hale), XXXVII (Meyer Bloomfield), and LVI (both, in ad for Feakins agency), https://books.google.com/books?id=FXAfAQAAIAAJ&source=gbs_navlinks_s.

[428] Hazel Canning, "Being a Woman Big Adventure," *Brooklyn Daily Eagle*, May 29, 1927, 74 (contains factual errors about Beatrice's background); *Boston Globe*, January 17, 1931, 14.

[429] *Boston Globe*, March 18, 1931, 19.

[430] Lyle Nyberg, "Origins of The Glades in Scituate, Massachusetts," memo, 2017, on file, SHS, and submitted to Massachusetts Historical Society; "Glades Association Records," Collection Guide, MHS, http://www.masshist.org/collection-guides/view/fa0139?terms=%22glades%20club%22. Thanks to Daniel Hinchen, Reference Librarian, MHS, for suggestions leading to this chapter.

[431] *Boston Globe*, March 15, 1914, 62.

[432] Mary B. Hunnewell, *The Glades* (Boston: E. O. Cockayne, private printing, 1914), 32, 34-35 (Saltonstalls evidently sold their interests in 1904); "Prominent Lawyer is Taken by Death," *Boston Globe*, April 18, 1922, 4; "Eleanor Saltonstall," Geni.com website, https://www.geni.com/people/Eleanor-Saltonstall/6000000010486563641; "Self Portrait [William Morris Hunt]," Boston Museum of Fine Arts website, https://collections.mfa.org/objects/31835; "Saltonstall, Leverett (1892-1979), Biographical Directory of the United States Congress, website, http://bioguide.congress.gov/scripts/biodisplay.pl?index=s000021; "Saltonstall-Brooks-Lewis Family Photographs," Collection Guide, MHS, http://www.masshist.org/collection-guides/view/fap019?terms=%22glades%20club%22. A photo of Richard with his son, grandson, and father-in-law, is in the MHS, https://www.masshist.org/database/2134.

[433] Harper, *History of Woman Suffrage*, vol. 6, 273 fn 81; "The Anti-Suffrage Campaign; Annual Meeting of the Association," *The Remonstrance* (Boston: Women's Anti-Suffrage Association of Massachusetts), July 1915, 6, https://books.google.com/books?id=0S5JAQAAMAAJ&source=gbs_navlinks_s; "Suffragists Promise a Record Turnout," *Boston Globe*, October 16, 1915, 3 (continued from 1), col. 4 ("Antis Complete Plans"); Derek Strahan, "Hotel Somerset, Boston," Lost New England website, posted October 27, 2015, https://lostnewengland.com/2015/10/hotel-somerset-boston/.

[434] Massachusetts Association Opposed to the Further Extension of Suffrage to Women Records, 1894-1920, MHS, http://www.masshist.org/collection-guides/digitized/fa0121/b2-f39#9; "Antis Held 600 Rallies," *Boston Sunday Globe*, October 31, 1915, 45; Marshall, *Splintered Sisterhood*, 73.

[435] "Eleanor Saltonstall Papers, 1911-1919," Guide to the Collection, MHS, https://www.masshist.org/collection-guides/view/fa0064; Nora Saltonstall (author), Judith S. Graham, ed., *"Out Here at the Front": The World War I Letters of*

Nora Saltonstall (Boston: Northeastern University Press, 2004), 21, preview, https://books.google.com/books?id=vSnAsG73vscC&source=gbs_navlinks_s;
[436] US Congress, House of Representatives, Committee on Woman Suffrage, "Hearings Before the Committee on Woman Suffrage," 65th Cong., 2d sess., January 3, 4, 5, and 7, 1918, 196, https://books.google.com/books?id=O0kuAAAAYAAJ&source=gbs_navlinks_s.
[437] Hunnewell, *The Glades*, 82 (T. Nelson Perkins and family spent the summer in 1914); Committee on Woman Suffrage, "Hearings," 197; *The Remonstrance*, July 1917, 1, 2, https://books.google.com/books?id=0S5JAQAAMAAJ&source=gbs_navlinks_s; "Mrs. S. S. Fitzgerald Antisuffrage Head," *Boston Globe*, April 27, 1917, 16; "Table Gossip," *Boston Globe*, February 21, 1915, 48.
[438] Abigail Adams Homans, *Education by Uncles* (Boston: Houghton Mifflin Company, 1966), 128-129; Massachusetts Association Opposed to the Further Extension of Suffrage to Women Records, 1894-1920, MHS, http://www.masshist.org/collection-guides/digitized/fa0121/b2-f39#9.
[439] *The Remonstrance*, January 1911, 1, https://books.google.com/books?id=0S5JAQAAMAAJ&source=gbs_navlinks_s; "Mrs. Charles D. Homans, 1832-1914)," *The Remonstrance*, October 1914, 7, https://books.google.com/books?id=0S5JAQAAMAAJ&vq=cohasset&source=gbs_navlinks_s.
[440] Massachusetts Association Opposed to the Further Extension of Suffrage to Women Records, 1894-1920, MHS, starting at http://www.masshist.org/collection-guides/digitized/fa0121/b2-f38#1; and http://www.masshist.org/collection-guides/digitized/fa0121/b2-f39#9.
[441] Author research and draft Form B, 180 Border Street, Scituate, not yet submitted for MACRIS; Boston Art Guide and Artists' Directory (Boston: The Wheat Publishing Company, 1893), 33, 36, https://archive.org/details/bostonartguidear00bost/page/n13/mode/2up/search/parker; *Boston Globe*, November 6, 1910, 54.
[442] John Galluzzo, "The Fight for the Right to Vote," *South Shore Living* magazine (November 2015); MAOFESW records cited above.
[443] "Plan Burial of Centenarian," *Boston Traveler*, December 14, 1921, clipping in Smith McLauthlin Collection, Drew Archival Library, Duxbury Rural and Historical Society [*SMC*]; "Mrs. Judith W. Smith Buried," *Boston Transcript*, December 15, 1921, clipping, *SMC*; "Mrs Smith, Suffragist, Leaves 36 Descendants," *Boston Globe*, December 14, 1921, 5; [Alice Stone Blackwell], "Mrs. J. Winsor Smith 98 Years Old Nov. 24; Is Still Active for Suffrage Cause, Despite Her High Age," *Boston Record*, November 20, 1919, 7, clipping, *SMC*; Lucy Stone to Judith W. Smith, July 22, 1892, transcription and notes at Oberlin College Libraries website, http://www2.oberlin.edu/archive/teaching/projects/hist213/stone/document3.html.
[444] Most of Judith Smith's papers, including her diaries, are in the Massachusetts Historical Society: "Judith Winsor Smith Papers," Guide to the Collection, MHS, http://www.masshist.org/collection-guides/view/fa0063, and "Judith Winsor Smith family photographs," Guide to the Collection, Photo. Coll. 161, Massachusetts Historical Society Photo Archives, MHS,

http://www.masshist.org/collection-guides/view/fap031. Some of Judith Smith's reminiscences are in "Papers of Judith Winsor Smith in the Woman's Rights Collection, 1915," collection overview, *WRC* 1048, M-133, reel D49, SL, https://id.lib.harvard.edu/ead/sch01038/catalog. The Drew Archival Library of the Duxbury Rural and Historical Society has an excellent archive of family papers in the Smith McLauthlin Collection; see partial finding aid, https://drewarchives.org/finding-aids/smith-mclauthlin-collection/. Judith Smith's family name has been variously spelled McGlauthlen (*Vital Records*), McLaughlin, Maglauthlin, and McLauthlin (most common, and appears on her gravestone). Email July 2, 2019 from Carolyn Ravenscroft, archivist, Drew Archival Library, Duxbury Rural and Historical Society. Judith's husband's name has also been spelled Silvanus, and that is the way he spelled it in his letters.

[445] "Vote! And Thank You Judith Winsor Smith," posted November 6, 2012, updated November 6, 2018, Drew Archival Library, Duxbury Rural and Historical Society, https://drewarchives.org/tag/judith-winsor-smith/; *Vital Records of Duxbury, Massachusetts, to the Year 1850* (Boston: New England Historic Genealogical Society, 1911), 158, 309, https://archive.org/details/vitalrecordsofdu00duxb/page/n7.

[446] "Judith Winsor Smith," Paper Trail blog (source of quote), posted October 12, 2008, http://paper-trail.blogspot.com/2008/10/judith-winsor-smith.html; family chronicle, *SMC*, including Sidney Smith, "The Varied Career of Silvanus Smith 1817-1901, by his Son, Sidney Smith," August 26, 1926, revised 1939. The Smith family chronicle is in a photocopied typewritten manuscript that includes photos taken by Erasmus F. Smith in 1890, all or portions of which are in the *SMC*, as well as in box 8 of 8, *JWS*; it appears to have been compiled by Zilpha Drew Smith, given to Erasmus Smith, then to his son Silvanus Smith, then to his son Herbert in 1965. It appears the additional family papers containing the language quoted in the text were purchased by the Massachusetts Historical Society, according to its annual report for 2011, at 49, https://www.masshist.org/2012/juniper/assets/about/reports/mhs_annual_report_2011.pdf.

According to the family chronicle (as of 1926 or 1939), the farmhouse was gone, but the barn Sylvanus built still stood. Deeds for purchase and later sale of the farm, of about 30 acres, in which Sylvanus (or Silvanus) is described as "of Duxbury" and a "Ship Carpenter," include: John P. Turner to Sylvanus Smith 2d, deed, May 21, 1844, PCRD, book 212, page 224; and Silvanus Smith to James Ford 2d, deed, October 23, 1854, PCRD, book 262, page 233. The adjacent Collamore property and house are still there. "Barker, Thomas - Collamore, Dr. Anthony House," 225 Washington Street, Pembroke, PEM.16, MACRIS (per author's continuation sheet submitted March 2020, the address is now 191 Washington Street, and the house appears to be original).

[447] Judith Smith to Miriam (granddaughter), July 11, 1912, *JWS*.

[448] Family chronicle, *SMC*, including Sidney Smith, "The Varied Career of Silvanus Smith 1817-1901, by his Son, Sidney Smith," August 26, 1926, revised 1939; Jonathan Smith to Silvanus Smith, November 28, 1853, offered on eBay, copied at "Sylvanus Smith (1817 - 1901)," Wikitree website (source of quote), https://www.wikitree.com/wiki/Smith-1597; Glenn A. Knoblock, *The American Clipper Ship, 1845-1920: A Comprehensive History, with a Listing of Builders and Their*

Ships (Jefferson, NC: McFarland & Company, Inc., Publishers, 2014), generally, preview, https://books.google.com/books?id=k3lkAgAAQBAJ&source=gbs_navlinks_s. An excellent photographic panorama of the East Boston shipyards, about 1877. is at the Boston Public Library, https://www.digitalcommonwealth.org/search/commonwealth:cn69mt96f. See also "View of Boston in 1848 (from East Boston)," photo of lithograph, https://www.digitalcommonwealth.org/search/commonwealth:cn69mt66q. Sylvanus Smith is mentioned (as "Silvanus Smith") in William L. Crothers, *American-Built Packets and Freighters of the 1850s: An Illustrated Study of Their Characteristics and Construction* (Jefferson, NC: McFarland & Company, Inc., 2013), 14, 79, 87, 106, including a ship built for Robert Bennett Forbes and others for operation in Chinese coastal waters, preview, https://books.google.com/books?id=qTZPsctuutwC&source=gbs_navlinks_s.

[449] "Smith, Sylvanus House," 76 White Street, Boston, BOS.14278, MACRIS. A copy of the photo is in the family chronicle with a note that it was taken by Erasmus Smith in 1889. Another photo of the house, taken October 1906, is in the Judith Winsor Smith family photographs, MHS.

[450] "Eagle Hill Historic District," area form BOS.JK, MACRIS; see also "24-82 White Street," BOS.U, MACRIS; G. M. Hopkins, *Atlas of the County of Suffolk, Massachusetts, vol. 4: including East Boston, City of Chelsea, Revere and Winthrop* (Philadelphia: G. M. Hopkins & Co., 1874), plate K (Hall's Ship Yard, and Hall's East Boston Drydock Company), page 48, and plate L, page 53, http://hdl.handle.net/2452/205983; Boston Redevelopment Authority (drafted by The Cecil Group), "Amendment of the East Boston Waterfront District Municipal Harbor Plan; 6-26 New Street, Boston East and 125 Sumner Street," May 15, 2008, Attachment A, including introduction ("East Boston Maritime History"), 9.2.2, page 82, and A1.1.2, page 96, http://www.bostonplans.org/getattachment/880aada3-4e4b-429d-8749-16521369069e.

[451] Dr. Regina Marchi, *Legendary Locals of East Boston, Massachusetts* (Charleston, SC: Arcadia Publishing, 2015), 26 (quote), and see 25 (Smiths), preview, https://books.google.com/books?id=ZX4cCgAAQBAJ&source=gbs_navlinks_s. Marchi notes that the McKay house, at 78-80 White Street, is listed in the National Register of Historic Places.

[452] Family chronicle, *SMC*, including Sidney Smith, "The Varied Career of Silvanus Smith 1817-1901, by his Son, Sidney Smith," August 26, 1926, revised 1939; "24-82 White Street," BOS.U, MACRIS; Thomas W. Davis, city surveyor, and J.H. Bufford's Lith., "Plan of East Boston," scale 400 ft. to an inch (Boston: Boston Engineering Dept., 1880), Boston Public Library, *Digital Commonwealth*, https://ark.digitalcommonwealth.org/ark:/50959/js956k32k. An 1880 bird's-eye-view map shows shipyards in the foreground and even the Smith and McKay homes, and a nice detailed note accompanies the plan in BPL/Digital Commonwealth. O.H. Bailey & Co., "View of East Boston, Mass." (Boston: O.H. Bailey & Co., 1879), BPL/Digital Commonwealth, *Digital Commonwealth*, https://ark.digitalcommonwealth.org/ark:/50959/3f4634491, and State Library of Massachusetts.

[453] "Vote! And Thank You Judith Winsor Smith," posted November 6, 2012, updated November 6, 2018, Drew Archival Library, Duxbury Rural and Historical Society, https://drewarchives.org/tag/judith-winsor-smith/; family chronicle, *SMC*, including Sidney Smith, "The Varied Career of Silvanus Smith 1817-1901, by his Son, Sidney Smith," August 26, 1926, revised 1939; 1860 US Census, AncestryHeritagequest.com; Knoblock, *The American Clipper Ship,* 76-77.
[454] Judith Smith diary entries, July 6 (wreck) & 22 (sale), 1876, *JWS*. It was, however, reported that the ship was fully insured for tens of thousands of dollars. *Boston Globe*, July 6, 1876, 6, and July 7, 1876, 6. According to the Smith family chronicle, listing vessels built by Sylvanus, the *Puritan* was built in 1866, and two ships were built in 1876: the *South American* (or *South America*), and the *Paul Revere.*
[455] DAR, *Old Scituate*, 257-258; "A Badly Neglected Gun," *Boston Globe*, February 15, 1894, 4; *Twenty-Fifth Annual List of Merchant Vessels of the United States* (Washington, DC: US Treasury Department, Bureau of Navigation, 1893), 201, https://books.google.com/books?id=FCcpAQAAIAAJ&source=gbs_navlinks_s ; Humane Society of the Commonwealth of Massachusetts, *Report:1899 and 1900* (Boston: Nathan Sawyer & Son, 1900), 124 (life-saving awards), https://books.google.com/books?id=bEYDAAAAMAAJ&source=gbs_navlinks_s. Judith later viewed the shipwreck, as mentioned below.
[456] "She'll Vote Even if it Rains," *Boston Globe*, August 29, 1920, 61 (source of quote); *The Liberator* (Boston: William Lloyd Garrison), vol. 32, no. 7, February 14, 1862, 28, col. 5, about ¼ of the way down from top, https://www.digitalcommonwealth.org/search/commonwealth:mc87rg78r and http://fair-use.org/the-liberator/1862/02/14/the-liberator-32-07.pdf.
[457] Various papers, *JWS*; Jennie Cunningham Croly, *The History of the Woman's Club Movement in America* (New York: Henry G. Allen & Co., 1898), 627–628, preview, https://books.google.com/books?id=OFJKn1HaKiAC&source=gbs_navlinks_s; Mary Ashton Rice Livermore, *The Story of My Life* (Hartford, CT: A. D. Worthington & Co., 1897), chapters 22 and 23, https://quod.lib.umich.edu/cgi/t/text/text-idx?c=moa;idno=4728109.
[458] "Papers of Judith Winsor Smith in the Woman's Rights Collection, 1915," collection overview, *WRC* 1048, M-133, reel D49, SL, https://id.lib.harvard.edu/ead/sch01038/catalog; "Elect Officers, Review the Year's Work and Lunch at the Vendome," *Boston Globe*, May 31, 1891, 9 (Judith at club's annual meeting at Chauncy Hall Building); Caroline M. Seymour Severance, *The Mother of Clubs* (Los Angeles: Baumgardt Publishing Co., 1906), 15, 24, 28, https://books.google.com/books?id=BEVIAAAAIAAJ&source=gbs_navlinks_s; Katie Ana Baca, *Beyond the University: Elite Bostonian Women's Organizations as Sites of Science Learning, 1868-1910* (Doctoral dissertation, Harvard University, Graduate School of Arts & Sciences, 2019), 134-138, http://nrs.harvard.edu/urn-3:HUL.InstRepos:42013065.
[459] Chauncy Hall Building, 585-591 Boylston Street, Boston, BOS.2651 (author's continuation sheet), MACRIS; Maud Wood Park, "Busy Hive Full of Workers for Women," *Boston American*, February 23, 1913, 2W, clipping in *WRC*, SL. In addition to attending meetings at the old Chauncy Hall Building, Judith Smith attended a meeting of BESAGG at the new Chauncy Hall building in 1910. "Equal Suffrage Tea Held," *Boston Herald*, March 12, 1910, 7. From 1916 through 1918, BESAGG's headquarters were in leased rooms at 167 Tremont Street (building since

demolished), where they met and ran the Sunflower Lunch Room, and then they moved to the Little Building at 74-94 Boylston Street, based on a search of the *Woman's Journal*, *The Woman Citizen*, and Maud Wood Park Papers. Little Building, 74-94 Boylston Street (author's second supplement sheet), MACRIS; *The Woman Citizen*, November 10, 1917, 462 (ad), for example, https://babel.hathitrust.org/cgi/pt?id=inu.30000098651049&view=1up&seq=346.

[460] Judith Smith diary (extract), May 30, 1871, MS N-123, folder 1 of 21, Box 7 of 8, *JWS*.

[461] "The Woman Suffrage Petitions," *WJ*, February 17, 1877, 52; "Woman Suffrage Petitions," *WJ*, February 23, 1878, 60; "Good News from East Boston," *WJ*, January 5, 1878, 4; "Send In Your Petitions," *WJ*, February 22, 1879, 61.

[462] "Faithful Worker Goes to Rest," *WJ*, January 27, 1917, 23, col. 4 (obituary); *WJ*, March 28, 1891, 97, col. 2 (promotion to editor); *WJ*, July 7, 1906, 105, col. 5; Wilde Family Collection finding aid, Drew Archival Library, Duxbury Rural and Historical Society, https://drewarchives.org/finding-aids/wilde-family-collection/. Catherine was the daughter of Dr. James Wilde and Zilpah Smith Wilde (Sylvanus Smith's sister) of Duxbury. Carolyn Ravenscroft email, March 6, 2020. Catherine joined the New England Woman's Press Association in 1890, five years after its founding, and she later became an officer, along with Floretta Vining and Alice Stone Blackwell. "Newspaper Women," *Boston Globe*, March 6, 1890, 2; "Woman's Press Association," *Boston Globe*, January 4, 1894, 6; Myra B. Lord, *History of the New England Woman's Press Association, 1885-1931* (Newton, MA: The Graphic Press, 1932), 45, 65, 68, 76, 77, 104, 109, 116, 123, 139, 143, https://babel.hathitrust.org/cgi/pt?id=wu.89098887490&view=1up&seq=9 and https://hdl.handle.net/2027/wu.89098887490?urlappend=%3Bseq=9. Catherine was secretary of the Boston Women's Suffrage League. "Woman Suffrage League Meets," *Boston Globe*, February 27, 1894, 6. Caroline and Judith Smith were on the executive committee of the New England and Massachusetts Woman Suffrage Associations. "Woman Suffragists," *Boston Globe*, May 29, 1903, 2; "Menace in Bridge Whist," *Boston Globe*, May 9, 1908, 11; "Officers Are Elected: New England Woman's Suffrage Association Holds Annual Meeting in Park-St Church," *Boston Globe*, May 26, 1909, 11; "Miss Blackwell Elected," *Boston Globe*, January 10, 1911, 10.

[463] "A Massachusetts Heroine," *WJ*, July 13, 1878, 224. The tale was again mentioned in "A Point For Woman Suffrage," *WJ*, July 21, 1894, 228, which also described the Smith family's vacation at Cedar Point. In addition, the tale appeared in a *Boston Transcript* article reprinted in the *Woman's Journal*, "Not From the West, But From the East," *WJ*, August 24, 1889, 272. The article opined that the activity of the woman suffrage leaders was "a case of Scituate drumming, two patriot daughters sounding long rolls behind the lighthouse for an army that does not exist."

[464] Harriet H. Robinson, *Massachusetts in the Woman Suffrage Movement: A General, Political, Legal and Legislative History from 1774, to 1881* (Boston: Roberts Brothers, 1881), 62 (Mrs. J. W. Smith one of three on a committee that arranged the two-day MWSA convention in 1881), https://archive.org/details/massachusettsinw00robi/page/n6; "A Pleasant Reception," *Boston Globe*, February 13, 1881, 8; Maud Wood Park Papers, *WRC*,

#Pa 144, copy of HBB list, SL; Stanton, et al, *History of Woman Suffrage*, vol. 3: 273, fn (School Suffrage).
[465] "Woman Suffrage Convention!" broadside, box 8, folder 25 (ephemera), SL; Neuman, *Gilded Suffragists*, 51-53 (Belmont); *WJ*, August 13, 1887, 260.
[466] *Boston Directory for 1887* (Boston: Sampson, Murdock, & Company, 1887), 920, https://babel.hathitrust.org/cgi/pt?id=mdp.39015074624456&view=1up&seq=15; "William Notman Biography," Notman Photographic Society website, https://notmansociety.wordpress.com/william-notman-biography/; R. Staudenbaur, Engraver, James Notman, photographer, "Oliver Wendell Holmes / photographed by Notman, Boston; R. Staudenbaur sc.," June 5, 1886, Library of Congress, https://www.loc.gov/item/2012649668; Notman Photo. Co., 480 Boylston St. and 3 Park St., Boston, "Lucy Stone with daughter Alice Stone Blackwell, half-length studio portrait, sitting, facing front," c. 1858, Library of Congress, https://www.loc.gov/item/2005677274/; J. A. Bullt [?], engraver, J. Notman, photographer, "Lucy Stone," in Elizabeth Cady Stanton, Susan B. Anthony, and Matilda Joslyn Gage, *History of Woman Suffrage, vol. 2, 1861-1876* (Rochester, NY: Susan B. Anthony, 1887), 760-761 (portrait of Lucy Stone), https://archive.org/details/historyofwomansu02stanuoft/page/n5/mode/2up; Eugène L'Africain, engraver, Notman Photo Boston, photographer, "Eminent Women," photographic collage of twelve women, J. Paul Getty Museum website, http://www.getty.edu/art/collection/objects/44165/notman-photograph-company-james-notman-eugene-l'africain-eminent-women-canadian-1884/?dz=0.5000,0.6190,0.66; photo of Sylvanus Smith (shown at beginning of Smith chapter), which appears to be a carte de visite or cabinet card version of a photograph photocopied and described in the Smith family chronicle as "photo by Notman – 1887." A similar carte de visite or cabinet card of Judith Smith (shown at the beginning of the Smith chapter) was taken, but she had at least six portraits taken by Boston-area photographers before one taken by Notman in the 1890s, when daughter Zilpha also had her pictures taken by Notman. Judith Winsor Smith family photographs, MHS. An 1895 Sanborn map indicated there was a photo studio on the fifth floor of 4 Park Street, and a picture frame facility in the basement. *Sanborn Fire Insurance Map from Boston, Suffolk County, Massachusetts,* vol. 1 (New York: Sanborn Map Company, 1895), sheet 24 (image 36 of 97), Library of Congress,
https://www.loc.gov/resource/g3764bm.g03693189501/?sp=36&r=0.431,0.208,0.256,0.102,0. Boston directories published by Sampson & Murdock Co. listed Notman studios at 3 Park Street (1916, page 313), and later at 4 Park Street, 4th floor (1922, page 410). A Notman photo of Julia Ward Howe lists both 480 Boylston Street and 3 Park Street as the studio's addresses. Cabinet card photo of Julia Ward Howe, c. 1885, in "Between the Covers Rare Books, Catalog 215: Women," https://www.betweenthecovers.com/images/upload/c215.pdf.
[467] *Sanborn Fire Insurance Map from Boston, Suffolk County, Massachusetts*, vol. 5 (New York: Sanborn Map Company, 1888), Library of Congress, https://www.loc.gov/item/sanborn03693_006/; Anthony Sammarco, "East Boston Ferries," in *Lost Boston* (London: Pavilion Books, 2014, 2016), 90-91.
[468] 50th anniversary guest book, *SMC*; "Archibald Henry Grimké," Boston Athenaeum website,

https://www.bostonathenaeum.org/collections/archive/archibald-henry-grimke; *WJ*, December 5, 1891, 394.
[469] "How to Make a Happy Home," typed manuscript, *SMC*.
[470] Judith Winsor Smith handwritten note, Christmas 1912, on typed manuscript, SMC; *WJ*, January 16, 1892, 32.
[471] Lucy Stone to Judith Smith, letter, July 22, 1892, Oberlin College Archives, http://www2.oberlin.edu/archive/teaching/projects/hist213/stone/document3.html, also in Leslie Wheeler, ed., *Selected Letters of Lucy Stone and Henry B. Blackwell, 1853-1893* (New York: The Dial Press, 1981), 343-344; Alice Stone Blackwell, *Lucy Stone: Pioneer of Woman's Rights* (Boston: Little, Brown, and Company, 1930), 273 (source of quote), https://babel.hathitrust.org/cgi/pt?id=uc1.$b21517&view=1up&seq=301.
[472] *Christian Science Sentinel* (Boston: Christian Science Publishing Society), February 2, 1899, 2, https://books.google.com/books?id=1mC-ODJgymkC&source=gbs_navlinks_s; "Equal Suffrage Tea Held," *Boston Herald*, March 12, 1910, 7; Harper, *History of Woman Suffrage*, vol. 6, 267, 279 (1915), 280 (spoke at MWSA luncheon August 13, 1918), https://chswg.binghamton.edu/docs/historyofwomansuffrage_vol6.pdf; A. S. B. [Alice Stone Blackwell], "98 Years Young," *The Woman Citizen* (New York: The Woman Citizen Corporation), December 13, 1919, [2], https://books.google.com/books?id=qtYRAQAAMAAJ&pg=PT483#v=onepage&q&f=false.
[473] Henry B. Blackwell to Mrs. Smith and daughter, May 5, 1905, *JWS*.
[474] Alice Stone Blackwell to Judith Smith, December 25, 1916, *JWS*, for example; Alice Stone Blackwell, "Lagoon Pond and Vineyard Haven Harbour, Vineyard Haven, Mass." color postcard, October 1, 1914, addressed to Mrs. Judith W. Smith (source of quote), quoted in "Lucy Hargrett Draper Center and Archives for the Study of the Rights of Women in History and Law Hargrett Rare Book and Manuscript Library Special Collections Libraries University of Georgia, Index," note 213, https://www.libs.uga.edu/hargrett/manuscrip/draper/lhd_cat.pdf; "Three manuscript poems on signed postcards to Smith" (1907, 1914, & undated), offered for sale by Glenn Horowitz Bookseller, http://www.glennhorowitz.com/dobkin/manuscript_three_manuscript_poems_on_signed_postcards_to_smith; documents referenced in American History, 1493-1945, website, http://www.americanhistory.amdigital.co.uk/Documents/Details/Alice-Stone-Blackwell-to-Judith-W--Smith-sharing-news-and-poems/GLC06975.
[475] Lyle Nyberg, "Scituate Lighthouse Was Once Abandoned But Not Vacant," *The Keeper's Log* (Hansville, WA: U.S. Lighthouse Society, November 2019), 12; Judith Smith diary entries, including July 3, 1873, *JWS*.
[476] Robert Fraser, "Scituate Lighthouse," typed manuscript, undated, 4, on file, SHS; Robert Fraser, "Scituate Lighthouse," *The Keeper's Log* (US Lighthouse Society, Winter 1987), 5; Jeremy D'Entremont, "History of Scituate Light, Massachusetts," New England Lighthouses: A Virtual Guide, http://www.newenglandlighthouses.net/scituate-light-history.html.
[477] Nyberg, "Scituate Lighthouse Was Once Abandoned." Fraser's manuscript said government records were destroyed in a fire in 1922, but index cards for the records from 1859 to 1875 survived, and they showed that the government rented

the quarters (or allowed them to be rented), and later hired Samuel Hall as a live-in caretaker.

[478] "Sad Death of William Hall," *Boston Globe*, July 30, 1875, 2 ("was brother to the late Samuel Hall, the famous ship-builder"); Briggs, *History of Shipbuilding on North River* (1889), 356-357 (Hall), 197-198 (Smith); Sidney Smith, "The Varied Career of Silvanus Smith 1817-1901, by his Son, Sidney Smith," August 26, 1926, revised 1939, third page ("foreman") and fourth page (Samuel Hall d. 1870), in family chronicle, *SMC*; Plymouth Archaeological Rediscovery Project, "Site Examination Fieldwork at the Second Meeting House Site in Duxbury, Massachusetts" (April 2009), 24-25, http://www.plymoutharch.com/wp-content/uploads/2014/11/49705059-Report-on-the-Archaeological-Investigations-at-the-Site-of-the-Second-Meeting-House-in-Duxbury-Massachusetts.pdf; Sydney [Sidney] Smith, "In a Gale off Cape Cod 1863," 1934, *SMC*; Hall family file, SHS; Daniel T. Rogers, "Daniel T. Rogers(b. 1943) - all my relatives," (Luke born 1797 begat Luke born 1830 begat Luke born 1854 who married Mary Hathaway Smith), https://sites.rootsweb.com/~dantrogers/pafg3924.htm; D. Hamilton Hurd, "Samuel Hall," *History of Plymouth County, Massachusetts, with Biographical Sketches of Many of its Pioneers and Prominent Men*, part 2 (Philadelphia: J. W. Lewis & Co., 1884), 1169, https://archive.org/details/historyofplymout01hurd/page/n775; *The Boston Directory for the Year Commencing July 1, 1868* (Boston: Sampson, Davenport, & Co., 1868), 277, https://books.google.com/books?id=SFwJAQAAIAAJ&source=gbs_navlinks_s; G. M. Hopkins, *Atlas of the County of Suffolk, Massachusetts, vol. 4: including East Boston, City of Chelsea, Revere and Winthrop* (Philadelphia: G. M. Hopkins & Co., 1874), plates I, K, & L; Massachusetts Secretary of State "Search for Citations to Vital Record (1841 - 1910)" website. See Knoblock, *American Clipper Ship*, 282 (Hall), 285 (Smith). George H. Hall (1825-1905) was the first keeper of the Gurnet Light in Plymouth from 1874 to 1878, about when the junior Samuel Hall (probably a distant relative) was caretaker at the Scituate Light. "Station Gurnet, Massachusetts," US Coast Guard history program website, https://media.defense.gov/2017/Jul/03/2001772698/-1/-1/0/GURNET.PDF, Lysander Salmon Richards, *History of Marshfield*, vol. 2 (Plymouth, MA: The Memorial Press, 1905), 110, https://books.google.com/books?id=AgHMDwAAQBAJ&source=gbs_navlinks_s; Duxbury Rural and Historical Society Facebook post, February 14, 2019, https://www.facebook.com/293774423291/photos/happy-valentines-day-from-the-drhs-this-lovely-couples-photograph-was-taken-at-n/10156536371698292/. ; "George H. Hall, FindAGrave memorial, https://www.findagrave.com/memorial/140217506/george-h_-hall; Lighthouse keeping seems to have been a family business.

[479] Emails from David Ball, July 15-17, 2019, including text of framed document entitled "Cedar Point Club" listing officers, directors, and members; "Scituate Boys Aid Aged Man in Building 'Friendship House,'" *Boston Globe*, November 13, 1935, 3 (meetings); David Ball, *To the Point: The Story of Scituate Light and Cedar Point* (n.p.: David Ball, 1994, 6th printing, 2000), 30.

[480] Judith Smith diary entries, various, *JWS*.

[481] Judith Smith diary, July 1, 1876, *JWS*; "Elijah T. Clapp," *Biographical Review, Vol. XVIII: Containing Life Sketches of Leading Citizens of Plymouth County, Massachusetts* (Boston: Biographical Review Publishing Co., 1897), 498, https://archive.org/details/biographicalrevi1897biog and https://books.google.com/books?id=7qd5EML7tYYC&source=gbs_navlinks_s; Massachusetts Secretary of State "Search for Citations to Vital Record (1841 - 1910)" website (Clapp 1860 marriage); "George Horace Manson," FindAGrave memorial, https://www.findagrave.com/memorial/158065759/george-horace-manson; *Vital Records of Scituate Massachusetts to the Year 1850, vol. I – Births* (Boston: New England Historic Genealogical Society, 1909), 80 (Mercy Ford Clapp birth, 1836), https://archive.org/details/vitalrecordsofsc01newe. John Bradford signed the guest registry for the Smith's 50th anniversary in 1891, *SMC*.
[482] Judith Smith diary entries, July 3, July 6 (water), July 10, July 21, 1876, *JWS*.
[483] *Boston Globe*, July 13, 1875, 8; *Boston Globe*, August 21, 1875, 5 (clipper).
[484] Mary [Smith] to "everybody," transcript of letter from Philadelphia, July 18, 1875, Hall family file, SHS; *Boston Globe*, July 14, 1875, 6. It seems Uncle Rufus was Rufus H. McLauthlin, Judith's brother, who (according to a photo in the Smith family chronicle), lived next to the Smith family when they were on Eutaw Street in East Boston. See "A Brief Record of the Ancestors, Nearest Relatives and Descendants of Miller McGlathlen, Born March 13, 1780," *SMC*.
[485] Judith Smith diary, July 13-14, 1875, *JWS*; Mary [Smith] to "everybody," July 18, 1875 (source of quote); Sylvanus [Smith] to wife and children, transcript of letter, probably July 1875, Hall family file, SHS; *Boston Globe*, July 19, 1875, 7 (ship arrived in Philadelphia July 19). The ship was cleared for departure from Philadelphia on August 19, *Boston Globe*, August 20, 1875, 7.
[486] Judith Smith diary, July 13-14, 1875, *JWS*.
[487] Judith Smith diary, July 20, 1875, *JWS* (finest ship); Sylvanus [Smith] to wife and children, transcript of letter; Sylvanus Smith to Judith Smith, July 24, 1875 (centennial folks), Hall family file, SHS. See *Boston Globe*, July 27, 1875, 7 (Crowell).
[488] Sylvanus Smith to Judith Smith, July 24, 1875, *JWS*.
[489] Sylvanus Smith to Judith Smith, August 1, 1875, *SMC*. The trip is documented with sources from three separate collections: MHS (Judith's diary), SHS (Mary's letter and Sylvanus's letters), and DRHS (Sylvanus letter of 8/1/1875). It brings these pieces back together for the first time in 145 years.
[490] Judith Smith diary, July 10, 1882, *JWS*.
[491] See Fred Freitas, *Humarock: Hummocks, Humming Rocks, and Silver Sands* (Scituate: Converpage, 2019), 63-75, 101-114, 217 (photo of shingle beach); Bryant F. Tolles, Jr., *Summer by the Seaside: The Architecture of New England Coastal Resort Hotels, 1820-1950* (Hanover, NH: University Press of New England, 2008), 69-70 (replacement hotel burned down in 1901). The beach road was labeled "highway" at both ends on a plan drawn after the storm of 1898. Massachusetts Board of Harbor and Land Commissioners, *Plan of New Mouth of North River, Scituate: Opened by Storm of November 1898*, July 1899, URI http://hdl.handle.net/2452/48567, from *Public Document No. 11, Annual Report of the Board of Harbor and Land Commissioners for the year 1899* (Boston: Wright & Potter, 1900), see 48-49, Digital Commonwealth. The bridge was enabled by "An Act to Incorporate the White's Ferry Bridge Company," Ch. 90 of the Acts and Resolves of Massachusetts, 1882, 70-71, approved March 17, 1882,

https://archive.org/details/actsresolvespass1882mass/page/70/mode/2up/search/marshfield. Subdivision into lots is shown in H. G. Ford, C. E., *Plan of Land in Scituate Mass. Belonging to Humarock and North River Land Assn, scale 80 ft = 1 in, August 1898*, in two sections with supplementary plan, PCRD, plan book 2, pages 249 (Section 1), and 492 (Section 2), and plan book 1, page 219, sheet 4 of 4.

[492] "Hotel Humarock Burned," *Boston Globe*, August 21, 1882, 4; "Scituate," *Boston Globe*, May 27, 1883, 3, col. 4.

[493] Nyberg, "Scituate Lighthouse Was Once Abandoned;" US Department of Commerce, Bureau of Lighthouses, "Scituate Breakwater Light Station, Massachusetts," photo, March 7, 1902, National Archives, 26-LG-9-1A, https://catalog.archives.gov/id/45692249; illustration accompanying text in this chapter. The ribs of the canopy also appear in two photos by the US Department of Commerce, Bureau of Lighthouses, both titled "Scituate Breakwater Light Station, Massachusetts," undated (probably 1902), National Archives, Record Group 26, 26-LG-9-1D (left side of photo), https://catalog.archives.gov/id/45692255, and 26-LG-9-1B (right side), https://catalog.archives.gov/id/45692251.

[494] Judith Smith diary, July 5 & 10, 1890, *JWS*; Sidney Smith, in booklet accompanying a memorial meeting for Zilpha D. Smith, December 11, 1926, 19, Hall family file, SHS.

[495] Family chronicle, typewritten manuscript with photos from 1890, *SMC*. The group photo is in the same collection, and on the back is a list of most of the people in the photo, including Sylvanus and Judith, and their children.

[496] Judith Smith diary entries, July 9, 1889 (fish), July 16, 1889 (trip), July 30, 1889 (mail), July 13, 1890 (kite), July 23, 1891 (moonlight sail; sand hills), *JWS*. Locals listed in the text are mentioned July 12 & 15, 1882; July 16, 1889; and July 29 & 31, 1890. Many of the names appear in an 1894 directory and the 1903 map. *Directory of Cohasset, Scituate, Marshfield, Duxbury and Norwell* (Quincy, MA: J. H. Hogan Co., 1894), 152, on file, SHS, and https://archive.org/details/directoryhistory00quin. For more on the Hammonds, the only ones listed in the 1894 directory, and the Colonial Inn, see "25 Meeting House Lane," SCI.__ (filed January 2020), MACRIS.

[497] Judith Smith diary, July 27, 1890, *JWS*; "Dr. Collamore Receives," *Boston Globe*, December 8, 1905, https://www.newspapers.com/clip/9768865/boston-globe-8-dec-1905/; family chronicle (house gone), *SMC*; Samuel Deane, *History of Scituate, Massachusetts, from Its First Settlement to 1831* (Boston: James Loring, 1831), 239-240, https://archive.org/details/historyofscituat00deane; "CPT Anthony Collamore," FindAGrave memorial, https://www.findagrave.com/memorial/8650522/anthony-collamore; Karen Cross Proctor, *Pembroke*, Images of America series (Charleston, SC: Arcadia Publishing, 2008), 110, preview, https://books.google.com/books?id=Z_UKe647CwAC&source=gbs_navlinks_s; "Barker, Thomas - Collamore, Dr. Anthony House," 225 Washington Street, Pembroke, PEM.16 (address is now 191 Washington Street, and the house appears to be original), MACRIS; Parker to Smith deed and Smith to Ford deeds noted above, which refer to adjacent property and house of Doctor Anthony Collamore,

[498] Judith Smith diary, July 22, 1891; "Died in the Saddle," "Steam Flyer," and related articles in different editions, *Boston Globe*, June 2, 1896, 1; Pete Gagan, "The First American Motorcyclist," Earliest Steam Cycles website (source of quote and

information on names of steam launches),
https://www.stanleysteamers.com/gagan.htm.
[499] Judith Smith diary entries, July 24 (source of quote) & 27, 1891, *JWS*.
[500] "Where the Breezes Are; Many are the City People at Scituate," *Boston Globe*, July 31, 1892, 9. Probably Emma McLaughlin was a relative of Judith (McLauthlin) Smith.
[501] Judith Smith diary entries, July 4 & 5, 1893, *JWS*.
[502] Judith Smith diary, early July 1894, *JWS*; Smith family chronicle (built in stable, named by Sidney as a joke).
[503] C. W. [Carolyn Wilde], "A Point For Woman Suffrage," *WJ*, July 21, 1894, 228, col. 3.
[504] Judith Smith to cousin, August 19, 1894 (source of quote), box 1, *JWS*; Judith Smith diary entry between July 14 and July 16, 1894, *JWS*.
[505] Judith Smith diary entries for the first three weeks of July 1894, *JWS*.
[506] Judith Smith diary entry between July 21 and July 23 (milk "to the beach"), and other entries for the first three weeks of July 1894, *JWS*. An 1894 directory listed 22 Clapps, many of whom were farmers, but Rufus was the only one listed as farmer and milkman. His site is shown on the 1903 map, and was not far from the lighthouse.
[507] Judith Smith diary, first three weeks of July 1894, and late July to early August (novel) 1894; see "The Heavenly Twins," University of Michigan Press website, https://www.press.umich.edu/9963/heavenly_twins. The novel came out in 1893.
[508]"Playing Peggotty," *WJ*, July 25, 1896, 236 (source of quote). The Smith family chronicle suggests the new cottage was prompted by Samuel Hall's death.
[509] Fraser, "Scituate Lighthouse," *The Keeper's Log*, 5; 1894 directory, 146 (Prouty, "undertaker, light keeper," with home on Front Street, Scituate Harbor); 1900 US census, sheet 20 (Prouty, who prepared the sheet, listed as undertaker). The wooden spar can be seen in old photos of the lighthouse.
[510] Mary Hathaway (Smith) Hall to Roy Hall (probably son), copy of letter, postmarked September 4, 1900, Hall family file, SHS.
[511] Hall to Hall, postmarked September 4, 1900; *The South Shore Blue Book, Containing Lists of the Summer Residents of the Principal Resorts Along the South Shore including Hull, Nantasket, Jerusalem Road, Cottage City, Falmouth, Marshfield, Duxbury, Scituate, Woods Hole, Cohasset, Etc.* (Boston: Boston Suburban Book Co., 1906), 42.
[512] *WJ*, September 15, 1900, 293.
[513] Sylvanus Smith to Judith Smith, July 5, 1901, *SMC*.
[514] Sylvanus Smith to Judith Smith, July 5, 1901, *SMC*.
[515] *Boston Globe*, July 31, 1901, 2; Henry B. Blackwell and Alice Stone Blackwell to Judith Smith, August 2, 1901, and Julia Ward Howe to Judith Smith, August 3, 1901, *SMC*; *WJ*, August 3, 1901, 245.
[516] "Silvanus Smith," *WJ*, August 10, 1901, 253.
[517] Susan B. Anthony Memorial Fund Extension Plan notice and contribution form (n.d.), Library of Congress,
https://www.loc.gov/resource/rbcmil.scrp7004201/?st=text.
[518] "Mrs. J. W. Smith's 88th Birthday," *WJ*, December 4, 1909, 196; Helen M. Winslow, "The Story of the Woman's Club Movement," *The New England Magazine*, vol. 38 (Boston: The New England Magazine Company, 1909), 543, at 553-554,
https://books.google.com/books?id=pLAVAAAAYAAJ&vq.

[519] "Thousands View Great Parade of Suffragists," *Boston Record*, May 2, 1914, 1, clipping, *SMC*.
[520] "Suffrage Rally in Postoffice Sq; Big Crowd Attentive to Several Speakers; Mrs Judith W. Smith, Aged 91, Makes Address From Auto." *Boston Globe*, August 1, 1914, 14. A year later, Judith, then 93 and "the oldest speaker in the suffrage ranks," evidently returned to Liberty Square to speak for suffrage. "Aged Woman Wants Vote: 93 Years Old, She Speaks for Suffrage," clipping from unknown newspaper (not the *Boston Globe*), marked Aug 4, 1915, in "Papers of Judith Winsor Smith in the Woman's Rights Collection, 1915," *WRC* 1048, M-133, reel D49, SL, https://id.lib.harvard.edu/ead/sch01038/catalog.
[521] "92-Year-Old Woman Addresses Crowd in the Cause of Suffrage," unknown newspaper, c. August 1914, probably August 1, clipping (with photo), *SMC*.
[522] "Aged Woman a Speaker; Mrs Judith Smith, 92 Years Old, at a Meeting in Liberty Sq." *Boston Globe*, August 25, 1914, 5.
[523] Google Maps; author's visit.
[524] "Meeting in Honor of Mrs Julia Ward Howe," *Boston Globe*, May 27, 1915, 3; "Bronze Tablet Unveiled; Suffragists Meet at the House in Worcester Where Lucy Stone Blackwell Was Born," *Boston Globe*, August 14, 1915, 6; "Over 10,000 Women March," *Boston Globe*, October 16, 1915, 1, at 2; "Suffragists Promise a Record Turnout," *Boston Globe*, October 16, 1915, 1, at 3; "Judith Winsor Smith Dead," undated clipping from Boston newspaper, obituary, *SMC*.
[525] "Suffrage 'Pilgrims' Flock to the Historic Lucy Stone Homestead," *Boston Globe*, September 12, 1916, 8; "Suffrage Workers to Celebrate," *Boston Post*, August 7, 1916, clipping in Lucy Stone Papers, *WRC*, folder 1052, SL.
[526] Little Building, 74-94 Boylston Street, Boston, BOS.2249 (with author's continuation sheets), MACRIS; "Suffragists Open New Headquarters on Fifth Floor of the Little Building," clipping (with photo), unknown newspaper, Maud Wood Park Papers, *WRC* #Pa 108, Schlesinger Library (2690_038_0433 from 1 to 39); "Boston Suffragists Receive," *Boston Globe*, January 15, 1919, 14.
[527] Alice Stone Blackwell to Judith Smith, January 15, 1918, *JWS*.
[528] "Suffragists to Observe Lucy Stone's Centenary," *Boston Globe*, July 31, 1918, 6; "Two Aged Suffragists to Honor Lucy Stone," *Boston Globe*, August 5, 1918, 9; "Coworkers of Lucy Stone Present at Observance," *Boston Globe*, August 13, 1918, 4; "Honor Lucy Stone on Her Centenary," *Boston Globe*, August 14, 1918, 8 ("active worker"). Speakers included Maud Wood Park, "Speech of Maud Wood Park at the Lucy Stone Anniversary 1918," typed manuscript, Maud Wood Park Papers, *WRC*, folder 1052 (Lucy Stone [?], 002695_018_1321_From_1_to_32), SL.
[529] Alice Stone Blackwell to Judith Smith, January 20, 1919, *JWS*: 11 Roanoke Avenue, BOS.10115 (continuation sheet February 2020), MACRIS.
[530] "Oldest Suffragist in Massachusetts," *Boston Post*, November 26. 1919, clipping (with photo) in Maud Wood Park Papers, folder 1052, *WRC*, SL.
[531] "She'll Vote Even if it Rains," *Boston Globe*, August 29, 1920, 61. See also "Mrs Judith W. Smith 100 Years Old Today; One of the Pioneers in the Woman's Movement," *Boston Globe*, November 26, 1921, 8.
[532] "Women's Club Pays Tribute to Mrs Smith, 100 Nov 26," *Boston Globe*, November 1, 1921, 14; "'Plymouth Day' - President Day - August 1, 1921 - The Parade," Plymouth Public Library website, https://pplma.omeka.net/exhibits/show/president-day---august-21--192.

[533] M. E. Hennessy, "Edwards Given Warm Greeting," *Boston Globe*, August 2, 1921, 12.
[534] "Smith, Sylvanus House," 82 Lighthouse Road, SCI.519, and Cedar Point Area, SCI.V (Cedar Point), MACRIS.
[535] *1896 Valuation List*, 111 (Sylvanus Smith penciled in for house $900, stable $100, no lot); *1897 Valuation List*, 108 (Sylvanus Smith, same as 1896); David Ball, *To the Point: The Story of Scituate Light and Cedar Point* (n.p.: David Ball, 1994, 6th printing, 2000), ch. 4 (99-year leases of lots), and 1907 plan marked up with dates of construction (1885 for lot 108).
[536] "Columbia Wrecked," *Boston Globe*, November 28, 1898, 1 at 4, col. 2.
[537] 1903 map, plate 32, inset for Barker Farm Beach.
[538] *WJ*, June 30, 1906, 103, col. 3; *WJ*, April 10, 1915, 117, col. 5.
[539] *Boston Globe*, June 22, 1913, 14, col. 8; Frances (daughter) to Judith Smith, September 27, 1914, *JWS*; Judith Winsor Smith family photographs, MHS.
[540] George O. Allen to Judith W. Smith, deed, November 27, 1908, PCRD, book 1013, page 81, conveying lots 108, 118, and 119, per George H. Wetherbee Jr., Civil Engineer, *Plan of Land at Sand Hills, Scituate, Mass., Owned by George O. Allen, September 29, 1908*, scale on plan, PCRD, plan book 1, page 506 (showing buildings on each of the three lots); *1908 Valuation List*, 123 (Sylvanus Smith heirs, includes La Casita); *1922 Valuation List*, 165 (last for Judith Smith, with house $1,300 on lot 108, house $100 on lot 119, stable $150 on lot 118); "Smith, Sylvanus House," 82 Lighthouse Road, SCI.519, MACRIS; "She'll Vote Even if it Rains," *Boston Globe*, August 29, 1920, 61; *SMC* (generally). See also "Descendant of Alden, a Century-Old, Tells Girls to 'Get Married,'" *Boston Post*, August 14, 1921, 35, https://www.newspapers.com/clip/7572552/100_year_old_alden/.
[541] "Mrs Smith, Suffragist, Leaves 36 Descendants," *Boston Globe*, December 14, 1921, 5; "Oldest Clubwoman," *Brooklyn Daily Eagle*, December 14, 1921, 29; "Vote! And Thank You Judith Winsor Smith," posted November 6, 2012, updated November 6, 2018, Drew Archival Library, Duxbury Rural and Historical Society, https://drewarchives.org/tag/judith-winsor-smith/; zoomurray, FindAGrave memorial, https://www.findagrave.com/memorial/173667196/judith-winsor-smith.
[542] Judith W. Smith by executors to Catherine L. Campbell, deed, June 13, 1922, PCRD, book 1410, page 575 (lot 118 with the building thereon and all household furniture and personal property); Catherine L. Campbell to Erasmus F. Smith, deed, June 13, 1922, PCRD, book 1410, page 576; Judith Winsor Smith by executors to Margaret M O'Hare, deed, June 13, 1922, PCRD, book 1410, page 576 (lot 108 with the building thereon and all household furniture and personal property); Judith Winsor Smith by executors to Sidney Smith as trustee for his grandson Lothrop Smith, deed, June 26, 1922, PCRD, book 1416, page 175 (lot 119 with the building thereon and all household furniture and personal property); author's visit July 13, 2019.
[543] Smith, "The Varied Career of Silvanus Smith," August 26, 1926, revised 1939, Smith McLauthlin Collection.
[544] *Scituate Herald*, May 17, 1940, 4, col. 3 & 4; "Sidney Smith of Scituate Died at Norwood; Oldest Resident of the Town Passed Away Thursday, Aged 94 Years – Had Very Noted Career," *Scituate Herald*, June 27, 1941, 5, col. 5; Sidney Smith by trustee to Lothrop Smith (born January 10, 1917), deed, December 4, 1942, PCRD,

book 1841, page 97, and see confirming deed, April 23, 1954, book 2337, page 385. The *1926 Harold Howard Directory*, 112, lists Erasmus F. Smith and his wife Lucinda C. Smith of Roslindale at their cottage on Lighthouse Road. The town's 1937 street listing of persons in Scituate, page 29, lists Sidney Smith on Lighthouse Road, age 90, retired.

[545] *Town of Scituate Valuation List 1944* (Town of Scituate, 1944), 118 (Roy), 193 (Erasmus), 194 (Lothrop).

[546] The Hall family lived two doors away from the Smith cottage on Lighthouse Road. Chris Hall email, November 16, 2019. Family trees in the Hall family file, SHS, and deed research, show they were descended from Sylvanus and Judith Smith (as well as the brother of shipbuilder Samuel Hall of Duxbury and East Boston). The Smiths' daughter Mary married Luke Hall, and they had children including Luke (married Effie Clark) and Roy (married Gertrude E. McLaughlin). Luke and Effie owned property in the Shore Acres section of Scituate from 1927 to 1933, but not on Lighthouse Point. Luke Hall and Effie C. Hall, both of Sharon, to Arthur V. Garland and Ebba A. Garland, deed (portion of lot 18), June 3, 1933, PCRD, book 1645, page 239. Roy Hall owned property at 65 Lighthouse Road from 1919 until his death in 1956, and then it passed to his descendants, including his son Roy Hall, Jr., and Roy Hall, Jr.'s son Roy Hall III. Then, in 1997, it was sold to a family trust whose trustee was Janet F. Winter, the sister of Roy Hall, Jr. See Roy Hall III, of Lunenberg, son of the late Roy Hall, Jr., late of Waltham, to Janet F. Winter, Trustee of Winter Family Trust, deed (lot 126 on plan), November 7, 1997, PCRD, book 15790, page 340. The deed refers to a plan by George H. Wetherbee, Jr., *Plan of Sea Shore Lots, Jericho Beach*, likely the plan, undated but probably April or October 1910, recorded in PCRD, April 5, 1945 (online version says January 1, 1900), plan book 6, page 706. The plan is similar, with similar lot numbers, to the 1908 plan referenced in the Judith Smith deeds. In 2009, the Winter Family Trust sold the property to another family trust, whose trustee was Janet F. Winter's daughter. Janet F. Winter, Trustee of the Winter Family Trust, to Lisa M. Richardson, Trustee of Scituate Winter Family trust, deed (reserving a life estate for Janet F. Winter), July 1, 2009, PCRD, book 37467, page 311. Janet F. Winter died September 11, 2016. "Janet F. Winter," Croswell Funeral Home website, http://www.croswellfuneralhome.com/janet-f-winter/. Janet's brother William R. Winter died December 28, 2019. "William R. Winter," Croswell Funeral Home website, https://www.everhere.com/us/obituaries/ma/reading/william-r-winter-10209221.

[547] GTMYS [?] L. Smith, card, *SMC*.

[548] See woman suffrage map, *History of Woman Suffrage*, vol. 6, page 627. A similar map is at "Map: States grant women the right to vote," National Constitution Center website, https://constitutioncenter.org/timeline/html/cw08_12159.html.

[549] "Suffragists' Efforts Turn to Legislatures; Only Five Now in Session – Doubt if Women Can Get Votes in Next Election," *Boston Globe*, June 5, 1919, 7; Irwin, *Story of the Woman's Party*, 420 (four states); "Woman Suffrage Finally Ratified," *Boston Globe*, June 26, 1919, 1; "19th Amendment to the U.S. Constitution: Women's Right to Vote (1920)," website by a cooperative effort among National History Day, the National Archives and Records Administration, and USA Freedom Corps, https://www.ourdocuments.gov/doc.php?flash=false&doc=63; Harper, *History of Woman Suffrage*, vol. 6, 301-302 (Massachusetts); Ware, *Why They Marched*, 265-277;

"On this day … June 25, 1919 – Massachusetts Ratifies the 19th Amendment," Massachusetts Secretary of State website, http://www.sec.state.ma.us/mus/pdfs/Suffrage-June-25-panels.pdf; *Journal of the House of Representatives of the Commonwealth of Massachusetts 1919* (Boston: Massachusetts General Court, House of Representatives, 1919), June 25, 1919, 1264-1267, State Library of Massachusetts, https://archives.lib.state.ma.us/handle/2452/796143.

[550] Margaret C. Robinson, ed., "Anti-Suffrage Notes," *The Woman Patriot*, vol. 4, no. 12 (Washington, DC: The Woman Patriot Publishing Co., March 20, 1920), 8, https://books.google.com/books?id=J9NBAQAAMAAJ&source=gbs_navlinks_s. Tennessee was listed with Florida as "Sessions in 1921. Constitutions Prohibit Ratification by Present Legislature."

[551] "Senator Harding 'Listens' and Evades," *The Suffragist*, vol. 8-9, July 1920 (Washington, DC: National Woman's Party, 1920), 127 & 143, https://books.google.com/books?id=nJszAQAAMAAJ&source=gbs_navlinks_s.

[552] Elaine Weiss, *The Woman's Hour: The Great Fight to Win the Vote* (New York: Viking Press, 2018); Fred Schwarz, "Suffragette City," *National Review*, July 9, 2018, online, June 21, 2018, https://www.nationalreview.com/magazine/2018/07/09/suffragette-city/; Irwin, *Story of the Woman's Party*, 451-463; *History of Woman Suffrage*, vol. 6, 616-625 (Tennessee).

[553] "Colby Proclaims 19th Amendment," *Boston Globe*, August 27, 1920, 16.

[554] "Colby Proclaims Woman Suffrage," *New York Times*, August 27, 1920, 1, http://movies2.nytimes.com/learning/general/onthisday/big/0826.html; Walton, *A Woman's Crusade*, 244; "Wilson Rejoices at Suffrage Ratification," *Boston Globe*, August 27, 1920, 14; Alice Paul, Interview by Amelia R. Fry, 1972-1973, 82-83 ("not one of us"), Suffragists Oral History Project, Conversations with Alice Paul: Woman Suffrage and the Equal Rights Amendment, University of California Calisphere website, http://content.cdlib.org/view?docId=kt6f59n89c&doc.view=entire_text. Mary Moore Forrest's role was reported in "Women's right to vote now official in United States," August 26, 1920, UPI Archives, https://www.upi.com/Archives/1920/08/26/Womens-right-to-vote-now-official-in-United-States/4867437115190/. See shorter UPI story, "Women's Right to Vote Now Part of the Constitution," *The Evening Missourian* (Columbia, MO), August 26, 1920, 1, Chronicling America: Historic American Newspapers, Library of Congress, https://chroniclingamerica.loc.gov/lccn/sn89066315/1920-08-26/ed-1/seq-1/.

[555] Woloch, *Women and the American Experience*, 354; Weiss, *The Woman's Hour*, 325; J. Kevin Corder and Christina Wolbrecht, "Was women's suffrage a failure? What new evidence tells us about the first women voters." *Washington Post*, August 26, 2017, https://www.washingtonpost.com/news/monkey-cage/wp/2016/08/26/was-womens-suffrage-a-failure-what-new-evidence-tells-us-about-the-first-women-voters/?noredirect=on; "Electoral College Box Scores 1789-1996," National Archives and Records Administration website, https://www.archives.gov/federal-register/electoral-college/scores.html#1920; Jennifer Remare, "Women Voters in Beverly, Massachusetts During the 1920 Election in Connection to the Woman's Suffrage Movement," 1997,

http://primaryresearch.org/women-voters-in-beverly-massachusetts-during-the-1920-election-in-connection-to-the-womans-suffrage-movement/.

[556] Robert C. Brooke, *Political Parties and Electoral Problems* (New York: Harper & Brothers, 1923), 409-410, https://books.google.com/books?id=JI0FAAAAMAAJ&source=gbs_navlinks_s; J. Kevin Corder and Christina Wolbrecht, "Was women's suffrage a failure? What new evidence tells us about the first women voters." *Washington Post*, August 26, 2017, https://www.washingtonpost.com/news/monkey-cage/wp/2016/08/26/was-womens-suffrage-a-failure-what-new-evidence-tells-us-about-the-first-women-voters/?noredirect=on.; Lyle Nyberg presentation (recent analysis), "After Women Got the Vote," in panel discussion sponsored by the League of Women Voters, "The Fight for the Vote: South Shore Women Make Their Voices Heard (1800s-1920s)," January 23, 2020, https://www.youtube.com/watch?v=4JLakdo_a_E&list=UUyeOxAghmVylv0umWkyIZUw&index=3&t=0s; Christina Wolbrecht, "Women Voters, 1920-2016," talk, January 30, 2020, Boston Athenaeum, C-SPAN, https://www.c-span.org/video/?468431-1/women-voters-1920-2016. Christina Wolbrecht and J. Kevin Corder are authors of *A Century of Votes for Women: American Elections Since Suffrage* (Cambridge: Cambridge University Press, 2020).

[557] Nyberg, "After Women Got the Vote;" J. Kevin Corder & Christina Wolbrecht, "Did Women Vote Once they had the Opportunity?" ABA website, posted December 2, 2019, https://www.americanbar.org/groups/public_education/publications/insights-on-law-and-society/volume-20/issue-1/did-women-vote-once-they-had-the-opportunity-/; Wolbrecht, "Women Voters, 1920-2016;" Elizabeth Cascio and Na'ama Shenhav, "A Century of the American Woman Voter: Sex Gaps in Political Participation, Preferences, and Partisanship Since Women's Enfranchisement," January 2020, NBER Working Paper No. w26709, https://ssrn.com/abstract=3530680, and *Journal of Economic Perspectives*, vol 34(2), 24-48; Derek Thompson, "Why Men Vote for Republicans, and Women Vote for Democrats: The gender gap is larger than ever," The Atlantic, February 9, 2020, https://www.theatlantic.com/ideas/archive/2020/02/how-women-became-democratic-partisans/606274/.

[558] *Town Records, vol. 12, 1906-1925*, 529, March 8, 1920, Town Archives.

[559] *Town Records, vol. 12, 1906-1925*, 531-532 (primary), April 27, 1920, Town Archives.

[560] *Town Records, vol. 12, 1906-1925*, 544, November 2, 1920, Town Archives.

[561] Town Records, mainly Town Reports, 1920 and 1921; Nyberg, "After Women Got the Vote."

[562] Nyberg, "After Women Got the Vote," citing Commonwealth of Massachusetts, The Decennial Census, 1915, Tables 1 & 2, and Decennial Census, 1925, Tables 2 & 3, State Library of Massachusetts.

[563] "Primary Documents From The Archives," Alice Paul Institute website, https://www.alicepaul.org/primary-documents-archives/; Finding aid for the Alice Paul Archive, https://www.alicepaul.org/documents-from-the-alice-paul-archives/; "Papers of Alice Paul, 1785-1985 (inclusive), 1805-1985 (bulk)," Biography in Collection Overview, SL, https://hollisarchives.lib.harvard.edu/repositories/8/resources/5012.

[564] "Suffragists' Body Adopts New Name; 'League of Women Voters' Effective Next Year," *Boston Globe*, March 28, 1919, 18; "Carrie Chapman Catt," article, Library of Congress, https://www.loc.gov/collections/national-american-woman-suffrage-association/articles-and-essays/carrie-chapman-catt/; Harper, *The History of Woman Suffrage*, vol. 5, ch. 22 "The League of Woman Voters."
[565] "Election of League of Women Voters," *Boston Globe*, April 1, 1921, 18; "Suffrage Organizations," Research Guide, Schlesinger Library on the History of Women in America, https://guides.library.harvard.edu/c.php?g=512561&p=3562670; *The Woman Citizen*, November 15, 1919, 487, https://books.google.com/books?id=qtYRAQAAMAAJ&source=gbs_navlinks_s.
[566] Lumsden, *Rampant Women*, 46-49; "History of Women in Massachusetts Government," Massachusetts Caucus of Women Legislators website, http://www.mawomenscaucus.com/history-of-women-in-massachusetts-government; "Women Legislators Had Busy Morning With Caucus and Photographers," *Boston Globe*, January 3, 1923, 1; "In Flourishing Condition," *Boston Globe*, March 27, 1908, 8; Susan W. FitzGerald, "Women in the Home," Papers of Inez Milholland, 1906-1916, Newsclippings, some re: Inez Milholland: Suffrage and women's rights, 1910-1915, n.d., SL, http://schlesinger.radcliffe.harvard.edu/onlinecollections/milholland/item/52043473/16; "P. E. U. Moved on Beacon Hill," *Boston Globe*, January 25, 1913, 5; "Jamaica Plain," Boston Women's Heritage Trail, https://bwht.org/jamaica-plain/; 11 Roanoke Avenue, BOS.10115 (continuation sheet February 2020), MACRIS.
[567] "National Register of Historic Places Program: Women's History Month 2018," National Park Service website, https://www.nps.gov/nr/feature/wom/;
[568] Judith Wellman, "Commemorating Suffrage: Historic Sites and Women's Right to Vote," National Park Service website, last updated April 10, 2019, https://www.nps.gov/articles/commemorating-suffrage-historic-sites-and-women-s-right-to-vote.htm. For a more detailed discussion of historic sites relating to women and woman suffrage, see Page Putnam Miller, ed., *Reclaiming the Past: Landmarks of Women's History* (Bloomington: Indiana University Press, 1992), especially Page Putnam Miller, ch. 1 "Landmarks of Women's History," and Joan Hoff, ch. 6, "Women and Politics."
[569] Emily Conklin, "Women's suffrage statue finally approved for Centennial unveiling," *The Architect's Newspaper*, October 25, 2019, https://www.archpaper.com/2019/10/central-park-womens-statue-approved/.
[570] The Boston Women's Heritage Trail started in 1989, and it has over 10 trails including "Ladies Walk," according to the trail's website, https://bwht.org/. The Ladies Walk says Judith Winsor Smith presented a bust of Lucy Stone in 1904 to the Boston Public Library, where it is still displayed, alongside with one of her daughter Alice Stone Blackwell.
[571] National Collaborative for Women's History Sites website, https://ncwhs.org/; Steve Bodnar, "First Historic Marker Celebrates Women's Suffrage History in United States," Pomeroy Foundation website, February 25, 2019, https://www.wgpfoundation.org/first-historic-marker-celebrates-womens-suffrage-history-in-united-states/. An ambitious blog covers the history of suffrage in South Dakota. Liz Almlie, "Women's Suffrage in SoDak,"

https://historysouthdakota.wordpress.com/womens-suffrage-in-sodak/, and see http://www.sdmuseums.org/news/7285277.

[572] "Women's Rights National History Trail Feasibility Study: Final Study Report 2003" (Boston: National Park Service, Northeast Region, 2003), 4, 49 (source of quote), https://books.google.com/books?id=IDOmQGWpEG8C&source=gbs_navlinks_s. Interestingly, Nantucket was considered but not Martha's Vineyard, as shown on the map on pages 22-23, and the appendix, page 74. In Plymouth County, only the Odd Fellows Lodge (Universalist Church) in Hingham was considered, page 74. Of all the possible summer suffragist sites, only Newport was considered, page 77.

[573] Chauncy Hall Building, 585-591 Boylston Street, BOS.2651 (continuation sheet February 2020). MACRIS.

[574] See list of documented historic suffrage sites at the author's website, www.lylenyberg.com, particularly tab for "Historic Suffrage Sites" at https://www.lylenyberg.com/historic-buildings-suffrage.

[575] Caleb Gayle, "Think the Constitution guarantees your right to vote? Think again," *Boston Globe*, January 5, 2020, K1, also posted January 1, 2020, https://www.bostonglobe.com/2020/01/01/opinion/think-constitution-guarantees-your-right-vote-think-again/; Ann D. Gordon, "Looking for a Right to Vote: Introducing the Nineteenth Amendment," National Park Service website, last updated April 2, 2019, https://www.nps.gov/articles/introducing-the-19th-amendment.htm.; "Women's Suffrage Rights," Legal Information Institute website, Cornell Law School, https://www.law.cornell.edu/constitution-conan/amendment-19; Corder and Wolbrecht, "Was women's suffrage a failure?"; Lisa Tetrault, "Winning the Vote: A divided movement brought about the Nineteenth Amendment," *Humanities* (Summer 2019), https://www.neh.gov/article/winning-vote-divided-movement-brought-about-nineteenth-amendment.; Joshua A. Douglas, "The Right to Vote Under State Constitutions," 67 *Vanderbilt Law Review* (2014), 89, https://wp0.vanderbilt.edu/lawreview/wp-content/uploads/sites/89/2014/01/Douglas-67-Vand.-L.-Rev.-89.pdf; Corder & Wolbrecht, "Did Women Vote Once they had the Opportunity?".

[576] Corder and Wolbrecht, "Was women's suffrage a failure?"

[577] Susan W. Ware, "The Long 19th Amendment," Schlesinger Library Newsletter (source of quote), posted 2018, https://www.radcliffe.harvard.edu/news/schlesinger-newsletter/long-19th-amendment; "Conclusion" chapter of Berenson, *Massachusetts Suffrage*, 165-166; Weiss, *The Woman's Hour*, 327-329.

[578] "Suffrage," Encyclopedia.com, updated June 5, 2020 ("overshadowed"), https://www.encyclopedia.com/social-sciences-and-law/political-science-and-government/political-science-terms-and-concepts/voting-rights; Michael P. McDonald, "2016 November General Election: Turnout Rates," United States Elections Project, last updated September 5, 2018, http://www.electproject.org/2016g; Nyberg, "After Women Got the Vote;" Drew DeSilver, "U.S. trails most developed countries in voter turnout," Pew Research Center, posted May 21, 2018, https://www.pewresearch.org/fact-tank/2018/05/21/u-s-voter-turnout-trails-most-developed-countries/.

[579] *Kill Chain: The Cyber War on America's Elections*, HBO documentary, YouTube (source of quote), https://www.youtube.com/watch?v=3c8LMZ8UGd8, and HBO website, https://www.hbo.com/documentaries/kill-chain-the-cyber-war-on-americas-elections.
[580] Matt Stout and Victoria McGrane, "State House gears still grind slowly," *Boston Globe*, April 21, 2020, 1; Jada Yuan, "A month later, this New York City primary is still a train wreck and a warning to us all," *Washington Post*, posted July 25, 2020, https://www.washingtonpost.com/lifestyle/style/a-month-later-this-new-york-city-primary-is-still-a-train-wreck-and-a-warning-to-us-all/2020/07/25/1c19f9c4-cb68-11ea-b0e3-d55bda07d66a_story.html; Ian Millhiser, "Democrats' risky plan to ensure Congress can vote during the pandemic, explained," Vox.com, posted May 29, 2020, https://www.vox.com/2020/5/29/21272260/democrats-house-pelosi-mccarthy-proxy-voting-supreme-court-constitution. Allowing voting by mail may actually reduce turnout for some Native Americans. Ella Nilsen, "For Native Americans, voting rights were hard-won. Mail-in voting could undo the gains," Vox.com, updated June 22, 2020, https://www.vox.com/the-highlight/21261058/vote-by-mail-native-americans-voting-rights-covid-reservations-ballot.
[581] Christina A. Cassidy and Nicholas Riccardi, "Trump: Mail-in voting presents 'biggest risk' to reelection," *Washington Post*, June 19, 2020, https://www.washingtonpost.com/politics/trump-mail-in-voting-presents-biggest-risk-to-reelection/2020/06/19/80cdc4de-b251-11ea-98b5-279a6479a1e4_story.html; Elise Viebeck, "Minuscule number of potentially fraudulent ballots in states with universal mail voting undercuts Trump claims about election risks," *Washington Post*, June 8, 2020, https://www.washingtonpost.com/politics/minuscule-number-of-potentially-fraudulent-ballots-in-states-with-universal-mail-voting-undercuts-trump-claims-about-election-risks/2020/06/08/1e78aa26-a5c5-11ea-bb20-ebf0921f3bbd_story.html.
[582] Irwin, *Story of the Woman's Party*, 232-233; Aaron C. Davis, Carol D. Leonnig, Josh Dawsey and Devlin Barrett, "Officials familiar with Lafayette Square confrontation challenge Trump administration claim of what drove aggressive expulsion of protesters," *Washington Post*, posted June 14, 2020, https://www.washingtonpost.com/politics/officials-challenge-trump-administration-claim-of-what-drove-aggressive-expulsion-of-lafayette-square-protesters/2020/06/14/f2177e1e-acd4-11ea-a9d9-a81c1a491c52_story.html; Alex Horton, "Use of medical helicopter to target protesters is under investigation, National Guard says," *Washington Post*, posted June 2, 2020, https://www.washingtonpost.com/national-security/2020/06/02/helicopter-protest-dc/.
[583] John Lewis, interview by Zak Cheney-Rice, "The Long View," *New York* Magazine, posted June 8, 2020, https://nymag.com/intelligencer/article/john-lewis-good-trouble-interview.html.
[584] US Supreme Court Chief Justice Roberts, December 31, 2019, *2019 Year-End Report on the Federal Judiciary*. See analysis by Ian Millhiser, "Chief Justice Roberts warns we're taking 'democracy for granted.' His rulings haven't helped," Vox.com, posted January 3, 2020, https://www.vox.com/2020/1/3/21046493/chief-justice-roberts-annual-report-democracy.

INDEX

Note: Images are indicated by page numbers in *italics*.

A
abolition, 8, 14–16, 70, 146–147, 151
Adams, Charles Francis, III, 138
Adams, Franklin P., 35–36, 45
Adams, John Quincy, 140
Adams, Samuel Hopkins, 35, 45
Allen, C. M., 18
American Civil Liberties Union (ACLU), 131
American Telephone and Telegraph, 61
American Woman Suffrage Association (AWSA), 12, 15–16, 142
Americus Club, 5
Angels and Amazons: A Hundred Years of American Women (Irwin), 41
Anthony, Lucy E., 8
Anthony, Susan B., 8, 12, 15, 24, 150, 168, 186
Arden (estate), 46
Aug, Edna, 45

B
Babson, Roger, 73
Bacon, E. R., 94
Baldwin, Roger, 131
Barber, Marcus, 113–114
Bar Harbor, Maine, 9
Bates, Abigail, 4
Bates, Rebecca, 4, 149
Bay End Farm, 126–128, 133
Bearse, Horace L., 8
Beckington, Alice, 5, 37, 45, 90
Beckwith, Alice, 71
Belmont, Alva Vanderbilt, 9, 72, 85, 150
Berenson, Barbara F., 26
Bijou (house), 62
Bjorkman, Frances Maule, 6
Blackwell, Alice Stone, 2, 8, 12, 17, 25, 69–71, 142, 149–150, 152–153, 170–171
Blackwell, Henry B., 8, 12, 16, 69, 142, 149–150, 152, 168
Blatch, Harriot Stanton, 9, 13, 20, 22–24, 79
Bloomfield, Catherine Pauline, 74
Bloomfield, Joyce Therese, 74
Bloomfield, Lincoln, Jr., 75
Bloomfield, Lincoln Palmer, 74
Bloomfield, Meyer, 1, 7, 21, 62, *65*, 65–75, 134
Bloomfield, Sylvia, 1, *65*, 66, 70–71
Bonney, Louisa F., 18
Bonney, Margaret Cole, 51
Boston Equal Suffrage Association for Good Government (BESAGG), 1, 7, 13, 19–20, 41, 44, 67, 69–70, 72, 147, 171, 185, 187
Boston Red Sox, 39
Boston, suffrage sites in. *See* Chauncy Hall Building; Little Building; Kensington Building (anti-suffrage)
Bourne, Fred, 166–167
Bradford, John, 155
Brandeis, Louis, 72
Brannan, Eunice Dana, 24
Broadwalls (house), 54
Brown, Olympia, 28–29
Burgess, Gelett, 5, 32–33, 35, 43
Burns, Lucy, 13, 22
Buzzards Bay, 126–129, *127*

C
Carman, Bliss, 35, 60
Carson, Mary A., 184

Catt, Carrie Chapman, 13, 94, 134, 180–181, 184
Centennial (ship), 155–156
Chace, Elizabeth B., 8
Chauncy Hall Building (Boston), 19, 147, *148*, 187
Chautauqua, New York, 96–98, 104, 110, 113
Chilmark, Massachusetts, 9
Civic Service House (Boston), 66–67, 69, 71
Civil War, 14–15, 52
Clark, Frank, 139
Clarkin, Franklin, 35
Cleveland, Grover, 127
Cohasset, Massachusetts, 3, 139–140
Colby, Bainbridge, 180–181
Colgate, Margaret, 63
College Equal Suffrage League, 1, 7, 27, 147, 187
College Women's Suffrage League, 12, 20
Committee on Public Information (CPI), 48
Congressional Union for Woman Suffrage (CUWS), 13, 22, 41
Conroy, George B., 94
Copeland, Charles H., 31–32, 34–35, 46
Copeland, Elberta, 31–32
Covid-19 pandemic, 189
Cox, James M., 183–184
Crothers, Rachel, 85
Curley, James Michael, 170
Cushing, H. Warren, 94

D
Dana, Charles A., 24
Davis, James J., 73
Demon's Notebook (Hale), 131–132, *132*
Dietrick, Ellen B., 8
Dix, Roger S., 94
Doak, William N., 73
Donaldson, Sylvia, 185
Dugan, Maude, 110
Dugan, Phyllis, 45, 109
Duganne, Maude, 50, 54
Duganne, Phyllis, 45
Duxbury, Massachusetts, 58–59, 62, 142, 147, 154, *161*, 176

E
East Boston Woman Suffrage Club, 148
Eastman, Crystal, 130–131
Eastman, Max, 34, 81, 130
Emerson, Ralph Waldo, 145
Equality League of Self-Supporting Women, 79
Equal Rights Amendment, 184
Evans, Rowland, Jr., 62

F
Feakins, William, 91, 93, 102
Fenway Park, 39
Fifteenth Amendment, 15–16
Filene, A. Lincoln, 72
Filene's (department store), 72
Fish, Frederick P., 61, 138
Fitzgerald, John F., 25
Fitzgerald, Richard Y., 70
Fitzgerald, Susan Walker, 69, 184–185
flu pandemic. *See* influenza pandemic
Flynn, William, 110
Food Administration, 100–102
Forbes-Robertson, Johnston, 79
Ford, Mary Ann, 52–53
Forrest, Mary Henderson, 59–60, *60*
Forrest, Mary Moore, 1, 7, 20, 38, 57–63, 58, *60*, 180–181
Foxcroft, Frank, 19
Franchot, Stanislaw, 134
Frye, Howard, 109
Futrelle, Jacques, 5, 31–32, 34

G
Gardner, Isabella Stewart, 140
Garland, James A., 128
Garland, Marie Tudor, 126–127.133, 126–129
Garrison, Francis J., 70
Garrison, William Lloyd, 8, 70, 147

Garrison, William Lloyd, Jr., 70, 147, 151
Gawthorpe, Mary, 85, 98–99
Gibran, Kahlil, 127
Gideon (Irwin), 55
Gillmore, Rufus H., 29, 35–37, 87–88
Gilman, Charlotte Perkins, 6, 21, 37, 41, 49–50, 78–79, 81
Glades, 3, *137,* 137–140
Great Depression, 73
Green, Frances Cushing, 128
Greenwald, Richard, 71
Grimké, Archibald H., 151

H
Hale, Beatrice Forbes-Robertson, 1–2, 6–7, 21, 37–39, 63, *77, 80*
arrives in Scituate, 87–91
attacks on, 94
at Chautauqua, 96–97, 104
on marriage, 95–96
marriage of, 115–124
Swinburne's affairs and, 124–129
tours America, 92–106
on Will Irwin, 90–91
Will Irwin on, 45
Woman Patriot and, 133–134
World War I and, 48
at "Writers' Roost," 35
Hale, Clemency, 91, 106–107, *108*
Hale, Robert Swinburne, 35
Hale, Rosemary, 91, 106–107, *108*
Hale, Sanchia, 87, 91, 106–107, 134
Hale, Swinburne, 1–2, 77–135, *79–80,* 99, 103, 110–111, 114–115
marriage of, 115–124
mental health of, 132–133
other women of, 124–129
as writer, 131–132
Hall, Luke, 154, 166
Hall, Roy, 177
Hall, Roy, III, 177
Hall, Roy, Jr., 177
Hall, Samuel, 154
Hall, Samuel, Jr., 155
Harding, Warren, 172, 182–183
Harrington, William, 166–167
Harvard University, 67
Haynes, Christina, 50
Haynes, Gideon, 50–51
Haynes, Harry E., 30, 32, 43, 52, 89–90
Haynes, Margaret J., 51
Haynes, Rose, 51
Haynes, Walter, 46, 51, 112, 180
Herron, Catherine W., 63
Herron, Schuyler F., 63
Heterodoxy (club), 2, 6, 21, 36, 80
Holmes, Oliver Wendell, 150
Homans, Abigail Adams, 139
Homans, Charles D., 139
Home Club of East Boston, 147
Hoover, Herbert, 73
Hoover, J. Edgar, 130
Hovey, Richard, 35
Howe, Julia Ward, 2, 8, 10, 12, 15, 128, 139, 142, 147–148, 150–151, 168, 170, 187
Howe, Maud, 128
Hull, Josephine, 36
Humane Society, 53

I
Idle Hour Theatre, 38, 39, 46, 48, 51
Immigration Act of 1924, 73
influenza pandemic, 41, 105
Irish moss, 167
Irwin, Agnes, 19
Irwin, Inez Haynes Gillmore, 1, *27,* 27–41, 44, 72
artists and, 5
as author, 5
Beatrice Hale and, 78, 83–84, 88–90
College Women's Suffrage League and, 12, 20
death of, 55
importance of, 2, 10
lodgings of, 6, 30–32, *32*, *34*, 54–55
Park and, 7, 53–54
picketing and, 23
in Scituate, 50–55
on Scituate, 53–54
Will and, 43

Irwin, Will, 1, 39, *42,* 42–50, 82
Beatrice Hale on, 90–91
Burgess and, 5, 32–33, 43
Jennings and, 89
in Scituate, 50–55
on Scituate, 45
in World War I, 47–49

J
Jennings, Al, 89

K
Keith, Randolph, 180
Keller, Helen, 41
Kelly, Annie, 94
Kensington Building (Boston), 19
King, Henry, 55

L
Lady of the Kingdoms, The (Irwin), 37
La Follette, Fola, 6, 36
Laidlaw, Harriet Burton, 85
Laidlaw, James Lees, 85
Lawson, Thomas, 38–39, 49, 140, 167, 184
League of Women Voters, 54, 71, 134, *181,* 185
Lewis, John, 190
Lewis, Josephine, 5, 45
Lewis, Matilda, 5
Lewis, Sinclair, 36
Liberty Bonds, 105
Liberty Loans, 105
lifesavers, 51, 53, *53,* 113
Lighthouse Point, 166, *166*
Litchfield, Carrie, 18
Little Building (Boston), 171
Livermore, Clara, 61
Livermore, Joseph, 61
Livermore, Mary A., 8, 15–16, 29, 147, 150–151, 168
Long, John D., 70
Longfellow, Henry Wadsworth, 145
Lovering, Frances, 138

M
Mackay, Katherine Duer, 79
Malone, Maud, 13
Manson, George, 155
Marguerite (house), 74, *74,* 75
Massachusetts Antisuffrage Association, 139
Massachusetts Association Opposed to the Further Extension of Suffrage to Women (MAOFESW), 18–19, 21–22, 138–140
Massachusetts in the Woman Suffrage Movement (Berenson), 26
Massachusetts Woman Suffrage Association (MWSA), 12, 63, 69, 96, 141, 147, 170–171, 187
Mayflower, 142
McCall, Samuel W., 38, 40, 52
McKay, Donald, 144–145
Men's League for Woman Suffrage, 21, 34, 38, 40, 59, 62, 70, 81–82, 85, 130
Merrick, Miriam, 175
Merritt, Fanny, 51
Merwin, Samuel, 36, 45, 90
Meteyard, Thomas Buford, 5
Milholland, Inez, 6, 37, 72, 79
Milholland, John E., 79
Milne, W. A., 102
Minnie Rowen (ship), 146, 164
Moore, Caro, 1, 7, 20, 38, 52, 57–63, *60*
Moore, William, 7, 21, 52, *58,* 58, 62, 70, 74
Morey, Agnes H., 24
Morey, Katherine, 24–25
moss, Irish, 167
Mott, Lucretia, 12
My Scituate (Bonney), 51

N
names, married, 17
National Advisory Council, 1
National American Woman Suffrage Association (NAWSA), 7, 12, 17, 79, 150, 152, *181,* 184–185
National Woman's Party (NWP), 1, 13, 22, 24–25, 27, 41, 62, 181, 184

National Woman Suffrage Association (NWSA), 12, 15–16, 168, *168*
Neal, M. J., 94
Nelles, Walter, 129, 131
New England Home Economics Association, 63
New England Woman's Club, 176, 187
New England Woman Suffrage Association (NEWSA), 12, 15–16, 149–150
New England Women's Club (NEWC), 147
Newport, Rhode Island, 9, 150
New York, 20–21, 37, 44, 80–82, *82,* 83, *83,* 84
Nineteenth Amendment, 13–14, 25–26, 52, 179–182, 188, 190
Norris, Mary Livermore, 29–30
Notman, William, 150

O
O'Hare, Margaret, 176
O'Keefe, Georgia, 133
"Old Oaken Bucket, The" (Woodworth), 4
O'Neil, Christopher, 46, 51
O'Neil, Margaret, 49, 51
O'Neill, Rose, 84, *84,* 116, *116, 132*

P
Page, Mary Hutcheson, 41, 69
Palmer, A. Mitchell ("Palmer raids"), 130
pandemic. *See* Covid-19 pandemic; influenza pandemic
Park, Maud Wood, 1, 7–8, 10, 12–13, 20, 29, 43–44, 69, 106, 134
Parker, Elizabeth, 140
Parker, William L., 140
Parsons, Frank, 67
Paul, Alice, 13, 22–23, 66, 72, 180–181, 184
Pearson, Ralph M., 131
Peggotty Beach, *4,* 30–31, *36,* 46, *47, 53,* 91
Perkins, Frances, 52
Perkins, Thomas Nelson, 139
Peterson, Reuben, 155
Picaroons, The (Irwin and Burgess), 43
picketing, *11,* 13–14, 23–25, 97
Preis, Englebert, 130
Prophet, The (Gibran), 127
Prouty, John E. O., 161, 165
Prouty, Mary F, 18

R
race, 15
Radcliffe College, 1, 7, 29
Remonstrance Against Woman Suffrage, The, 19
Renault, Ralph, 35
Rhode Island Woman Suffrage Association, 8
Roberts, John, 190
Robinson, Boardman, 33–35, 45, 90, 130
Robinson, Carl, 34
Ruggles, Carl, 33–35, 45, 90

S
Saltonstall, Eleanor, 138–139
Saltonstall, Leverett, 138
Saltonstall, Richard M., 138, 140
Satuit Playhouse, 51
Saturday Evening Post, 42, 45
Schauffler, Robert Haven, 46
Scituate, Massachusetts, 3–6, *4*
  artists in, 5
  Beatrice Hale arrives in, 87–91
  Hale family in, 86–87
  Irwins' life in, 50–55
  Will Irwin on, 45
  writers in, 5
Scituate Historical Society, 52
Scituate Light, 153–154, *154*
Scott, Miriam Finn, 35
Seaver, Etta, 38
Seiberling, F. A., 99
Seneca Falls convention, 12, 15
Shaw, Anna Howard, 8, 94
Shaw, Pauline Agassiz, 66–70, 85, 106, 185
Shaw, Quincy Adams, 67–68
Shaw, Robert Gould, II, 106

Shepard, Hannah, 175
Shoreham, New York, 9
Shuman, Mary Keegan, 184
Simpson, Marcus, 103
slavery, 14–15
Smith, Erasmus F., 176
Smith, Frances, 143
Smith, Judith Winsor, 2, 6, 8, 52, 58, *141,* 141–177, *173,* 185–187
Smith, Lothrop, 176–177
Smith, Mary, 154, 166, 177
Smith, Sidney, 143, 176–177
Smith, Sylvanus, 2, 6, 58, 141–177, *143, 173*
Smith, Zilpha, 143, 171, 185
Spadoni, Adriana, 45
Stanton, Elizabeth Cady, 9, 12, 15, 22, 186
Stimson, Henry, 61
Stone, Lucy, 2, 8, 10, 12, 15–16, *16,* 17, 69, 142, 150, 152, 170
Story of the Woman's Party, The (Irwin), 41
Stuart, Mabel, 5
Stuart, William G., 72
suffrage movement
- in 1900s, 18–26
- early years of, 14–18
- historic sites, 185–187
- as ongoing, 188–189
- suffrage map, *179*
- timeline of, 12–14

Suffragist, The (newspaper), 41
Supple, W. E., 30–32

T
Tague, Peter F., 24–25, 107
Thayer, Helen G., 184
Thayer, Theodora, 5
Thomas, Al, 45
Thompson, Edith "Daisy," 6, 35–36, 48, 50–51, 75, 80, 85, 89
timeline, of suffrage movement, 12–14
Titanic, 34
Tudor, Frederic, 127
Tudor, Frederick, 127

U
Una, The (newspaper), 12

V
Van Winkle, Mina C., 100, *101,* 101–102
Villard, Oswald Garrison, 70
voting, *181,* 181–185, 189–190

W
Wadsworth, William Austin, 61
Walsh, David, 24, 40, 49, 170
Waltham Equal Suffrage League, 94
Ware, Susan, 26, 188–189
War of 1812, 4, 149
Warren, George C., 94
Warren, Maude Radford, 35, 37
Watson, Dawson, 5, 35
Weeks, John W., 24, 49
Weiss, Elaine, 14, 180
Welch, George, 63, 75
Welch, Sarah E., 18
Welch Company, 108, 111
Wells, Bettina Borrmann, 13
White, Trumbull, 98
White House, *11,* 13–14, 23–25, 97
Whitehouse, Vira, 48
Why They Marched: Untold Stories of the Women Who Fought for the Right to Vote (Ware), 26
Wianno, Massachusetts, 8–9
Wilde, Catharine, 148–149, 151, 163
Williams, Jesse Lynch, 45
Wilson, Woodrow, 13–14, 22, 24–25, 181
Winter, Janet F., 177
Woman Patriot, 133–134, 180
Woman's Journal, 9–10, 12, 16–17, 67, 69, 82, 94–96, 142, 147–148, *149,* 151, 153, 168–169, 175
Woman's Suffrage Party of Maryland, 93
Women's Anti-Suffrage Association of Massachusetts (WASAM), 138
Women's Political Union, 79
Woodworth, Samuel, 4
World War I, 13, 24, 41, 47–48, 52, 63, 97, 99–102, 105, 124, 139

"Writers' Roost, The," 35
Wyoming, 14

Y
Yellow Wall Paper, The (Gilman), 78

Z
Ziffrin, Marilyn, 35

ACKNOWLEDGMENTS

This book would not have been possible without the support of my wife and family. Special thanks to Janet Paraschos and Alix Stuart for editing. Thanks to my reviewers: Carolyn Ravenscroft, Jim Glinski, James Conroy, and especially David Dixon. Thanks also to Johanna Neuman and other historians and writers who showed me the way and whose work enlightens us all, particularly about the movement for women's suffrage. Thanks to Dave Ball for his help, comments, and foreword, Susannah Green for the cover illustrations and help on interior design, and John Roman for creating the map — they are examples of the amazing people who live in Scituate.

Thanks to my neighbors and my teachers. They have inspired my history search and have made Third Cliff and Scituate such a great place in which to live.

Thanks to the Duxbury Rural and Historical Society. Its Judith Smith collection was the spark that led to this book. Thanks to the Scituate Historical Society, Scituate Town Archives, Scituate Town Library, and State Library of Massachusetts, for their invaluable help. (Thank you Carol, Mary, and Betty.) Thanks to the Scituate Historical Commission and the Massachusetts Historical Commission for their support as I documented historic places in Scituate and elsewhere. Thanks to the Massachusetts Historical Society, particularly for the "Brown Bag Lunch" opportunities for talking and feedback.

Thanks to the Library of Congress and its staff, which provided great photos online, and (in response to my request) copies of letters to and from Inez Haynes Irwin. Thanks to the Schlesinger Library, Radcliffe Institute, Harvard University, for the help of its librarians and permission to use information from the Inez Haynes Irwin collection and other women's rights collections. Thanks also to the librarian at the Fray Angelico Chaves History Library, who accessed the Ralph M. Pearson collection for me during Covid-19 time. Many went out of their way to help, it seemed to me. We are fortunate to have these institutions and their people.

I relied on primary source materials at these institutions and online, including the Internet Archive, HathiTrust Digital Library, and *Boston Globe* archives. The Plymouth County Registry of Deeds, with its online database back to colonial times, was a fantastic resource. I relied on a wide range of other sources. Google's search engine, books, maps, and other resources were invaluable. Many thoughtful authors have written about the woman suffrage movement, and I have cited them in my extensive notes. Readers who want to explore this subject in more detail may consult those notes at the end, and review materials at my website.

Thank you to everyone who helped me on this book. Please forgive me if I forgot to mention someone or some institution who helped.

I dug deep and ruthlessly sought accurate information. But in a work like this, it is only natural for mistakes to occur. They are my responsibility. Let me know and I will try to fix them.

ABOUT THE AUTHOR

Lyle Nyberg graduated from Dartmouth College and Boston University School of Law. Like Will Irwin (featured in the book), he met and married a summer resident of Scituate, and came to love the town, and to write of the town's history. Lyle retired to Scituate after a career as a corporate lawyer. He is an independent scholar and historian.

He is a member of the Scituate Historical Society and the Massachusetts Historical Society.

Lyle has spent years researching, writing, and speaking about the history of Scituate. He has documented more than 50 historic buildings, published in the state's online MACRIS database. His work includes sites in Boston that were nationally important for women's suffrage. In January 2020, he was a panelist for a League of Women Voters program on women's suffrage.

Reach him at lylenyberg@comcast.net, or www.lylenyberg.com.

Made in the USA
Middletown, DE
02 September 2020

18211693R00159